Global Money, Capital Restructuring and the
Changing Patterns of Labour

Global Money, Capital Restructuring and the Changing Patterns of Labour

Edited by
Riccardo Bellofiore

Department of Economics,
University of Bergamo, Italy

Edward Elgar
Cheltenham, UK • Northampton, MA, USA

Published by
Edward Elgar Publishing Limited
Glensanda House
Montpellier Parade
Cheltenham
Glos GL50 1UA
UK

Edward Elgar Publishing, Inc.
136 West Street
Suite 202
Northampton
Massachusetts 01060
USA

A catalogue record for this book
is available from the British Library

Library of Congress Cataloguing in Publication Data

Global money, capital restructuring, and the changing patterns of
    labour / edited by Riccardo Bellofiore.
        Papers presented at a conference held in Bergamo, Dec. 3–5, 1997.
        1. Labour market—Congresses. 2. Saving and investment-
    –Congresses. 3. Money—Congresses. I. Bellofiore, R. (Riccardo)
    HD5701.3.G575   1999
    331.12—dc21   99–14861
                                                                            CIP

ISBN 1 85898 848 9

Typeset by Manton Typesetters, Louth, Lincolnshire, UK.
Printed and bound in Great Britain by MPG Books Ltd, Bodmin, Cornwall

Contents

Figures

Tables

Contributors

Giovanna Altieri is director of IRES-CGIL in Rome, Italy. Recent publications include 'Lavoro nero e irregolare: eterogeneità del fenomeno e differenzione delle politiche per favorire l'emersione', *L'Assistenza Sociale*, 3, July–September, 1997, and 'Route counselling for disadvantaged groups on the labour market: exploratory study in six member states', final report, HIVA (Hoger institut voor de arbeid), Università di Lovanio (1998).

Riccardo Bellofiore is Associate Professor at the University of Bergamo, Italy, where he teaches monetary economics, macroeconomics and history of economic thought. He is the editor of *Marxian Economics: A Reappraisal* (London: Macmillan, 1998) and has contributed to *John Maynard Keynes: Language and Method*, edited by Alessandro Marzola and Francesco Silva (Aldershot: Edward Elgar Publishing, 1994). He has published in academic journals on Marxian value and monetary theory, the monetary aspects of the Schumpeterian system, Wicksell's and Keynes's circuit theory of money, Mises and Hayek on banking and the cycle, Sraffian price theory, and about economic epistemology.

Suzanne de Brunhoff, Honorary Research Director, Centre National de la Recherche Scientifique, Paris. Author of *Marx on Money* (1976), *The State, Capital and Economic Policy* (1978) and 'L'instabilité monétaire internationale' in F. Chesnais (ed.), *La mondialisation financière. Genèse, coûte et enjeux* (Paris: Syros, 1996).

Guglielmo Carchedi is Senior Research Fellow in the Faculty of Economics and Econometrics at the University of Amsterdam, The Netherlands. He is the author of several books and articles. His two most recent books are *Frontiers of Political Economy* (Verso, 1991) and, with A. Freeman (eds), *Marx and Non-equilibrium Economics* (Edward Elgar, 1997).

Sergio Cesaratto teaches economics at the Faculty of Economics of the University of Rome 'La Sapienza'. He has published articles on the theory of economic growth, technical change and methodology in various international journals including *Cambridge Journal of Economics, Review of Political Economy* and *Research Policy*.

Carl H.A. Dassbach is in the Department of Social Sciences, College of Sciences and Arts, Michigan Technological University, USA.

Gérard Duménil is Director of Research for CNRS, LAREA-CEDRA at the University of Paris X-Nanterre.

Joseph Halevi teaches economics at the University of Sydney and at the Université Pierre Mendès France in Grenoble where he is a member of the Institut de Recherches sur la Production et le Développement (IREPD).

Dominique Lévy is Director of Research for CNRS, CEPREMAP, France.

Mike Parker is an industrial electrician and industrial computer controls specialist and has helped design a number of skilled trades electrical/electronics training programmes. He writes for the Detroit-based publication, *Labor Notes* and is the co-author, with Jane Slaughter, of a number of widely-used books and articles for unionists on the ideology and practice of management cooperation and work-reorganization schemes. The latest book in this series is *Working Smart: A Union Guide to Participation Programs and Reengineering*. He has just completed a book, co-authored with Martha Gruelle, *Democracy is Power: Rebuilding Unions from the Bottom Up*, available from *Labor Notes*.

Michael Perelman teaches economics at California State University, Chico. His most recent books are *The Natural Instability of Markets: Expectations, Increasing Returns and the Collapse of Markets* (New York: St Martin's Press, 1999), *Class Warfare in the Information Age* (New York: St Martin's Press, 1998) and *The End of Economics* (London: Routledge, 1996).

Hugo Radice, Lecturer in Economics, Division of Industrial and Labour Studies, Leeds University Business School. The main areas of Hugo Radice's research, teaching and publication are international and comparative political economy, transnational corporations, industrial policies and transitional economies.

Vittorio Rieser has been teaching industrial sociology at the University of Modena for a number of years, and is currently working as a researcher in IRES-CGIL, Turin – a research centre connected with the Italian union CGIL.

Franklin Serrano is Associate Professor at the Instituto de Economia, Universidade Federal de Rio de Janeiro, Brazil.

Antonella Stirati is Associate Professor at the Università del Sannio, Benevento, Italy. She has published various papers on labour economics and the interpretation of the classical economists in Italian and international journals and is the author of *The Theory of Wages in Classical Economics*, Edward Elgar Publishing, 1994.

Vittorio Valli, Professor of Economic Policy, Faculty of Political Sciences, University of Turin, Italy. Former president of the European Association for Comparative Economic Studies (EACES). Author of several books and essays on labour economics, economic growth, comparative economic systems and economic policy.

Introduction

Riccardo Bellofiore

The 1990s have seen a radical weakening in the conditions of the working class, together with the reshaping of the international economy. The implementation of new productive techniques and new methods in the organization of labour has gone hand-in-hand with the growing importance of financial capital, with the search for new markets in new areas and with a wider spread of the capitalist relationship. Everything has seemed to conspire against employment, the welfare state and active national economic policies. Employment has become increasingly precarious and fragmented, the welfare state is being regarded as too expensive, and the nation-state has been sentenced to powerlessness. All too often, mass unemployment has been declared to be our imminent and unavoidable fate, the only way out being some kind of 'escape' from the economy. Labour should no longer be seen as (even one of) the essential arena(s) where human beings' sociality is constructed.

A powerful interpretation of these processes has been coming to increasing prominence, and is even hegemonic in some European countries, such as Italy and France. It is articulated along three lines. First, concerning the world economy's trends, it is argued that, with the completion of the globalization of capitalism, we are facing a qualitative and irreversible change. Not only the financial markets, but also those in commodities and labour, together with production are, by now, fully interconnected and interchangeable. As a consequence, the sovereignty of the nation-state is reduced to an empty simulacrum. Second, concerning the labour processes, it is argued that we have entered post-Fordism, a new stage in the regulation of capitalism. According to some commentators, 'Toyota-type' organization of labour may contribute to the expression of the worker's creativeness, though, in the view of others, it carries alienation to its extreme consequences. Finally, the two circumstances together, global competition and the new productive order, after the end of the Keynesian era and of the political management of aggregate demand, have brought about an increase in the productivity of labour, so much greater than the pace of growth of production as to lead us to expect, within a short time, the end of (wage) labour.

1

The chapters of this volume propose a critical appraisal of this position, and at the same time provide an alternative reading of contemporary capitalism. Though plural and perhaps sometimes conflicting, these interpretations share the ideas that the changes affecting contemporary capitalism still revolve around the nature and the quality of labour, and that they are the effects of political choices which require political answers.

The first chapter is by Riccardo Bellofiore, who surveys the evidence for and against the aforementioned interpretation according to which capitalism is now truly global, the organization of the labour process has abandoned Fordism, and the labour embodied in capitalist production as a whole is shrinking. According to this author, the conditions that allowed for the golden age of full employment capitalism after the Second World War (above all, US hegemony and social peace within the factories) started to fade away in the mid-1960s. Globalization has been one of the capitalist strategies to counter the structural crises within valorization. However, the growth of internationalization is a limited and contradictory process. Not only are markets and production much less globalized than finance is: the same short-term mobility of hot money, which increases the risk of systemic crises and which compels governments to follow the path of deflationary monetary and/or budgetary policies, is itself the result of social conflicts and of political support from individual states (especially from the USA and the UK). It is neither natural nor irreversible. Discussing post-Fordism, Bellofiore does not deny that innovations in the organization of labour may have led to a restricted requalification of labour and to a partial autonomy of workers within production. The crucial point, however, is to understand that nowadays technological restructuring, with low and variable demand, calls for more committed labour, and that job enrichment has been precisely the means for a higher intensity of work. Thus the increased instability in working conditions is the outcome of pressures springing both from production and from the markets. Bellofiore closes by contesting the end-of-work thesis: recent inquiries confirm that wage labour is still growing on the world scale, and that capitalism since the mid-1970s has been more, and not less, job-intensive than in the Keynesian years.

In Chapter 2, Gérard Duménil and Dominique Lévy look at the same issues by means of a comparison between the US and European experiences. The 1970s saw a massive wave of unemployment in both areas. While its effects are still felt in Europe, the unemployment rate in the USA declined from 1982 onward. The rapidity of technical change does not explain the rise of unemployment, since technical change slowed after 1970 both in the USA and in Europe. Rather, structural unemployment was caused by the sluggishness of accumulation because of the diminished profitability of capital in the early 1970s, the fall in profits being in its turn brought about by the change in the rapidity and the form of technical change. In fact, the lower US unemployment, relative to Europe, was due to the dynamics of technical change, but not in the way put forward by the usual interpretation: the main point here is that, in the USA, the growth in labour productivity was lower than in Europe, while both were declining. These determinants acted in concert with macroeconomic and financial developments. The new conservative policies, in particular the high rates of interest, added to the severity of unemployment and prolonged its effects.

Chapter 3, by Suzanne de Brunhoff, concentrates on the globalization of financial capital and on its consequences in Europe. According to de Brunhoff, the internationalization of finance is limited, and is not purely economic, being supported by the most powerful developed capitalist countries. The result has been the preservation of US financial hegemony. As this author explains, the 'triadic' nature of the emerging global economy does not affect the foreign exchange market, where most Asian and some European countries make reference to the dollar. Against the background of the free mobility of financial flows, the euro/dollar exchange rate will be much more volatile than that between the D-mark and the dollar. Following Paul M. Sweezy, de Brunhoff shows that the current 'financialization' is the offspring of a renewed coalition among financial interests, central bank monetary policies and governments. A 'financialization' process of this sort imposes some finance-linked standards of capital accumulation on productive capital: searching for high and quick profitability, capitalist restructuring accelerates and reduces the employment base. The situation cannot but weaken workers *vis-à-vis* capital. However, according to de Brunhoff, nation-states which deregulated could reregulate finance. The most urgent measure is to reduce the unfettered mobility of short-term financial capital.

The relationship between globalization and restructuring is also at the heart of Chapter 4, where Hugo Radice looks critically at the experience of the UK, the country that was the pioneer in deregulating, with Mrs Thatcher, and that has now seen the emergence of a New Labour, which is no less concerned about flexibility. An important element of flexible Britain has been an ultraliberal policy towards both inward and outward investments. Among the European big four, Britain has by far the highest foreign ownership of capital, while British-owned capital has the highest proportion of assets located abroad. Economic policies and performance have therefore been shaped by global economic forces to a much greater extent than elsewhere in Europe. According to Radice, the Anglo-Saxon model of capitalism is a particularly suitable vehicle for the project of globalization. Though this model seemed hopelessly in crisis only 20 years ago, it recovered afterwards and now dominates politically the competing models. One of the reasons for the success of this model – a model which includes, as its defining features, deindustrialization, deskilling and growing inequality – is the fact that it replaces the negotiated relations with the banking system or with stakeholders with a larger base for economic and political support, such as the multitude of anonymous shareholders investing on the stock market. Blair's New Labour does not resist the ideology of globalization, it simply adds the ideology of modernization, namely, a flexibility of labour and a squeeze of wage costs mitigated, more in theory than in practice, by much talk about skills.

Globalization is again the focus of Chapter 5, by Guglielmo Carchedi, in connection this time with the European economic and monetary union. In the first part of his chapter, Carchedi argues that the internationalization of capital, the victory of capitalism over 'communism' and the alleged progressive disappearance of the working class as a result of the introduction of new technologies are ideological renderings of real developments which are better understood as the contemporary forms taken on by world imperialism, rather than following the globalization thesis. One of these forms is discussed in the second part of the chapter, namely the emergence of the European Union as an imperialist power rival of the USA, under the leadership of German oligopoly capital. It is a process still in the making, full of limits and contradictions. What must be stressed is that the deregulation of financial flows, and monetary and budgetary austerity in Europe are not merely functional to speculative capital; rather, they are the means for a greater creation of value and surplus value at the expense of workers.

The analysis put forward by Joseph Halevi in Chapter 6 starts from the role of Germany in Europe, presenting a historical perspective in relation to Europe and to Asia of the Baran–Magdoff–Sweezy neo-Marxian conception of monopoly capital. Since the 1970s, Germany has ceased to be the growth engine for European effective demand. Since then, German strategy has had two aims: to keep European competitors from devaluing against the D-mark and to finance foreign direct investments thanks to net exports within Europe. As a consequence, stagnation in effective demand and industrial restructuring are the model imposed on the whole region. These constraints compelled Germany to increase external competitiveness: the price, however, was the quantitative and qualitative degradation of employment in other European countries. This deflationary trap still works, even after the decline of real interest rates in the last few years, as a consequence of the stability pact signed in Amsterdam and Dublin. According to Halevi, a similar stagnationary tendency has been going on in East Asia. For more than 40 years, the productive dynamics of Japan's periphery has been characterized by some structural and monetary asymmetries. The most conspicuous have been (a) the role of the USA in generating effective demand and in supplying the liquidity needed to fund the current account deficit of the area, and (b) the pegging to the dollar of East Asian currencies (with the exception of the yen). Because of the former, East Asian countries have been able to overcome the constraint of their structural current account deficit with Japan, which (like Germany for Europe) is the monopolistic supplier of advanced capital goods. Because of the latter, they could export to the USA even when the expansionary effects of American support for Japan's reconstruction and of the Korean war ended. However, the collapse of the Japanese economy since the early 1990s, and the consequent devaluation of the yen, have eventually made Japan a competitor for the other East Asian countries, breaking what seemed to be a virtuous circle. Halevi concludes that neither East Asia and Japan nor Germany and Europe are capable of generating dynamic demand internally, so that both depend on net exports to the USA. However, the USA is too small, relative to Japan and Europe together, to provide the external demand the other two poles needed to avoid a state of long-term stagnation.

The three following chapters are all about the USA. In Chapter 7, Michael Perelman compares the present situation with the emergence of Fordism, in relation both to working conditions and to capitalist competition. In the USA, Fordism arose out of the resistance of workers to a new form of industrial work. The new system won because of the higher labour productivity and of the initial monopoly rents, which allowed higher wages to be paid. This original Fordism became known as the era of private 'high wage' capitalism, or as 'Welfare Capitalism'. The welfare capitalists believed that (relatively) high wages would make workers more productive and less resistant to the demand of capital. As the Great Crisis worsened in 1931, the welfare capitalists gave up their pretences and began cutting wages severely. In the process, business became discredited, and came to look to government to rescue the economic system. After the disappearance of the Keynesian boom, which guaranteed outlets but reduced the forces of competition, business successfully shifted resources from the government and labour in order to bolster profits. In addition, new markets and new source of cheap labour made profits recover. Disadvantaged groups and labour are bearing the brunt of competition, just when the new emerging industrial system is protected in the name of intellectual property rights. According to Perelman, however, nowadays we are seeing the first signs of a saturation in demand. For this reason, a new 'high wage' capitalism would be welcome. But there are other reasons as well: for instance, high wages are a less socially destructive way than deregulation and flexibility to force business to innovate.

Carl Dassbach, in Chapter 8, debunks the myths of lean production, the last and most typical instance of post-Fordism. In the last 10 years, the Japanese system of production has been touted by many as the cure for the problems confronting the motor industries of Western Europe and the USA. Lean production, its supporters claim, is a 'win–win' situation for management and labour. Management benefits from increased productivity, improved quality and lower inventory levels, while labour benefits from improved working conditions and more interesting, varied and satisfying work. Sassbach observes that, while the implementation of lean production in the USA has proved to be beneficial for management, it has failed to provide any of the promised benefits to labour. Workers in lean factories have not experienced any measurable improvement in their working conditions. Their work has not become more interesting, varied or satisfying. If anything, when compared with existing Fordist practices, lean production appears to have had the opposite effect on working conditions: lean practices have intensified the tempo of work, reduced the number of workers and increased stress and injury levels. Workers in lean factories are not, as advocates of lean production would have us believe, thinking team members who autonomously determine their activity, but living robots, whose every move is controlled and observed.

The critical attitude towards the recent changes in work organization sweeping the global economy is shared by Mike Parker in Chapter 9. The new production system is seen, at least potentially, as 'high-wage/high-performance': high skill levels and high worker involvement combined with new technology and modern workplace reorganization create high productivity which can sustain high wages and excellent working conditions. Parker carefully reviews the issue of skills in lean production, and through this 'micro' inquiry is able to reach general conclusions. The new production system is best described, from the workers' vantage point, as 'management by stress'. Management exercises tighter control, not by increasing direct observation of employees at work or by micromanaging shopfloor decisions, but by maintaining continued pressure on the total system with nested fast-response internal feedback mechanisms. In this system, management control and workers' ability and willingness to adapt quickly to shifting management demands (called 'flexibility') take priority over skill. Indeed, while the system in some cases may raise the skills floor, it also tends to retard the ability of the top skilled workers in the union bargaining unit from keeping up with changes in technology. Changes in technology both allow and are partly driven by management's ability to shift key skills from the union bargaining unit to management categories, outside vendors and non-union subsidiaries of the parent corporation. Parker acknowledges the difficulty in identifying trends: no common definition of skill exists; there is no standard to evaluate training and retraining programmes; a technology-driven change of skill requirements and training does not mean an increase in skill requirements; union involvement in institutionalized training programmes creates interests which disguise the reality on the shop floor; the distribution of skills within and outside the bargaining unit is a sensitive political question in unions; the technical content of the skills make it difficult for those without the technical background to evaluate training and skill requirements.

Chapter 10, by Antonella Stirati, Sergio Cesaratto and Franklin Serrano focuses again on the relationship between innovation and employment. It is generally recognized that the recent rate of job creation in the industrialized countries has been rather poor, particularly in Europe, and, in the last 15 years or so, unemployment has reached levels unknown in the preceding post-war period. Is technological change a cause of the current disappointing rate of job creation and high unemployment levels? This question entails a discussion of the existence of automatic, endogenous 'compensation effects' to the reduction of labour inputs per unit of output determined by technical progress. The analytical and empirical strength of some of them are assessed by the authors, in particular that of the neoclassical approach, on which the prevailing views are based, and the Schumpeterian. Stirati, Cesaratto and Serrano think that the soundest view is that of the non-conventional tradition of Keynes, Kalecki, Kaldor and Sraffa, which they call the 'long-period effective demand approach': innovation may create persistent, structural unemployment whenever the growth of effective demand is not such as to compensate for the growth of labour productivity caused by technical change. Looking at post-war experience, the chapter concludes that the very slow rate of job creation in recent years, particularly in Europe, is the result, not of an abnormally high growth of labour productivity, but of an excessively slow growth of aggregate demand. In recent years, technical change may have been of a kind particularly unfavourable to demand growth, for it seems that there has been a concentration on process innovations (which tend to destroy jobs) at the expense of product innovations (which favour job creation). However, according to the authors, this conclusion must be qualified. It is possible, for example, that radical changes in consumption patterns, and less concentration on process innovations, could have been observed had monetary policy and hence consumer credit conditions been looser over the period, and income distribution more favourable to the working classes. The policy implications drawn in the final part of the chapter include a brief discussion of the service sector and of the reduction in working time as an aid to job creation.

On the same theme, Vittorio Valli, in Chapter 11, takes as his starting point the observation that, in the period 1973–96, and in particular in the 1990s, several countries in the European Union (EU) have failed to increase labour input, that is, the total number of hours worked, whereas in the same period the USA and most East Asian countries have considerably increased their labour input. The stagnation of labour input in most EU countries has brought about a reduction of working time or of employment, or both. According to Valli, an important factor that contributes to explaining the stagnation of labour input in the EU is associated with the drop in the investment ratio and with the high proportion of intensive investment, partly induced by a sharp catching-up process in productivity. In the period of the partial demise of the Fordist model, extensive investment, product innovation, efforts in research and development (R&D) and in the upgrading of education have been too limited in most EU countries. Valli stresses that working time reduction schemes can contribute in a substantial way to reducing unemployment and to improving the quality of life. However, a greater effort to invest in human capital and to create favourable conditions for product innovation, both in industry and in the tertiary sector, as well as a less restrictive macroeconomic policy, are essential in order to re-establish a positive trend in labour input.

Again on unemployment, Giovanna Altieri, in Chapter 12, concentrates on the peculiarities of the Italian experience. Low activity rate, high female unemployment and the strong exclusion of young people from the world of work, as well as insufficiency in the employment base, are the main features of the social model on which the Italian record is grounded. This model, which gives priority to the adult male in guaranteeing jobs and welfare provisions, went into crisis when it showed itself less and less capable of adapting to the new economic and social dynamics. The novelty of the current situation is that, in some social groups, unemployment and the precariousness of all aspects of working conditions are normal in people's life experience, but this risk situation is affecting an increasing number of individuals. Moreover, increasing unemployment is accompanied by the rise in work opportunities that differ from the 'standard' work model, in terms of both working hours and contractual forms. Instead of producing a new work standard, the result has been the segregation of these segments of the labour supply. As a consequence, the social employment difficulties do not only come down to the lack of work but also imply the degradation of the quality of employment itself, as well as of the system of social and labour guarantees.

In the closing chapter, Vittorio Rieser deals with the segmentation of the labour force from the viewpoint of the changing patterns in the division of labour (both 'micro', within the firm, and 'macro', among firms). The empirical reference is again the Italian framework: namely, big firms like Fiat and small firms producing directly for the market. According to Rieser, the new kinds of work organization, implying changes in the division of labour within the firm, determine changes in the skill composition of the labour force. Flexibility requirements, just-in-time and the drive for cost reduction converge in bringing about, on the one hand, an increased exploitation (centred on the reduction of slack) and, on the other, a more unstable and diversified labour force. Divisions between 'make' and 'buy', and also in the division of labour among firms, give way to new patterns of growth in smaller firms and in other forms of (seemingly) autonomous labour. All this leads to a new and more diversified map of the labour force, where self-employment may often be a form concealing conditions of other-directed work. If the dependence of labour on capital is not shrinking, and if the potential demand for union organization and collective bargaining is larger than before, it would be deceptive to hope for simplified solutions. The path that the trade union movement should follow is an experimental one, building up experiences of organization and struggle from below to answer the peculiar needs of different kinds of workers, while at the same time trying to connect them to forms of bargaining common to the various kinds of workers dependent on capital on the post-Fordist scene.

ACKNOWLEDGEMENTS

The papers collected in this volume were all presented at the conference, 'Which Labour Next? Global Money, Capital Restructuring and the Changing Patterns of Production', held in Bergamo, 3–5 December 1997. The conference was promoted by the Department of Economics of the University of Bergamo and by the local section of the FIOM-CGIL, the left-wing trade union representing the metal workers, in collaboration with IRES, an economics and social studies think-tank. I wish also to thank Marcello Gibellini, Evaristo Agnelli, Luciano Ongaro and Francesco Garibaldo, who discussed with me this initiative from the beginning; Giancarlo Graziola, the head of the Department, for his support; Rodolfo Di Stefano, at the time managing director of Abb Sace, Riccardo Leoni, professor of Labour Economics at the University of Bergamo, and Claudio Sabattini, the national secretary of FIOM-CGIL, who spoke at the round table closing the conference. Richard Davies checked the English of several of the contributions. Last but not least, my thanks to Eugenia Valtulina for her invaluable assistance before and during the conference, to Simona Locatelli, who helped during the conference, and to Laura Capelli, the secretary of the Department.

1. After Fordism, what? Capitalism at the end of the century: beyond the myths

Riccardo Bellofiore

INTRODUCTION

'Globalization', 'post-Fordism' and 'end of work' are buzzwords littering recent discussion about present-day capitalism and the conditions of the working class: words intended to identify a new, uncharted and epoch-making historical phase. In only a few years, these terms have come to dominate political, trade union and even academic reasoning. Their spread has been, in a way, ecumenical. It is enough to look around. It is almost impossible to read a speech by the secretary of any political party, by a member of the leading classes, or by intellectuals, whether of the left or the right, without finding these words right there at the crucial nodes of the reasoning, as if they were categories requiring no argument. Naturally, the conclusions drawn and therefore the social and political policies proposed for dealing with the new era vary widely. But few seem to doubt that these are the facts.

As we shall see, however, the meaning given to these words varies. They are, in fact, myths whose evocative force takes over from the reality that they are supposed to represent but often mystify. The success of these myths forces anyone who wants to criticize them to show that they offer a one-sided picture of (some of the) tendencies at work at the end of the twentieth century. We shall attempt to present here an alternative reading of the current phase. The task is made easier by the fact that critical views exist, offering a more convincing description of present-day capitalism than that based on the lines of the globalization–post-Fordism–end of work outlook.

THE NEW ORTHODOXY

In order to establish a reference point we should provide some overview of the dominant position. The most rigorous, and in some ways most fascinating, interpretation within the new orthodoxy is presented by some intellectuals on the left.[1] The starting point is the Taylorist–Fordist–Keynesian model dominant from the end of the Second World War right up to the mid-1970s, a social and productive paradigm which, as the adjectives used to describe it suggest, was built upon the scientific organization of work, on the rigid technology of the assembly line and on the state supplying aggregate demand to firms and social security to workers. According to this interpretation, the crisis occurred because the model of life and consumption typical of the system of mass production – a system requiring a continuous increase in the demand for consumer durable goods – reached a ceiling in the mid-1970s. Saturation showed that markets were 'bounded', 'restricted'. It is for this reason that capital is said to have been forced to globalize. To save on costs, production became worldwide, and the labour market extended to cover the entire planet. To search for additional outlets, aggressive behaviour among firms worsened, and competition became general. Displacing factories made productive capital an entity disembedded from given material spaces, workforces, policies, breaking the autonomy and the power of the national governments. Keynesianism was dead forever. This deepening of the 'abstraction' of capital reached its climax on the financial markets, where the free, unlimited mobility of global money is now able to bend any government to its will.

Growth slowed down and instability increased from the mid-1970s. Thus the main problem for business became how to survive. The answer was to 'downsize' (for example, to minimize the work time necessary for production), to 'shorten' (for example, to reduce the bureaucratic apparatus); to keep low inventories ('just-in-time'), to impose continuous improvements on workers ('*kaizen*'), to strive for 'total quality' and 'participation' from the workers. The joint effects of these organizational innovations have been, on the one hand, redundancies and therefore the firing of workers and, on the other hand, an almost 'organic' unity of the workers with their firms. Factories became monistic, cancelling all traces of social conflict. The Fordist virtuous circle between investment and employment was broken: post-Fordism capitalism has systematically destroyed jobs. Mass unemployment is the result.

This is a vision with dark overtones, but one which does not differ from that of many supporters of globalized and flexible capitalism, except from the ethical and political standpoint. For them, the globalization of capital brings to fruition a thousand-year-old dream of a common home for humankind. Post-Fordism increases efficiency in production, makes work more varied and autonomous, and improves consumer satisfaction. The end of work means freedom from work, more time available for activities outside the market arena.

DECONSTRUCTING GLOBALIZATION

The triad of globalization, post-Fordism and the end of work can thus be seen as a general and systematic reconstruction of the social and economic world we live in. Before accepting it at face value, however, it is better to look closely at each element of this sequence. We start with the globalization of capital.

The expression made its appearance in managerial literature, and was used in a variety of contradictory senses.[2] The first to introduce it, in 1983, was Theodore Levitt, of the Harvard Business School, arguing for the existence of a single world market, in which companies, which still have a national base, 'sell the same things, in the same way, everywhere' – something which, obviously, is not borne out by the facts. For years Ford has chased the dream of producing the world car; and when Fiat recently launched one, the Palio, it was, on close examination, no more than a car destined mainly for the regional market in which it is produced, and for other developing areas.[3] Kenichi Ohmae, ex-director of McKinsey, used the term again at the end of the 1980s. Global integration is here the fifth stage in the process of internationalization of firms, the last link in a chain which is preceded by export from a domestic base, by the direct sales and marketing overseas, by local production in foreign countries and, finally, by the transfer of financial departments, engineering and R&D. The global phase is that in which, according to Ohmae, planning, cash flows and the recruiting of personnel are effectively carried out on a worldwide scale.

Against the background, it is interesting that at the beginning of the 1990s the ex-president of Phillips, Wisse Dekker, defined globalization as a fairly primitive stage in the process of internationalization of a company: as the stage at which part of its production process is transferred abroad to avoid import barriers or to reduce the transport costs of the finished product. A stage followed by multinationalization (where the enterprise blends completely with the host nation: 'local amongst the locals') and transnationalization (where the company produces in a network, starting from a few worldwide production centres). Even more interesting is that Dekker's sequence is not linear, with the international presence of the enterprise growing steadily in the world arena. Quite the contrary, transnationalization means a withdrawal from global reach towards a concentration of effort into the trade blocs of the so-called 'Triad' (North America, East Asia, Western Europe), something which could perhaps represent better than globalization what is actually happening these days.

The rhetoric surrounding the globalization literature loves to present it as a new phase marked by absolute novelty, a true and irreversible epoch-making change, a qualitative break with the capitalism of the past. If this refers to the growing spatial extension of capitalistic relations and to the colonization of life from the values of 'production for production's sake', we are battering on an open door. What is meant, however, is something completely different: that the interdependence and openness within the capitalist world has grown out of all proportion, so that we now live in an economy without frontiers. This can be doubted. A good reference here is *Globalization in Question* by Paul Hirst and Graham Thompson. The authors present two ideal-types:[4] on the one hand, an international economy; on the other, a truly global economy. In an international economy, nations continue to be the principal agents. Trade is specialized by national areas and there is an international division of labour. Firms are multinationals with a strong national base: a large share of output and sales takes place in the original territory. The picture can be made more realistic by adding that, nowadays, the true subjects of the international economy are big nation-states, around which the regions of the Triad revolve. In global capitalism, things are quite the opposite. The space in which production, trade and the labour market operate is planetary. There is no division, but a diffusion of labour, because the same commodities are manufactured and sold in every corner of the world. The economic process does not have strong links with any particular area: firms are transnational, and more and more mobile, like financial capital.

A glance at the empirical evidence shows that what has occurred in the last decades is the return of the world economy to the degree of internationalization already reached at the end of the nineteenth century, and has not so far been a process of genuine globalization. Between 1870 and 1913, world trade grew at an average rate of 3.4 per cent (3.9 per cent between 1899 and 1911). The rate slowed down to 1 per cent between 1914 and 1950, picking up after the Second World War (9 per cent between 1950 and 1973). Between 1973 and 1990, the annual growth in trade, 3.6 per cent, was more or less the same as it was a hundred years ago. The ratio of total capital flows to GDP during the period of the gold standard was even higher at the beginning of the twentieth century than in the 1980s. The same can be said about trade openness. And, of course, migratory flows of nineteenth-century capitalism were larger than today's migrations to advanced countries: between 1815 and 1915, approximately 100 million people moved to countries that, far from setting up rigid controls and barriers, favoured immigration. Not only is present globalization not unprecedented, it is limited and contradictory: limited because, though the figure is rising for Europe and the USA (but falling for Japan), the openness of the major trading blocks still stands at about 10 and 14 per cent; contradictory because the trend towards a greater trade integration is weakening, and a tripartite regional division of world trade is becoming more and more apparent.

Despite the liberal legend, the capitalism of the gold standard at the end of the nineteenth century was no less managed than later capitalism, though the mechanism of governance was different. We shall return to this. What must be clarified immediately is that any country, except for the leaders, lost then, as it would lose today, its independence once it chose to join the gold standard, until it decided, or was forced, to leave. We can see here a parallel and a contrast with current capitalism. The parallel has to do with the restricted room for manoeuvre in an international economy and high capital mobility. The contrast lies in the fact that, nowadays, the international monetary system is on floating exchange rates, and only limited areas are on fixed exchange rates: the chances for the exit option are higher today than at the beginning of the century, as the examples of Italy and Britain in 1992 testify.

The return of the capitalist system to the interdependence and the international integration that obtained before the First World War has been favoured by the Fordist–Keynesian interlude. There is a strong temptation to answer the new orthodoxy about globalization by saying that, in various ways, Fordism was even more global than post-Fordism is. For contingent historical reasons, and on the edge of an unstable equilibrium, the economic, political and military hegemony was concentrated in the United States. The dollar was indeed the world currency. Keynesian policies were the universal model, improving firms' expectations and driving investments, growth and employment. The model was inherently unstable because the way that the Europeans and Japanese were catching up fostered intracapitalist conflicts, because the erosion of trust in US currency led to the collapse of the gold exchange standard, and because of the growing social antagonism that arose once labour markets tightened and production speeded up. Those years of high and continuous growth were characterized by fixed exchange rates, trade integration and control of capital movement. All these features are the opposite of what emerged from the crisis of the Fordist paradigm which broke down between 1971 and 1974, with the collapse of the Bretton Woods system and the oil crises: exchange rates became flexible, financial markets were deregulated, the liberalization of capital movements became the new credo. Behind this contrast are others. With the partial exception of the USA, national and international budgets were substantially balanced in the Keynesian years. From the 1970s, deficits exploded: because of the two oil shocks; because Germany and Japan insisted on having a surplus in their trade balances, which could only result in deficits for their partners; because of Reagan's policies; and because of US bank overlending in South America. And so on.

The last two decades have seen a dramatic displacement of manufacturing towards the new industrialized countries (NICs). Some authors see this phenomenon as a cause of mass unemployment, because of the growing penetration of these newcomers into the rich markets of advanced capitalism.[5] The share of the world market taken by NICs actually grew from 2 per cent (in 1980) to 4 per cent (in 1993); in manufacturing, imports even reached

10 per cent. The phenomenon is therefore real. It signals, incidentally, the effectiveness of active policies in East Asia, such as those of South Korea, in promoting internal accumulation with price controls, subsidies and credit rationing. The state has been able to monitor the industrial structure from above and to promote a strengthening of the international position of national firms. Western unemployment, however, has little to do with the globalization of production. The overall trade balance between old and new industrial countries at the beginning of the 1990s is more, and not less, balanced than it was in the early 1960s. The reason is that markets in NICs are growing with the accumulation of capital, and it is in these markets that the multinationals of the Triad increasingly find outlets. It is true that the situation is rapidly deteriorating, but the main cause seems to be the low growth plaguing the advanced countries, not NICs' high growth.

Our argument so far, highlighting the continuity between modern capitalism and Fordism and pre-Fordism which is revealed by quantitative data, should not be interpreted as denying that there are qualitative changes going on. A first distinctive feature is stressed by Ruigrok and van Tulder: though it is not yet a reality, nor is it the inevitable outcome of current tendencies, globalization is nevertheless just one of the rival internationalization strategies for firms.[6] The authors distinguish between globalization and 'glocalization'. The former term here refers to a worldwide intra-firm division of labour, to exploit comparative advantages of particular areas (such as the low cost of labour, the innovative environment of an industrial district, and so on). A strategy of this kind naturally tends to favour the 'free trade'. Glocalization, or global localization, on the other hand, refers to a geographical inter-firm concentration of labour within the three major trading blocs. Locating production near the product market produces a gradual decline in the volume of international exchanges. The authors note that globalization is a logical extension of the micro-Fordist form of direct control, and requires vertical integration, while glocalization is more akin to the 'Toyotist' form of structural control over local suppliers, dealers, workers and government, and goes hand-in-hand with vertical deintegration. Thus, paradoxically, there is a continuity between globalization and Fordism, whereas post-Fordist glocalization runs against a higher integration among the major trading blocs.

The revolution in telecommunications and computing and the rapidly falling cost of transport have been powerful factors in fostering foreign direct investment (FDI), which after the oil crisis became the leading factor for economic growth, taking the place that international trade had occupied during the Fordist era. The *Economist* reports that, over the past decade, trade has increased twice as fast as output, whereas FDI has grown three times as fast. This second distinctive feature is fundamental for François Chesnais, in *La mondialisation du capital*.[7] The growth in FDI is associated with multinationals having a substantial productive capacity and employment in foreign subsidiaries, and with the fact that nowadays a significant share of world trade is accounted for by intra-firm trade. The best-known example is from the USA, where intra-firm trade amounts to about 40 per cent of imports and exports. However, far from spreading production worldwide, FDI concentrates it within the Triad, and within the Triad in the most advanced countries; and the concentration is rising. Moreover, FDI flows are still a small (and declining) proportion of net domestic business investment. FDI flows in manufacturing are dominated by mergers and acquisitions, that is by existing ownership changing hands, rather than arising from the creation of new capacity; and a big share of FDI is non-productive, speculative and financial ventures. These processes are anything but spontaneous, because they have been made possible by political choices, such as the liberalization and deregulation of financial markets.

Also the thesis that big modern firms are footloose transnationals does not stand up to close scrutiny.[8] The empirical evidence on the hundred most important firms in the world shows that the executive boards of the multinationals are still firmly national. The same is true for research and development and corporate financial control. Multinationals' sales and production remain mostly stuck in the region of origin: according to Hirst and Thompson (1996) between 70 and 75 per cent of their value added was earned in the home base. Research into patents by major companies, used as a proxy for their technological activities and conducted by Patel and Pavitt for the Organization for Economic Cooperation and Development (OECD) and by Archibugi and Michie, confirms that we are not witnessing a globalization of technology either. Patenting is still dominated by domestic rather than by foreign applicants, with the exception of the individual Western European countries, but not of Western Europe as a whole.[9] Therefore the three major economic areas – each of which is still more similar to a single, closed economy than to a truly open one – seem to be moving towards some kind of a new and informal protectionism, thanks to direct subsidies, tax benefits, research grants, voluntary export restrictions, bilateral agreements on market quotas, and so on.[10] This looks more like managed trade rather than the pure laisser faire of the new orthodoxy about globalization. It is against this background that the internationalization strategies of multinationals, striving to exploit all the opportunities in commodity and labour markets, have to be assessed.

Globalization of finance capital, on the other hand, is not a fantasy. This is a process which has its origins in the imbalances of many economic factors from the end of the 1960s. These have been followed since the late 1970s by restrictive monetary policies in most capitalist countries. The rising demand for finance could only be satisfied by non-banking intermediaries. Such a situation was the result of two major institutional changes: first, in the early

1970s, the collapse of the Bretton Woods pegged (but adjustable) exchange rate regime, and the transition to fluctuating rates, which in only a few years produced the liberalization of capital flows and the abandonment of quantitative monetary control; and second, in the 1980s, the financial deregulation got going by Reagan and Thatcher, political leaders of the strongest financial power and of the largest capital market. The international monetary system and the international capital markets are indeed two sides of the same coin. A floating exchange rate system allows speculative yields to be gained and compels hedging to reduce the risks due to currency fluctuations thanks to the invention of new financial instruments. Institutional restraints in the way of the constitution of a capital world market very quickly faded away. Short-term capital mobility became almost perfect, and cross-border financial transactions exploded: the annual average growth rate of cross-border trading in bonds and equities was 10 times greater than output growth rate.

The high degree of short-term international capital mobility cannot be doubted; but

> the net mobility of capital measuring the inflow minus the outflow of capital in a given period of time (flows), or on an accumulated basis over time (stocks), give a very different picture. Data on net asset positions in the nineteenth and twentieth centuries (relative to GDP or their capital stock), which represent how much capital has been transferred from one country to others on a net basis over a long period of time, clearly show that there was much more capital mobility on a net basis in the late nineteenth century than there is in the late twentieth century. (Epstein, 1996, p. 212)

Other well-established findings are that international diversification of investments is very low; that the correlation between investments and domestic savings, though falling, is very high (implying a considerable degree of international independence); that identical assets in different countries gain unequal returns; and that there is no evidence in favour of an increased tendency towards profit rate equalization. As the *Economist* put it, 'There is no "world" interest rate, and, hence, no single global capital market.' Thus, once again the strong globalization view of the new orthodoxy exaggerates the integration in capital markets.[11] Nevertheless, the removal of capital restrictions and its consequences on currency parities and on interest rate volatility have had a tremendous impact on the real economy, promoting regional divergences and income inequalities all over the world and eroding states' willingness and power to enforce policies in favour of employment and social solidarity.[12]

Rising interest rates from the late 1970s benefited creditors and rentiers, establishing a convention[13] on the financial markets that only economic policies cutting budget deficits and squeezing the money supply were credible and could be sustained. These are self-fulfilling expectations, since the government moving alone against what the markets, autoreferentially, judge as the appropriate policies sets off capital flights and speculative attacks. National economic policies are thus deprived, at one blow, of the fiscal arm and of the monetary arm. This is particularly true for small countries, less so for the leaders within the Triad, and still less for the USA, whose hegemony was shaken in the 1970s and 1980s but never broken, as the 1990s testify. For the countries involved in the European monetary union, this negative spiral was worsened by the Maastricht criteria and by the Amsterdam Stability Pact. The only economic policy left to nation-states is to follow the pressures from the financial markets towards further flexibility in the labour markets and in the labour process.

It is important to realize that the cumulative mechanism that has in this way been set in motion will produce the opposite of a real globalization of productive capital: it fragments capitalism into a few trade blocs and a few centres of power, and it fragments societies by turning workers into the shock-absorbers of an ever more unstable and precarious economic environment. What is nowadays called globalization is nothing but the (temporary) victory of the US pole in intracapitalist competition, after the collapse of actually existing socialism and the Gulf War, and against the background of a longer-run defeat of progressive social forces. The rise in the power of finance is the most powerful weapon that US capital has against its competitors as well as of capital against labour. No wonder, then, that this cumulative mechanism has perverse global effects. Higher interest rates shrink productive investment, thus slowing down, on the one hand, output and income, and on the other the growth of world trade; consumption, employment and wages are compressed and the viability of the welfare state is impaired. Such a process cannot be stopped on a purely national or local level, nor can much trust be put in reforms of international organizations, which are nowadays either too weak, or themselves promoters of the negative tendencies that need to be reversed. Suzanne de Brunhoff is right when she underlines that the most urgent issue is to limit short-term capital flows: something that few economists and politicians dare to say or do, except in the case of peripheral currencies. And she adds, quite rightly:

> The stakes in a reform of the exchange rate regime are so high that interventions 'from above' are difficult to conceive without social movements 'from below' by the workers injured by current monetary policies, or without a major international crisis such as those which have periodically ended exchange regimes in the past.[14]

The heart of the matter, in my view, is uncovered by Barry Eichengreen in his *Globalizing Capital*.[15] Eichengreen updates the well-known argument of Karl Polanyi about the tension between capitalism and democracy. According to Eichengreen, the conflict today is between the high degree of democracy reached, through struggles and catastrophes, in the middle of the twentieth century, and the capitalism of recent decades. International capital mobility and pegged exchange rates are not incompatible by nature. They were not so, for example, during the gold standard. The fact is that, between the last quarter of the last century and the First World War, governments were, so to speak, insulated from domestic politics. Defence of the exchange parity was the priority; central banks and governments were totally committed to this aim; financial markets had no reason to guess that other objectives, such as employment, could interfere with the determination to support the external stability of the currency. Between the Great Crash of the 1930s and the collapse of the Bretton Woods agreements in the early 1970s, the situation was different, marked by the conjunction of free trade and fettered finance. Pegged (but adjustable) exchange rates went hand-in-hand with capital controls, and full employment became a goal to be pursued by governments. After the mid-1970s, with economic liberalization and free capital mobility, the question of priorities in economic policy became problematic, and the markets started to bet on governments' and central banks' boldness in defending the currency. The dilemma in front of us is, then, whether to limit the extent of capital mobility or to limit democracy.

POST-FORDISM?

The passage from the Keynesian era to the flexible capitalism of the 1990s is described by many authors as the transition from Fordism to post-Fordism. I have myself already used the term 'Fordism' to characterize the 30 years of high, continuous growth after the Second World War (the French call them *les trente glorieuses*). The label is attributable to the 'regulation school', which regarded the period as one in which growth in production was driven by mass consumption, thanks to demand management by big states, and to collective bargaining between vertically integrated big oligopolistic firms and big trade unions which allowed wages to keep in step with productivity. Whatever the merits of the regulation school in posing the problem of a historical understanding of the various phases of capitalism, and in putting at the heart of its explanation fundamental changes in the capital–wage labour relationship and in the monetary system, it must be stressed that the proposed reading of the 'glorious 30 years' is factually controvertible and theoretically ad hoc.[16] It is impossible to go further into the matter here. What is sure is that some followers within the school, very often going much further than the founders suggested, have started to call post-Fordism the new productive and economic paradigm which, in their view, resolved in the 1980s and 1990s the crisis of Fordism that had developed in the late 1960s and early 1970s.

'Post-Fordism' is a vague notion, embarrassing in its programmed, astute avoidance of every positive characterization. Moreover, the literature on post-Fordism ranges from the inquiry about changes in macroeconomic development and policies to the evolutionary approach to technological trajectories and paradigms; from the geographical transformation of industrial organization to the transformations within the labour process affecting industrial relations; from contemporary art to postmodern fantasy. Here we shall only follow one theme: the discussion on the new productive order and on the consequent changes in the working-class conditions.[17]

At the beginning of this chapter we recalled that the crisis of Fordism, with the term referring to the 'macro' regulation of the economy, is imputed, by the interpretation that we are criticizing, to the rigidity of the Taylorist organization of labour and of the micro-Fordist technology of the assembly line, both unsuited to the competitive struggle in markets which have become limited and variable. Taylorism and (micro-)Fordism would have been the cause of a growing 'deskilling' because of the separation of conception and execution. In his classic book, Harry Braverman made the tendency towards deskilling the distinctive feature of capitalism.[18] Deskilling, however, went side-by-side with a transparency of antagonism over the intensity of work. An alternative view is that a cause, if not the cause, of the crisis of macro-Fordism is rather to be found in workers' disaffection within the labour process and in the vulnerability of the Taylorist–Fordist flow of production to conflict within the shop floor. What is sure is that capitalist restructuring changed the terrain of production in the following decades.

According to Michael Piore and Charles Sabel,[19] new technologies, above all the use of computers in batch production, together with the increased variability in demand and the consequent greater attention to quality, made it possible for 'artisan' forms of production to re-emerge. Mass production requires special machine tools for universal products and unskilled work, whereas small-scale flexible production uses universal machines and skilled work; in craft production there is no division between conception and execution, and hence work is more varied and autonomous. This was the original divide for capitalist development, which now is again before us after the breakdown of mass production in the 1970s. As examples of the new trend towards a flexible-specialization model, Piore and Sabel cite Japan and the so-called 'Third Italy' – the socioproductive area located in the centre and in the north-east of Italy, particularly strong in shoes, textiles and precision mechanics, often interpreted as a typical Marshallian district with its network of small firms with old manufacturing and cooperative traditions, efficient local governments and cohesive social reality. In both cases, productive units are able to bring to the market with very short delays products of high quality and/or innovative design, and to make continual improvement in the products. In a timely review, published in *Challenge*, of Piore and Sabel's book, Hyman Minsky cast doubts on the possibility of generalizing their idealized model: its success, in Italy as well as in Japan, was based on the prevalence elsewhere (at the national or international level) of expansive macroeconomic policies, without which it would have given rise to a zero-sum game.[20]

Criticisms came also from industrial economists, who pointed out that the model cannot be extended to every industrial sector. Other commentators have underlined the partiality of the examples given by Sabel and Piore in support of the humanizing and reskilling properties of the flexible production model. Finally, others have noted that firms move towards standardized mass production whenever they have prospects for long-term growth of demand. The Italian experience confirms these criticisms. The 1970s were indeed marked by the rapid growth of the flexible specialization model. The 1980s, however, saw a recovery of the large firms; while the north-east 'miracle' in the 1990s has been partly due to the competitive devaluation of the exchange rate.[21]

In favour of their thesis, Piore and Sabel also refer in their book to the computerization of the big firms, accompanied by the redesigning of skills and teamwork in groups. In the same year, two German researchers, Horst Kern and Michael Schumann, reversing the outcome of their previous research in the early 1970s showing a growing polarization of skills, claimed that what was going in the Germany of the late 1970s and early 1980s was the 'end of the division of labour' in the hard core of manufacturing: machine tools, chemicals and motor vehicles.[22] The worker increasingly had technical autonomy and had taken on the role of controller of automatic systems, so that the continuous requalification of the workforce is an internal requirement of the new automated production. The German model, partly because of trade union pressure, had then chosen a diversification of quality in mass production. Large-scale companies, though producing in high volumes, committed themselves to making profits in the upper segments of the market. Microelectronics made it possible to reach the point where total profits match total costs at lower production levels, and to employ the same machine for distinct models. In this way, the German system has been able to compete with higher wages and shorter working hours than their competitors, as well as bearing the costs of intense legal regulation, and of constant retraining of the workforce, by avoiding price competition and taking refuge in quality competition. It must, however, be added that the 'enriching' of labour, though effective, has been mostly marginal, and has not improved the lack of control by workers over the overall production process.[23]

The attempt to marry the advanced computerization of large firms and the requalification of a workforce ever more involved in the active control of production processes is also to be noted in other experiences. One of the reasons has been the failure of the totally automated factory: a dream that has invariably ended up in technical bottlenecks and in lower yields than expected. The big firms that took this route (an example is the Fiat factory at Cassino) have realized, to their cost, that the choice of a capitalistic deepening of production increased the need for more intense and more careful use of the machinery, hence of a more active participation by workers in the production process. The rhetoric about the need for an increased involvement of the workforce gathered impetus between the mid-1980s and the early 1990s with the spread of the Japanese model of organization.

The race to imitate was already under way – first in the USA and in Britain, then in the rest of Europe (as in the case of the Fiat factory at Melfi) – when, in 1990, MIT published the results of a five-year research project, *The Machine that Changed the World*.[24] In the introduction to the Italian edition, Giovanni Agnelli proclaims that the book 'shows the extent of the agreement about the undeniable obsolescence of the principles and criteria which have guided, from Ford to now, the business logics in the US and in Europe', and the contrast 'between mass production, based on large volumes, excessive standardisation and the un-differentiation of work, and lean production, based on flexibility, agile structures, the creative contribution of the individuals who participate in the production process'. The Japanese experience (concludes Agnelli) is not based on deep cultural differences, and therefore can, and must, be imitated. Lean production refers to the just-in-time method of keeping inventories low, the continuous improvement through *kaizen*, total quality attained through the participation of a skilled workforce, and the streamlining of the hierarchical chain within the firm focusing on direct production.[25] Lean production, according to the MIT experts, combines the advantages of craft production with mass production, avoiding the high costs of the former and the rigidity of the latter, thanks to multispecialized employees and highly flexible, automated machinery; and it is 'lean' since it uses a lower quantity of everything with respect to mass production: half the human resources in the company, half the production space, half the investment in equipment, half the hours for the development of new products in half the time. Moreover it requires much less than half the stock in the warehouse, manufacturing defects are not so gross and it produces an increased and ever-growing variety of products.

The MIT report has been rightly condemned for its ideological exaggerations and its apologetic tone. It is interesting to look at some of the other extreme positions in the debate. The first is that of Martin Kenney and Richard Florida in their *Beyond Mass Production*, where they rechristen the

Japanese method as 'innovation-mediated production'.[26] It is not, they claim, a system based on the coercion and exploitation of the workers, but one based on the guarantee of lifelong employment, promotion based on seniority, company unions and on the proximity and the collaboration between workers and executives on the shop floor. It originates from a genuine class compromise which allows the Japanese workers to gain some fruits of their productive efforts. Knut Dohse, Ulrich Jurgens and T. Malsch offer a quite different outlook on what they call 'Toyotism', from the name of the company which is the principal reference point in the MIT research. In a paper published in 1985, they reached the conclusion that Toyotism was not a break with the old paradigm: it rather carried to an extreme the rationalization of work and the continual flow of production, typical of the principles of Taylorism and Fordism, in a situation where the power relationships were in favour of capital, owing to the workers' defeat in Japan just after the Second World War, and firms had a free hand and could impose more stringent working conditions.[27] In the book *Breaking from Taylorism*, the three authors admitted that, at the beginning of the 1990s, a convergence of managerial strategies was under way, but they confirmed their scepticism about the novelty of Japanese production methods and the need for national adaptation: the 'after Japan strategy' was more a shaking-off of the old model than the strengthening of a new one.[28] They also observed that, where direct control of times and methods of work have been abandoned, there has been an incorporation of the standards requested of workers into the structure and design of technology itself.

The success of the Japanese model depended on historical and social conditions very different from the legend surrounding its transplantation to the west: among these conditions was the powerful strategy of division on the part of Japanese employers against workers' struggles before and after the Second World War, which led to the exclusion of the female workforce from the advantages of the system and to a chain of suppliers with low wages and precarious job conditions.[29] Moreover, job rotation and teamwork create a mechanism where control is internalized by the worker collective. However, it would be wrong to deny that the Japanese model has led to a partial recomposition of work, but the idiosyncratic nature of reskilling is the pretext for one-sided evaluation by management. There is here a sort of silent exchange in which firms cannot but gain: they recognize and stimulate knowledge and control by the workers of parts of the production process, and get back increased saturation of the planet. Intensification of work is made higher, not only through the elimination of every superfluous pore in working time, but also through the partial job enlargement which is essential to fully exploit fixed capital: the two are, in fact, the same. The minimization of the buffers needed to avoid interruptions in the production cycle or to absorb market turbulence is viable only thanks to an increased surveillance over the production flow while it is under way; and this need – which, incidentally, makes Toyotism more fragile than Fordism – can only be satisfied by an ever more careful and flexible workforce, whose consent must then be guaranteed – with the carrot and the stick.[30]

Many criticisms from the left, such as those mentioned at the beginning of this chapter, suffer here, in the uncritical opposition between Fordism and Toyotism, from two errors, which are nowadays the consequence of an older conceptual limit, the improper identification of Taylorism and Fordism. The first error is the separation of organizational innovation from technological innovation, which paves the way to the reduction of the latter to the mere mechanical incorporation of the fragmentation and simplification of labour put forward by the former. The second error is the consequent identification of capitalist control with deskilling. The interpretation that sees Taylorism extend into Fordism (or, strictly speaking, micro-Fordism) and Fordism into Keynesianism (or macro-Fordism) mistakes exploitation for the pressure for a higher effort. On this view, the fragmentation of labour operated by Taylor was translated by Ford into the mechanical movements of the assembly line, while Ohno's Toyotism gets around the rigidity of micro-Fordism by annexing the 'souls' and 'brains' of workers. Commodification reaches its climax, and living labour is actually reduced to a commodity producing commodities.

Things are not like this. Taylorism, when it was implemented, made work more intensive on a given technical basis. Conflict over the intensity of labour became transparent: for this reason, Taylorism produced a bitter social conflict and risked failure. Fordism broke workers' resistance because the control over worker effort and the pressure for an increased intensity were brought about by a radical and impersonal change in the system of machines. Successful revolutions in the organization of labour often follow, rather than precede, process innovations. A similar story can be told for the 1970s and the 1980s, with the total automation (of some phases) of the manufacturing process and the successive 'Japanization' of the workplace. The current tendency towards a partial job recomposition does not mean the infringement of the capitalist logic. Skilled workers can be subordinated to the needs of capital accumulation no less than mass workers. Incidentally, the portrayal of Fordist workers as a homogeneous mass of deskilled labour is itself a caricature: the collective worker of mechanized mass production was complex, internally differentiated, and unequal in ability and skill, albeit within a narrow range.

To sum up, on the one hand the continuity between the old and new productive orders is as important as the discontinuity, if not more so; on the other, the overcoming of the separation between conception and execution of work and of the standardization of the production process is itself the means for increasing the subordination of the labour process to the valorization process. The participation of workers in the benefits and values springing from firms' increasing competitive behaviour must not be interpreted, as many would have us believe, as the obsolescence of class conflict or of the working class. It is rather the result of a passive revolution, thanks to which entrepreneurs have been able to put the labour movement on the defensive and win temporary agreement from workers.

It is perhaps worth adding the following. According to some, post-Fordism can be identified in a reduction of wage work in favour of self-employment.[31] Many of the new forms of self-employment are rich in relational and information content, unlike traditional wage labour; but this so-called 'autonomous' labour is in fact no less other-directed than wage labour, though mediated by a different mechanism. In this research there is much that is valid. What is unconvincing is the idea that self-employment is the paradigm for post-Fordist work, and that wage labour nowadays is merely a residual: an idea that very often boils down to the dubious political project of supporting the former against the latter. In my view, both wage-earners and autonomous workers are subject to the same process of exploitation, with the impersonal forces of the market and of relational networks taking the place of direct personal control in furthering the real subordination of labour to capital. The distinctive feature of capitalistic labour is not its juridical form or the method of retribution. It lies in a double circumstance: on the one hand, in being the object of a monetary submission, so that for workers access to liquidity follows the sale of labour power, whereas for entrepreneurs a prior provision of money precedes the starting up of production and the selling of the commodity output; on the other hand, in the control of human action – in making of labour an other-directed activity – precisely as a consequence of that monetary submission. The fact that in most of the new forms of self-employment the buyer (capitalist firms) has market power over the seller (the 'autonomous' worker) obviously produces the same results as the wage contract, with some bonuses for the capitalist firm: because capital anticipations must be paid by the 'autonomous' worker, and because the cost of external control disappears: exploitation becomes self-exploitation.

STILL WORKING

The re-emergence of mass unemployment in the 1990s is very often imputed either to the lack of flexibility in the labour market or to technological and organizational innovation. Here we will deal only with the second reading, which is the most widespread in the post-Fordist literature.

This reading is best summarized with the words of Giorgio Lunghini:[32]

The stable, bijective relation between commodity production and employment has changed. It is still true that if production decreases employment decreases, but the converse does not hold, that if production recovers employment increases. Unemployment is crystallized through technological and organizational restructuring and tends to become irreversible ... When production increases but positive long waves are not foreseen, all individual entrepreneurs will take advantage of technical and organizational changes which make it possible to reduce the number of workers, and will not employ new ones. Here we see at work the structural side of employment flexibility in capitalism: labour power is a commodity whose demand can only decrease.

Post-Fordism systematically destroys jobs. The number of hours worked in so-called 'global capitalism' is going down.

Recent research casts doubts on this picture. In the World Development Report 1995, published in 1996, the World Bank disproved the myth of the reduction of the working class on a world scale.[33] The workforce of the planet was equal to 1329 million workers in 1965, increasing to 2476 million in 1995, and is expected to reach 3656 million in 2025. Their distribution by country with high, medium and low incomes is changing. In the countries with high incomes the percentage is continually falling, from 21 per cent to 15 per cent to 11 per cent; in the countries with low income it is growing, by 52 per cent to 58 per cent to 61 per cent; in the countries with medium income it remained at 27 per cent in the first two years cited and rose to 28 per cent in the outlook for 2025. In the OECD countries it falls from 20 per cent to 15 per cent to 10 per cent.

The supporters of the end-of-work thesis sometimes speak about a tendency to the reduction of the working day. But this too is false: the OECD in its *Perspectives on Employment* has for years documented that, while the yearly hours of work have effectively decreased since the end of the 1970s/ beginning of the 1980s, according to the country, since then in many countries the tendency is for them to rise. The point is confirmed by the 1996/97 report on world employment by the International Labour Organisation (ILO), where it can be seen that weekly hours of work have been rising in the USA, Japan, Canada and Italy in the last decades; the situation is stationary, or decreasing, for the other European countries.[34] The rate of employment growth everywhere has been stable since 1960, and has not slowed down significantly since 1973. Dividing the 1960–95 period into the Fordist (1960–73) and post-Fordist (1974–95) eras, the figures go from 0.3 per cent to 0.2 per cent for Europe, from 2 per cent to 1.8 per cent for the USA and from 1.3 per cent to 0.9 per cent for Japan. Per capita employment growth, which takes into account the labour force growth, confirms that there is continuity between the two phases, if not a higher destruction of jobs in the Fordist relative to the post-Fordist era: there was an increase from 0.3 per cent to 0.6 per cent in the USA, and from –0.4 per cent to 0.2 per cent in Japan, while there was a decline in Europe from –0.3 per cent to –0.4 per cent. This last figure for Europe, the ILO remarks, was due to the fact that employment growth lagged behind the growth in the labour force because of a rise in activity rates, especially among women.

The most interesting result, however, is that economic growth since 1974 has been more, not less, job-intensive than the Fordist era. The rate of growth required for the economy to start creating jobs has indeed fallen everywhere: from 2.3 per cent to 0.7 per cent in the USA, from 8.1 per cent to 2.2 per cent in Japan, and from 4.5 per cent to 1.9 per cent in Europe (for Italy, the fall was from 5.7 per cent to 2.3 per cent). The explanation of mass unemployment that appeals to technological change as the principal cause certainly accounts for the unemployment of unskilled workers in the large manufacturing firms.[35] But it cannot be accepted for the economy as a whole: the rate of growth in productivity, measured as the ratio of gross domestic product (GDP) to employment, shows that between 1961–70 and 1981–90 this figure fell from 9.1 per cent to 3 per cent for Japan, from 4.3 per cent to 1.9 per cent for West Germany, from 5 per cent to 2 per cent for France, from 6.2 per cent to 1.9 per cent for Italy, from 3.3 per cent to 2.0 per cent for Britain, and from 1.9 per cent to 1.1 per cent for the USA. The question then becomes, in general, what is the quality of the jobs created by capitalist growth after the eclipse of the Keynesian era, and also, what explanation may be proposed for the upward trend of unemployment figures in Europe?

The answer to the first part of the question is that the jobs created by economic growth in recent years have often (thought not always) been of low quality: moreover, even when jobs have been at the high end of the skill range, the new employment has been precarious. The answer to the second part of the question is easily found: the reader has only to recall the global deflationary impact of financial liberalization, reinforced in Europe by the Maastricht Treaty, on demand, income and employment. If jobs are disappearing, the reason is to be found in the defeatist attitude that, even on the left, now considers it unfeasible actively to promote a new, coordinated wave of economic growth. The only way out of the crisis of labour which is offered by left- and right-wing governments is a renewed mercantilist fight on the world market and internal austerity programmes to win the confidence of the financial markets. Even granting such a dubious line of thought, the outcome cannot but be divisions among workers, political (if not military) tensions and regional crises, leading to overproduction and financial instability.

AGAINST THE TIDE

The globalization of capital is a legend of our times, whose hidden content is the unrestrained mobility of short-term financial capital through which capitalist restructuring is imposed all over the world. Post-Fordism is an empty notion which, giving the picture of a shop floor without conflict, hides the concrete means of exploitation of today and the dialectics of conflict and cooperation which have always being present in the labour process. Work is not ending, but growing, together with unemployment, in a mixture of precariousness and exclusion.

What must be clear is that, nowadays, on all fronts – from the cultural and academic, to the political and activist – it is necessary to swim against the stream: against the stream of the new orthodoxies, against the stream of capitalist restructuring, against the stream dividing workers one against the other. The picture is bleak indeed. The capitalism of a century ago saw a growing internationalization going hand-in-hand with the strengthening of the workers' movement. The capitalism of the end of the twentieth century couples a new internationalization with the disintegration of the workers' movement, on the wave of an ideological offensive which reinstates the values of the early Manchesterian capitalism. In this combination we have the true novelty of the 'modern times' that we are living in. There is plenty of work to be done – without, it must be clear, the consolation of thinking that our effort is moving in the spontaneous direction of events. After all, to change the way things are is the reason for the workers' movement being born in the first place.

NOTES

1. For a reading of this kind, amongst the many possible sources, see Aronowitz and Di Fazio (1994), Aronowitz and Cutler (1998), Brecher and Costello (1995), Rifkin (1995), Greider (1997), Martin and Schumann (1996), Forrester (1996), Ingrao, Rossanda *et al.* (1995). The clearest and most comprehensive account is Revelli (1995; 1997). A critique of the Italian version of this interpretation was Bellofiore (1997).
2. Ruigrock and van Tulder (1995, pp. 130–39).
3. It is worth quoting the *Economist* here ('A car is born', 13 September 1997): 'Only those firms that can build the right car for the emerging markets will be able to sell enough to make money in them. But the right car for Brazil or India is not necessarily a copy of those trundling off the lines in Detroit or Dagenham. Or, indeed, Turin. That, at any rate, is the conclusion of Fiat, which has gone to great lengths to build a car especially for poorer parts of the world. ... From the Palio's design through its manufacture, it was different from Fiat's European cars.' Comparing the success of the Fiat Palio with the fate of the Ford Fiesta, launched in Brazil a month later, the *Economist* writes: 'Ford has invested $1.1 billion in a new assembly line at its factory in São Bernardo, a São Paulo suburb. Its aim was to produce exactly the same car, in exactly the same way, as it does in Western Europe. But the launch was troubled: delays and two recalls because of minor defects dented Ford's Brazilian sales and profits last year'.

4. Hirst and Thompson (1996, pp. 1–50). Useful material for criticism of the new orthodoxy of globalization, along the lines of the following paragraphs, may be found in Krugman (1996), Berger and Dore (1996), Boyer and Drache (1996), Cohen (1997), Fouquet and Lemaître (1997) and Boyer *et al.* (1997).
5. The reasons why this view is mistaken are taken from John Eatwell (1996).
6. Ruigrok and van Tulder (1995, pp. 119–51).
7. Cf. Chesnais (1997). For qualifications about FDI, see Wade (1996), on which the first half of Weiss (1997) is mostly based (the second half summarizes her argument about the importance of domestic state capacities in exploiting the opportunities of international economic change, more fully developed in Weiss, 1998).
8. Ruigrok and van Tulder (1995, pp. 152–73).
9. Patel and Pavitt (1992); Archibugi and Michie (1994).
10. Cf. Graziani (1993, pp. 260–61).
11. Together with Epstein (1996) – who quotes the classic study by Feldstein and Horioka (1980) – see Obstfeld (1995) and Zevin (1992).
12. See again Chesnais (1997).
13. Ciocca and Nardozzi (1993).
14. De Brunhoff (1996, p. 57).
15. Eichengreen (1996), especially the introduction and the conclusion.
16. The founding text of the regulation school was Aglietta (1979); Boyer (1990) is a survey by one of the leading representatives. For criticism, see Brenner and Glick (1989).
17. For a general overview, see the reader edited by Ash Amin (1994).
18. Cf. Braverman (1974). For a criticism, relevant to what follows, see Elger (1979).
19. Piore and Sabel (1984). For brief and balanced assessments of the competing paradigms which we are going to review (flexible specialization, diversified quality production, Japanization) see the first part of Appelbaum and Batt (1994), and Tomaney (1994).
20. Minsky (1985).
21. Amongst the criticisms of the flexible specialization model, one of the best is Harrison (1994).
22. Kern and Schumann (1984).
23. On the German model of the 1970s and 1980s, see Streeck (1991).
24. Womack *et al.* (1990).
25. This last point is refuted, with reference to the application of Japanese methods to US industry, in the last book by the late David Gordon (1996).
26. Kenney and Florida (1993).
27. Dohse *et al.* (1985).
28. Jurgens *et al.* (1993). On lean production as 'management by stress', cf. Parker and Slaughter (1988; 1994).
29. For a historical reconstruction of the formation of the Japanese model, see Price (1997). Following Burawoy (1979; 1985), Price rightly underlines the dialects of conflict and consent within direct production.
30. On all this, good references are Elger and Smith (1994) and Smith (1994).
31. Cf. Bologna and Fumagalli (1997).
32. Lunghini (1995, pp. 41–2). Collin (1997) provides a Marxist critique showing the links between the end-of-work thesis and the new orthodoxy on globalization.
33. World Bank (1996).
34. ILO (1996).
35. Whether we want to use the ambiguous term 'globalization' or not, the current capitalistic dynamics creates a watershed between the groups which enjoy the skill and mobility necessary to win on world markets and the groups which lose work, income and security. Cf. Rodrik (1997).

REFERENCES

Aglietta, Michel (1979), *A Theory of Capitalist Regulation*, London: New Left Books.
Amin, Ash (ed.) (1994), *Postfordism. A Reader*, Oxford: Blackwell.
Appelbaum, Eileen and Rosemary Batt (eds) (1994), *The New American Workplace. Transforming Work Systems in the United States*, Ithaca, NY: ILR Press.
Archibugi, Daniele and Jonathan Michie (1994), 'The globalisation of technology: a new taxonomy', *Cambridge Journal of Economics*, **1** (19), 121–40.
Aronowitz, Stanley and Jonathan Cutler (eds) (1998), *Post-Work. The Wages of Cybernation*, London: Routledge.
Aronowitz, Stanley and William Di Fazio (1994), *The Jobless Future*, Minneapolis: University of Minnesota Press.
Bellofiore, Riccardo (1997), 'Lavori in corso', *Common Sense*, **22**, 43–60.
Berger, Suzanne and Ronald Dore (eds) (1996), *National Diversity and Global Capitalism*, Ithaca, NY/London: Cornell University Press.
Bologna, Sergio and Andrea Fumagalli (eds) (1997), *Il lavoro autonomo di seconda generazione. Scenari del postfordismo in Italia*, Milan: Feltrinelli.
Boyer, Robert (1990), *The Regulation School. A Critical Introduction*, New York: Columbia University Press.
Boyer, Robert and Daniel Drache (eds) (1996), *States against Markets. The Limits of Globalization*, London: Routledge.
Boyer, Robert *et al.* (1997), *Mondialisation au-delà des mythes*, Paris: La Découverte.
Braverman, Harry (1974), *Labour and Monopoly Capital*, New York: Monthly Review Press.
Brecher, Jeremy and Tim Costello (1995), *Global Village or Global Pillage*, Boston: South End Press.
Brenner, Robert and Mark Glick (1989), 'The regulation approach to the history of capitalism', *Économies et sociétés*, **11**, 89–131.
Burawoy, Michael (1970), *Manufacturing Consent. Changes in the Labor Process under Monopoly Capitalism*, Chicago: University of Chicago Press.
Burawoy, Michael (1985), *The Politics of Production. Factory Regimes Under Capitalism and Socialism*, London: Verso.
Chesnais, François (ed.) (1996), *La mondialisation financière. Genèse, coûte et enjeux*, Paris: Syros.
Chesnais, François (1997), *La mondialisation du capital*, Paris: Syros.
Ciocca, Pierluigi and Giangiacomo Nardozzi (1993), *L'alto prezzo del danaro*, Rome: Laterza.
Cohen, Daniel (1997), *Richesse du monde, pauvretés des nations*, Paris: Flammarion.
Collin, Denis (1997), *La fin du travail et la mondialisation. Idéologie et realité sociale*, Paris: L'Harmattan.
de Brunhoff, Suzanne (1996), 'L'instabilité monetaire internationale', in François Chesnais (ed.), *La mondialisation financière*, Paris: Syros, pp. 33–57.
Dohse, Knut, Ulrich Jurgens and Thomas Malsch (1985), 'From "Fordism" to "Toyotism"? The social organisation of the labour process in the Japanese automobile industry', *Politics and Society*, **2** (14), 115–46.
Eatwell, John (1996), 'Unemployment on a World Scale', in John Eatwell (ed.), *Global Unemployment. Loss of Jobs in the '90s*, New York: M.E. Sharpe.
Eichengreen, Barry (1996), *Globalizing Capital. A History of the International Monetary System*, Princeton: Princeton University Press.

Elger, Tony (1979), 'Valorisation and "deskilling": a critique of Braverman', *Capital & Class*, **7**, 58–99.

Elger, Tony and Chris Smith (1994), 'Introduction', in Tony Elger and Chris Smith (eds), *Global Japanization? The Transnational Transformation of the Labour Process*, London: Routledge.

Epstein, Gerald, (1996), 'International Capital Mobility and the Scope for National Economic Management', in Robert Boyer and Daniel Drache (eds), *States and Markets*, London: Routledge, pp. 211–24.

Feldstein, Martin and Charles Horioka (1980), 'Domestic saving and international capital flows', *Economic Journal*, June (90), 314–29.

Forrester, Vivianne (1996), *L'horreur économique*, Paris: Fayard.

Fouquet, Annie and Frédéric Lemaître (eds) (1997), *Démystifier la mondialisation de l'économie*, Paris: Les Éditions d'Organisation.

Gordon, David (1996), *Fat and Mean. The Corporate Squeeze of Working Americans and the Myth of Managerial 'Downsizing'*, New York: Free Press.

Graziani, Augusto, (1993), 'Domestic and international economic changes. Embarassing correspondences', *International Review of Applied Economics*, **3** (7), 253–66.

Greider, William (1997), *One World, Ready or Not. The Manic Logic of Global Capitalism*, New York: Simon & Schuster.

Harrison, Bennett (1994), *Lean and Mean. The Changing Landscape of Corporate Power in the Age of Flexibility*, New York: Basic Books.

Hirst, Paul and Graham Thompson (1996), *Globalization in Question. The International Economy and the Possibilities of Governance*, Cambridge: Polity Press.

ILO (1996), *World Employment 1996/1997. National Policies in a Global Context*, Geneva: ILO Press.

Ingrao, Pietro, Rossana Rossanda *et al.* (1995), *Appuntamenti di fine secolo*, Rome: il manifestolibri.

Jurgens, Ulrich, Knut Dohse and Thomas Malsch (1993), *Breaking from Taylorism. Changing Forms of Work in the Automobile Industry*, Cambridge: Cambridge University Press.

Kenen, Peter (ed.) (1995), *Understanding Interdependence: The Macroeconomics of the Open Economy*, Princeton: Princeton University Press.

Kenney, Martin and Richard Florida (1993), *Beyond Mass Production. The Japanese System and its Transfer to the U.S.*, New York: Oxford University Press.

Kern, Horst and Michael Schumann (1984), *Das Ende der Arbeitsteilung?*, Munich: Verlag C H Beck.

Krugman, Paul (1996), *Pop Internationalism*, Cambridge, Mass.: MIT Press.

Lunghini, Giorgio (1995), *L'età dello spreco. Disoccupazione e bisogni sociali*, Turin: Bollati Boringhieri.

Martin, Hans-Peter and Harald Schumann (1996), *Die Globalisierungsfalle. Der Angriff auf Demokratie und Wohlstand*, Reinbek bei Hamburg: Rowohlt Verlag.

Matzner, Egon and Wolfang Streeck (eds) (1991), *Beyond Keynesianism: The Socio-Economics of Production and Full Employment*, Aldershot, UK and Brookfield, US: Edward Elgar.

Minsky, Hyman (1985), '"Review" of Piore and Sabel (1984)', *Challenge*, July–August (28).

Obstfeld, Maurice (1995), 'International Capital Mobility in the 1990s', in P. Kenen (ed.), *Understanding Interdependence: The Macroeconomics of the Open Economy*, Princeton: Princeton University Press, pp. 201–61.

Parker, Mike and Jane Slaughter (1988), *Choosing Sides. Unions and the Team Concept*, Detroit: Labor Notes.
Parker, Mike and Jane Slaughter (1994), *Working Smart. A Union Guide to Participation Programs and Reengineering*, Detroit: Labor Notes.
Patel, P. and K. Pavitt (1992), 'Large Firms in the Production of the World's Technology: An Important Case of Non-Globalisation', in O. Granstrand, O. Hakanson and S. Sjolander (eds), *Technology Management and International Business*, Chichester: Wiley.
Piore, Michael J. and Charles F. Sabel (1984), *The Second Industrial Divide*, New York: Basic Books.
Price, John (1997), *Japan Works. Power and Paradox in Postwar Industrial Relations*, Ithaca, NY: ILR Press/Cornell University Press.
Revelli, Marco (1995), 'Economia e modello sociale nel passaggio tra fordismo e toyotismo', in Pietro Ingrao, Rossanda Rossana *et al.*, *Appuntamenti di fine secolo*, Rome: il manifestolibri, pp. 161–224.
Revelli, Marco (1997), *La sinistra sociale. Oltre la civiltà del lavoro*, Turin: Bollati Boringhieri.
Rifkin, Jeremy (1995), *The End of Work. The Decline of the Global Labor Force and the Dawn of the Post Market Era*, New York: G.P. Putnam's Sons.
Rodrik, Dani (1997), *Has Globalization Gone Too Far?*, Washington, DC: Institute for International Economics.
Ruigrock, Winfried and Rob van Tulder (1995), *The Logic of International Restructuring*, London: Routledge.
Smith, Tony (1994), *Lean Production: A Capitalist Utopia?*, Amsterdam: International Institute for Research and Education.
Streeck, Wolfang (1991), 'On the Institutional Conditions of Diversified Quality Production', in Egon Matzner and Wolfgang Streeck (eds), *Beyond Keynesianism*, Aldershot, UK and Brookfield, US: Edward Elgar, pp. 21–61.
Tomaney, John (1994), 'A New Paradigm of Work, Organization and Technology?', in A. Amin (ed.), *Postfordism*, Oxford: Blackwell, pp. 157–94.
Wade, Robert (1996), 'Globalization and Its Limits: Reports of the Death of the National Economy are Greatly Exaggerated', in S. Berger and R. Dore (eds), *National Diversity and Global Capitalism*, Ithaca, NY/London: Cornell University Press, pp. 60–88.
Weiss, Linda (1997), 'The myth of the powerless state', *New Left Review*, September–October: 3–27.
Weiss, Linda (1998), *The Myth of the Powerless State. Governing the Economy in a Global Era*, Cambridge: Polity Press.
Womack, James P., Daniel T. Jones and Daniel Roos (eds) (1990), *The Machine that Changed the World: The Story of Lean Production*, Cambridge, Mass.: MIT Press.
World Bank (1996), *Workers in an Integrating World*, Washington, DC: WorldBank/Oxford University Press.
Zevin, Robert (1992), 'Are World Financial Markets More Open? If So, Why and With What Effects?', in T. Banuri and J.B. Schor (eds), *Financial Openness and National Autonomy*, Oxford: Oxford University Press, pp. 43–83.

2. Structural unemployment in the crisis of the late twentieth century: a comparison between the European and the US experiences

Gérard Duménil and Dominique Lévy

We begin with some straightforward questions concerning unemployment.

Was unemployment a result of rapid technical change (the rise of labour productivity)? No, the growth rate of labour productivity, which measures the ability to produce with less and less labour, has been *slow* since the 1970s in comparison to the 1950s and 1960s, when full employment was achieved. Yes, the high rates of unemployment in Europe in comparison to the USA basically reflect the difference in the growth rates of labour productivity, which was *low* in Europe, but *very low* in the USA.

What was the main cause of the rise of unemployment? The slowdown of capital accumulation, which was part of the structural crisis of the 1970s.

What caused the structural crisis of the 1970s? The decline of the profit rate.

What was the original cause of the fall in the profit rate? The disappearance in the late 1960s and early 1970s of certain favourable features of technical change (rapidity and forms) since the Second World War.

Is this erosion of technical progress puzzling? No, the real issue is the records of the previous decades. They were the outcome of the managerial revolution in the early twentieth century, a real transformation of relations of production within capitalism.

What was the role of wages in the decline of the profit rate? The growth rate of wages (total compensation) was 'adjusted' with some delay to the diminished performances of technical change.

What was the major policy development? Fighting unemployment is not part of the economic programme of finance. The fight against inflation was achieved in the 1980s, independently of its costs in terms of employment. Inflation was fought by large interest rates.

What were the effects of this policy? (1) Inflation was defeated; (2) firms, the state, households and Third World countries went into debt; (3) lenders became richer, poor people became poorer; (4) welfare expenses were reduced on the pretext of deficits actually caused by high interest rates; (5) the effects of the low profit rate on unemployment were exacerbated and prolonged, despite worker concessions.

Did monetary and exchange rate policies in Europe aggravate unemployment? Yes, strong pressure was placed on the general level of activity in Europe, with comparatively high exchange rates (for some countries) and a restrictive monetary policy devised to maintain very low levels of inflation and to contain the public debt. Maastricht criteria are at issue. These policies had a negative impact on investment, and therefore also on employment.

Is a recovery under way? Strong indications are apparent, and confirmed by the most recent data now available for the USA.

Would such a recovery in Europe restore employment if it is confirmed? It could, after a considerable period of time.

Could this recovery benefit workers? Yes, if they fight for it.

Could the structural crisis of the 1970s rebound into a major clash, as did the crisis of the late nineteenth century into the Great Depression? Yes, if finance resists new forms of regulation. In case of emergency, finance will immediately call for the intervention of governments and international organizations, which could possibly stop the slide.

INTRODUCTION

The large and lasting wave of unemployment that engulfed the developed countries is of major proportions. It is also a challenge for economists. There are similarities among countries, but also differences. Moreover, each decade had its own traits. The impact is different for the various categories of workers: male, female, young, old and so on. Also it cannot be understood in isolation. Everything is potentially important: technology, finance, new rules on the labour market, globalization and so on. Where to begin and where to end?

This chapter does not begin with the orthodox dogma that the causes of unemployment lie in the obstacles to the mechanisms that supposedly ensure the clearing of the labour market.[1] We will not discuss what would happen if workers always allowed wages to decline to alleged 'adequate' levels. There are two basic reasons for this choice. First, realistically workers do not behave in this manner. We can surmise that wages would not have grown much historically if workers had always complied with the requirements of profitability. In spite of large concessions during the last decades of crisis, in terms of wages and working conditions, unemployment still exists in Europe and, as we will contend, if unemployment declined in the USA, it is not because labour became more flexible but for other reasons. Second, the deflationary consequences of wages adjusting downward during recessions are at issue. They have already been the object of much academic discussion, at least since the Great Depression of the 1930s.

Our point of departure is different. It is that the problems in our econo-mies, and their solutions, are the expression of the evolution of capitalism, the shock of productive forces against relations of production, their metamor-phosis, class struggle and the non-autonomous role of the state in these transformations. In the same tradition, we believe that much attention must be paid to the movement of the important variables accounting for technol-ogy and distribution, in relation to other categories of phenomena: economic in the strict sense, institutional and political. The present chapter does not accomplish the entire task.[2] The analysis is based on a rather extensive use of data series made available by national accounting frameworks and the OECD. The investigation of each field, considered in isolation, is rapid. What we want here is to provide an idea of the broad picture.

We first discuss unemployment as a component of the structural crisis that has affected major developed countries since the 1970s. What was the size of unemployment, its profile over time, its specific features in the USA and Europe? (This study only considers France, Germany, Italy and the UK, hereafter 'Europe'.) We show that the rate of accumulation is crucial in this analysis. This investigation must, however, be supplemented by that of the historical trends of technology and distribution, in particular the decline of the profit rate. These trends explain the slowdown of accumulation, and account for the differences between Europe and the USA, which are due to the specific features of technical change. This is the object of the second section. We then show, in the third section, how the policy of high interest rates accentuated the effects of the crisis, with consequences up to the present. A final section discusses the likelihood of a recovery. We contend that the 'fundamentals' support this hypothesis. Whether all categories of the popula-tion will eventually benefit from such a recovery is another issue.

This study does not question standard statistical figures as used within national accounting frameworks or OECD data bases. As is well known, depending on the measurements used, the unemployment rate in the USA may vary between 5.4 per cent and 10 per cent. Being employed does not mean a satisfactory standard of living for workers, as well as satisfactory working conditions. A very large fraction of employed persons live below the poverty threshold, work less than they want to, and under precarious condi-tions. This study is based on the conviction that already a lot can be derived from standard statistics.[3]

UNEMPLOYMENT IN THE STRUCTURAL CRISIS OF THE 1970s

The basic characteristics of the wave of unemployment are well known.[4] As shown in Figure 2.1, unemployment rates soared in Europe[5] and in the USA in concert, from about 1973 to 1982, the size of the increase being similar. The unemployment rate in the USA reached a maximum of 9.7 per cent in 1982, when the figure for Europe was 9.1 per cent. A sharp divergence in the two evolutions was then observed. The US rate began its decline, returning to levels similar to those observed in the 1960s, while Europe fluctuated at a high level, with a maximum of 10.9 per cent in 1994. Finally, unemployment rates in 1996 are as shown in Table 2.1.

Consider the overall movement of these two rates for the USA and Europe, the trends of 'structural' unemployment, abstracting for shorter fluctuations (concentrating on the trend lines in Figure 2.1). While the first episode of the

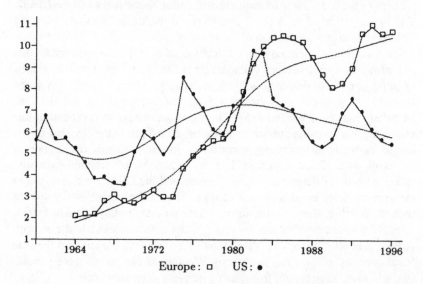

Europe: □   US: ●

Figure 2.1   Unemployment rates in the USA and all OECD European countries (per cent)

Table 2.1   Unemployment rates in 1996 (per cent)

France	Germany	Italy	UK	USA
12.4	10.3	12.2	7.6	5.4

drama was approximately the same in the two countries, the second act was quite different. Thus, a double question is posed.

- How can we account for the simultaneous rise, common to all countries?
- How can we explain the following divergence, and in particular, why has the USA fared better than Europe as regards unemployment since the early 1980s?

The first issue suggests a global approach in which we abstract as much as possible from individual differences. In the second case, the specificity of the US economy in comparison to Europe becomes a central issue. Still, each European country has its own traits.

There is obviously no 'explanation' for unemployment in isolation. The wave of structural unemployment that affected Europe and the USA from the 1970s onward can only be understood as one component of a broader phenomenon, *the structural crisis of the 1970s–1990s*. In a rather short period of time, many things went astray after 1970: the accumulation of capital and the growth of output underwent a considerable slowdown; comparatively frequent and severe recessions occurred; inflation soared; the growth of labour productivity was eroded; the profit rate declined; real wages entered a long period of stagnation.

It is difficult to pinpoint in such a system of interrelated phenomena any single factor as a *cause*. In our opinion, however, *the decline of the profit rate* has a special explanatory power and will be at the centre of our investigation. The reference to the declining trend of the profit rate raises several methodological issues. It has often been used dogmatically by Marxists. It is also clear that Marx's demonstration in *Capital* does not fully measures up to his remarkable insight into the features of technical change and distribution within capitalism. Nonetheless, we consider it a very powerful tool in the analysis of capitalism.[6]

Why is the profit rate so important to capitalism? Through what mechanisms is its influence exerted? It is rather intuitive that large profits in comparison to the funds invested in a business are favourable to the accumulation of capital; new investments are financed out of retained earnings and present profits augur well for the future. In turn, the construction of new productive capacity conditions the growth of output. The link between profitability levels and the instability of the general level of activity is more difficult to trace. Diminished profit rates reduce the cash flow of firms and put pressure on liquidity; they tend to react more sharply to disequilibria (such as a drop in demand); in this context of general 'nervousness', the macroeconomy becomes jerky. Concerning wages, the resistance of firms to the pressure for higher wages and better working conditions from workers is increased in periods of low profitability; firms actually fight to diminish the cost of labour and obtain more favourable employment conditions from the workers; high rates of unemployment tilt the balance in favour of employers; the rise of the purchasing power of wage-earners is consequently eroded or offset; actual declines might finally be imposed. There is a link between a stagnating labour cost and technical change; the stimulus to improve labour productivity is weakened.

The crisis of the 1970s was the outcome of a longer evolution. Abstracting from differences in timing between the USA and Europe, unfavourable trends of technology and distribution could be identified from the 1960s. Besides the slowdown in the growth of labour productivity and the declining profit rate, one central feature was the increasing 'burden' of fixed capital in comparison to labour and production.[7] Such a pattern of evolution is reminiscent of that described by Marx in Volume III of *Capital*. We denote this as a pattern *à la Marx*. It was also part of Marx's analysis that such trends would lead to crises. As shown in Figure 2.2, two such trajectories have been observed in the US economy since the second half of the nineteenth century, both followed by a structural crisis: the first one in the late nineteenth century and the second in the late twentieth century.[8]

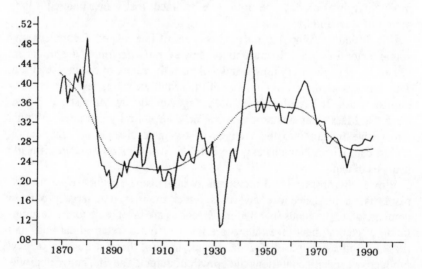

Figure 2.2   The profit rate in the USA, 1869–1993

THE FRAGILE DYNAMICS OF EMPLOYMENT

Unemployment does not only depend on the evolution of employment; it is also a function of the profile of the labour force. The relationship between employment and the labour force is complex, because they are interdependent. When employment approaches the limits of the labour force, as in the 1960s, several adjustments come into play to increase the population available for employment (immigration, participation of women in the labour force, and so on). Symmetrically, when unemployment develops for long periods of time, as in the 1980s, the labour force tends to contract; people are discouraged from seeking employment. This study does not investigate these relationships, but only considers the impact of basic economic evolutions on demand for labour.

The maintenance of full employment is a difficult process in which the major economic variables and many institutional and policy mechanisms are implicated. The sub-sections below discuss, first, the role played by the major variables accounting for accumulation and technical change in the dynamics of employment and unemployment; second, the consequences of the structural crisis, which unsettled the earlier fragile equilibrium; and third, the important differences between the USA and Europe with respect to technical change – quite slow in the USA as Europe was catching up – and the ensuing advantage for employment in Europe.[9]

Accumulation, Technology and Employment

The chain that links capital accumulation to employment (and finally unemployment) occurs through the capital–labour ratio, a measure of the mechanization of production, and the duration of labour.[10] In terms of rate of variation, this chain is as follows:

growth rate of capital
(growth of productive capacity)

−

growth rate of the capital–labour ratio
(mechanization)

−

rate of variation of the duration of labour

=

growth rate of employment

Thus, independently of the evolution of the labour force, accumulation, technical change and the duration of labour are all at issue. Consider, for example, the case of Germany in Table 2.2, which displays these rates of variation for two periods of time, before and after 1973. These figures show that full employment or unemployment follow from very fragile dynamic adjustments. The average rates of variation of employment were less than 0.3 per cent. They resulted from differences between rates of variations that were more than *10 times larger*. Consequently, any small dislocation between accumulation, technical change and the duration of labour has a large impact on the evolution of employment.

Table 2.2   Average rates of variation (per cent per year): Germany

	1960–73	1973–93
Capital	5.58	2.86
– Capital–labour ratio	6.94	3.26
– Duration of labour	–1.10	–0.63
= Employment	–0.26	0.24

As is intuitive, insufficient growth of employment of 0.5 per cent causes, independently of other changes, 10 per cent additional unemployment in 20 years! *This means that a rate of accumulation 0.5 per cent above what it was in Germany (compared to an average of 2.86 per cent after 1973 and 5.58 per cent before) from the 1970s onward would have eliminated unemployment in this country.* The same result would have been obtained with a growth rate of the capital–labour ratio 0.5 per cent below what it was (compared to 3.26 per cent after 1973 and 6.94 per cent before).

The Shock of the Crisis

Within this framework of analysis, we can address the first question raised above concerning the simultaneous rise of unemployment during the 1970s, comparing the role of accumulation and technical change. Our answer is unambiguous:

● There was a structural crisis, linked to a specific pattern of technical change – the disappearance of its earlier favourable features – leading to a decline in the profit rate. One major manifestation was the slowdown of accumulation. Because of this sluggish accumulation, too few jobs were created. The cause of unemployment was not the acceleration of technical change since, in all countries, technical change slowed.

Other competing explanations can also be dismissed. It was not the lack of demand since, with some qualification for short periods of time (as currently in Europe), productive capacity was used normally in the average. Labour was forced into large concessions: precarious and part-time employment, stagnating wages, diminished protection and so on. These concessions could have been even larger, but their limits must not be mistaken for the causes of the crisis. Conversely, finance[11] took advantage of the crisis to strengthen its grasp on society in general.

The history of capitalism shows that there is no automatic adjustment of the variables that ensure full employment. The perturbation that occurred during the last decades was actually rather small, and states were not able – in all countries in the 1970s and early 1980s, and in Europe to the present – to make the necessary adjustments. A 'little' stimulation of investment, of research and development, a degree of industrial policy, would have been required. The programme of finance does not exclude the intervention of the state, via legislation and policy. The new pro-merger attitude provides a striking example of such intervention. The same is true concerning research programmes, in computer technology, for example. *But these policies are not aimed at full employment.* Full employment will perhaps come in time, when firms' prosperity is re-established.

Catching Up

We now turn to the second question raised above: why did the USA fare better than Europe concerning unemployment after 1982? In a nutshell, abstracting from policies and politics, and considering only macro variables, the answer is simple: *there was more unemployment in Europe after 1982 because technical progress was more rapid within those European countries catching up with the USA (more mechanization, faster growth of labour productivity).* It was not because of the record performances of the USA concerning technical change, but quite the opposite. It was not because the USA grew faster than Europe, even in recent years, since growth rates in the USA were not significantly larger.

A key aspect in the analysis of technical change in major developed countries since the Second World War is catching up. Since the war, European countries (and Japan) have been gradually closing the gap that separates them from the USA. This is true for technology, management, wages, financial structures and so on. There is a very spectacular convergence of major developed countries. The term 'catching up' does not imply that these countries are simply copying the US model. There are obviously several creative elements in this process. In a world of multinational corporations, innovation goes around the world in every direction.[12] Figure 2.3 provides a striking illustration of this process. The variable displayed is the capital–labour ratio (the stock of fixed capital in volume divided by the total number of hours worked). It is a straightforward indicator of mechanization. The convergence is stunning. The series come from Angus Maddison's data base (Maddison, 1991; 1993).[13] The catching up gathered momentum around 1960, and remained very strong until the mid-1970s. Then the structural crisis is manifest, with its slow technical progress. Although this study excludes Japan, the series for this country is plotted because of its dramatic character that strengthens the general argument.

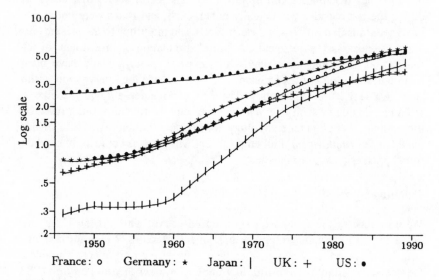

France: o   Germany: ⋆   Japan: | UK: +   US: •

Figure 2.3   The capital–labour ratio in Maddison's series

The main difference between the USA and Europe concerning unemployment lies in the unequal rhythms of mechanization depicted in Figure 2.3. Combining the European accumulation of capital with the profile of the American capital–labour ratio dramatically increases employment in Europe.[14]

This analysis must not be confused with the view that unemployment in recent decades was caused by the speed of technical progress. Looking at Figure 2.3, it is difficult to conclude that the wave of structural unemployment that developed from the 1970s was linked to rapid technical change. Globally, a central feature of the crisis was the slowdown in technical progress (notably the famous productivity slowdown). The rhythms of technical change explain the difference between the USA and Europe, not the aggregate phenomenon.

This analysis stresses a major feature of the present situation in the most developed countries. Once the choice of free trade and free capital mobility has been made, European economies must adjust, as fast as possible, to the most advanced technology and management. Improving their technology, they create unemployment by another channel. The moral of the story is as follows: *it is not good to catch up in times of structural crisis.*

There is obviously no automatic link between catching up and unemployment. After the Second World War, US technology was dramatically ahead of that of Europe. The capital–labour ratio in the USA was four or five times larger than that of Europe. The catching up was realized in a context of growth, in which state intervention played a crucial role. European states conducted active industrial and macro policies to stimulate development. Governments seized direct control of some segments of the economy. These countries enjoyed a rather large degree of autonomy, thanks to the Keynesian framework prevailing in those years, both domestically and internationally. Inflation was tolerated. The general circumstances were quite different during recent decades, under the pressure of international competition.

THE RULE OF FINANCE

Independently of the resistance to policies concerning unemployment, the rule of finance was also directly felt within its own field. We now turn to this issue. The financial picture of recent decades is not less complex than that obtained for technology and distribution.[15] In a sense, it is less 'fundamental' but it is also very important. Our major thesis in this study concerning monetary and financial mechanism is as follows: *the effects of the structural crisis in the 1970s, as it can be accounted for by the evolution of technology and distribution, were prolonged to the present by the policy of high interest rates and the subsequent indebtedness of firms.* This influence occurred primarily through the impact of interest rates on investment. The rise in interest rates discourages new borrowings and, therefore, investment. This is, however, only one aspect of the problem. Firms always hold a certain amount of debt. When old debts come to maturity, they can either be renewed at a greater cost, and firms go into greater indebtedness, or these debts can disappear without compensation. This latter outcome is also detrimental to accumulation.

The sudden rise in real interest rates after 1979 is well documented. In the 1970s, during the first steps of the crisis, traditional demand policies were used. They had been very successful during the 1960s in stimulating activity, investment and growth, but the situation was different after 1970. Inflation rates soared. A new phenomenon appeared, called *stagflation*, as inflation rates became larger during recessions. In 1979, in the USA, a sharp policy about-face occurred. Monetary authorities decided to fight inflation at any cost. Instead of directly rationing credits, the choice was made of allowing interest rates to rise to unprecedented levels. (As we will see, this policy gave finance significant advantages, independently of the fight against inflation.)

Looking at the larger picture, long-term interest rates (corrected for inflation, that is, real interest rates) fluctuated around 2.2 per cent until 1970, then declined dramatically to negative values, and finally soared after the 1982 recession to reach a plateau of about 5.2 per cent. There is no clear world-wide decrease in recent years. The same observation can be made for short-term interest rates, except for the US short-term rate that declined below 2 per cent from 1991.

It is not surprising in this context that, progressively, interest payments encroached more and more on the profits of non-financial enterprises. It is hard to imagine to what extent non-financial corporations were hurt by the rise in interest rates simultaneously with the decline in the profit rate. In 1982, the profit rate before interest payments was so low that more than 80 per cent of profits in France and Italy were, for example, pumped by interest. Only the new rise in the profit rate (before interest) allowed for some relief. It is also possible to relate the mass of net interest paid by firms to their capital stock. This ratio measures the number of percentage points of profit rates lost as a result of indebtedness. In France and the USA, where this ratio can be computed, it displays an upward trend. No restoration is clearly apparent up to 1990, then a sharp decline is observed in the USA, related to the decline of interest rates.

It is also useful in this analysis to consider the present burden represented by interest payments to the debt stock held by enterprises, the ratio of interest paid to the outstanding stock of debts. This variable can be called the *apparent interest rate*. Figure 2.4 presents its profile (corrected for inflation) for France and the USA.[16] It appears strikingly in this figure that the real cost of holding a debt has remained historically high in both countries since 1979. Under such circumstances, it is not surprising that firms primarily used their cash to pay back these debts. This is clearly confirmed by the recent evolution of the rate of self-financing of investment. In both France and the USA, this rate has remained above one since 1986 (1.27 in France in 1994). With the new recession following the 'boom' around 1990, most self-financing rates reached similar levels. The policy of high interest rates has prolonged the effects of the structural crisis up to the present time.

It is not difficult to imagine the immediate benefit of finance in this transfer of profits from non-financial enterprises, via interests, but this mechanism also used tax channels. The policy of high interest rates, besides its ruinous impact on Third World countries, actually *caused* public deficits – and not the reverse. When the flow of interest paid is subtracted from state expenses, public finance is in balance, sometimes above, sometimes below equilibrium,

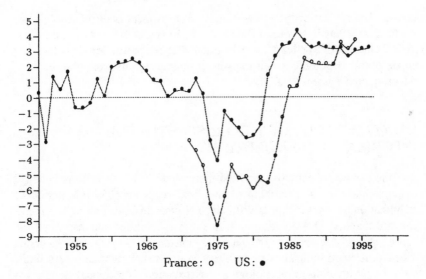

Figure 2.4 Real apparent interest rates on the debt stock

depending on business cycle fluctuations. States still held significant debts when the new policy was adopted after 1979. The short-term securities, which financed a large fraction of these debts, were renewed at the new high cost. No special device was implemented to shelter public finance from high interest rates. Although this is only indirectly related to unemployment, it is also part of the overall picture.

Another component of this analysis refers to the new financial structure that emerged under the leadership of finance.[17] We only focus here on a few quantitative aspects of this analysis. Although difficulties of measurement are particularly acute in this respect, a new feature of capitalism appears strikingly in the financial accounts of non-financial enterprises: a new network of financial relationships is progressively established; firms hold larger and larger portfolios of shares of other corporations. This is simultaneously the effect of tighter financial relationships (linked to the new wave of mergers and financial agreements) and standard financial investment. In the USA, non-financial enterprises have been consistently developing financial investment in shares or any other financial investment, paralleling their own traditional activity. This phenomenon is linked to the new prevalence of high interest rates. It seems clear that the strong heterogeneity among firms and the new financial network is central in this evolution. Large corporations, for example, enjoy a privileged access to credit channels, and they can lend under more favourable conditions to other firms (or take possession of them). The size of financial relations among firms of a same group is also well known. The impact of these new trends on investment is difficult to assess. Do firms arbitrate in favour of financial investment, at the cost of real investment? One should at least keep in mind that reciprocal lending does not create profits. But lending can transfer substantial profits from one sector of the productive system to another.

RECOVERY? OUT OF THE CRISIS WITH THE INFORMATION REVOLUTION?

As time passes, it becomes more and more obvious that something changed fundamentally in the aftermath of the 1982 recession.[18] Is it a period of stabilization or recovery? It is difficult to answer this question in a straightforward manner. The situation is different in the various countries, and the picture strongly depends on the variables considered. Nor is it easy to define a straightforward indicator of a recovery from a structural crisis, even limiting the investigation to technology and distribution. Is technical progress at issue? Is it distribution? In the latter case, the question is posed of the beneficiaries of the recovery: is a rise in the profit rate with stagnating wages a recovery?

A number of observations can be made. There is no improvement concerning wages, and the same is true for unemployment in Europe. The growth rate of labour productivity is still low. In the manufacturing sector of the economy, the profit rate stagnates at its present low levels. Capital accumulation and the growth of output are still slow, and the USA is no exception in this respect. A number of signs of improvement are, however, evident. The productivity of capital is increasing. *The profit rate is on the rise*[19] (also the share of profits in some countries). This restoration of the profit rate is illustrated in Figure 2.5 for the corporate sector in the USA. Two measures of the profit rate are plotted, the ratios to the stock of fixed capital of either profits in the broad sense (subtracting only the cost of labour from the total product), or after taxes (indirect and direct) and net interests. The recovery is striking in both cases, in particular for the first measure.

A process of economizing on fixed capital is currently under way. With stagnating wages, it has favourable effects on the profit rate. To date, this recovery has not led to faster accumulation (and growth). Consequently, no decline in unemployment is observable in Europe. One clue to help interpret this recovery is provided by the analysis of particular industries and goods. *The restoration of the productivity of capital relates to the information revolution.* Its magnitude is manifest in the proportions of the various components of investment. From 1970 to 1996, the share of information investment (computers, communication, photocopying), in constant dollars, rose from 5 per

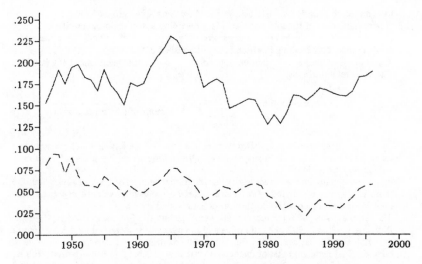

Note: Net domestic product minus total labour compensation over fixed capital stock, prior to taxes and interest payments (—) and after (– –).

Figure 2.5   The profit rate in the US non-financial corporate sector

cent to 42 per cent. This increased use of information technology was paralleled by a sharp decline in the relative price of this category of equipment.

As was noted in the previous section, this restoration in the USA also affected the financial situation of firms, in rather sharp contrast with the European countries. This is particularly clear in the relaxation of the proportion of net interest in profits.

NOTES

1. For such a demonstration, see Bean (1994).
2. A broader analysis can be found in Duménil and Lévy (1997).
3. On these issues, see Thurow (1996).
4. The analysis in this section relies on Appendix I of Duménil and Lévy (1997).
5. This is the only figure in this chapter where all OECD European countries are considered.
6. See Duménil and Lévy (1993; 1996) which discuss the origin of the bias of technical change *à la Marx* within capitalism, as well as the consequences of actual declines in the profit rate.
7. This can be measured by the ratio of fixed capital (after correction for inflation) to the number of hours worked: the capital–labour ratio; or the ratio of output to fixed capital: capital productivity.
8. See section 2 of Duménil and Lévy (1997). The existence of a downward trend of the profit rate in Europe in the late nineteenth century is not well documented. Most economic historians agree, however, concerning the existence of a 'great depression' at the end of

the nineteenth century. We also believe that there were some grounds for the insights of Adam Smith, David Ricardo and Karl Marx regarding a decline in the profit rate during the eighteenth and nineteenth centuries. Precisely during which period? Were there episodes of recovery? Nothing has been firmly established in this respect.

9. The analysis in this section relies on Appendices II and III of Duménil and Lévy (1997).
10. The basic relationship is:

$$\text{Employment} = \text{capital stock} \frac{1}{\dfrac{\text{capital stock}}{\text{total hours}}} \frac{1}{\text{duration of labour per worker}}$$

11. By 'finance', we mean the capitalist owners in a capitalist society in which property and management are separated (managerial capitalism). Finance in this sense refers to individuals and institutions.
12. Nor does catching up mean necessarily that the further behind the USA a country was, the more it progressed. Obviously, we consider here a group of developed countries. This convergence is not a worldwide phenomenon, as is well known.
13. The series ends in 1989. For recent years, see Appendix III of Duménil and Lévy (1997).
14. Between 1973 and 1992, the ratio of capital to employment increased by 1.3 per cent in the USA and 2.7 per cent in the four European countries. If technical progress in these countries had paralleled that of the USA, that is if no catching up had occurred, with no consequence for accumulation, employment in these countries would have reached 128.8 million, in excess of 30 million above present employment, also well above the labour force.
15. The analysis in this section relies on Appendices VIII and X of Duménil and Lévy (1997).
16. The average values of this rate may appear low. First, they are corrected for inflation; second, important fractions of the debt considered, such as trade credit, do not pay interest or only at a very low rate.
17. See section 2 of Duménil and Lévy (1997).
18. This section relies on Appendix VI of Duménil and Lévy (1997).
19. For the total private sector, not in manufacturing.

REFERENCES

Bean, C.R. (1994), 'European unemployment: a survey', *Journal of Economic Literature*, **XXXII**, 573–619.

Duménil, G. and D. Lévy (1993), *The Economics of the Profit Rate: Competition, Crises and Historical Tendencies in Capitalism*, Aldershot: Edward Elgar.

Duménil, G. and D. Lévy (1996), *La dynamique du capital. Un siècle d'économie américaine*, Paris: Presses Universitaires de France.

Duménil, G. and D. Lévy (1997), *Structural Unemployment in the Crisis of the Late Twentieth Century. A Comparison between the European and the US Experiences*, Paris: Cepremap, Modem.

Maddison, A. (1991), *Dynamic Forces in Capitalist Development. A Long-Run Comparative View*, Oxford/New York: Oxford University Press.

Maddison, A. (1993), 'Standardized estimates of fixed capital stocks: a six countries comparison', *Innovazione E Materie Prime*, April, 3–29.

Thurow, L. (1996), 'The crusade that's killing prosperity', *The American Prospect*, **25**, 54–9.

3. Which Europe do we need now? Which can we get?

Suzanne de Brunhoff

Economic globalization seems to be the main feature of the world today. International financial markets are its central character. According to most economists, it would now be impossible to control flows of finance across the borders of national countries. Even if it was possible, it would be inefficient. What prevails is a fatalistic economic ideology.

This chapter proposes another understanding of the relationship between globalization, nationally rooted capitalisms and political action. The most impressive form of economic globalization, the financial one, should rather be named 'internationalization' of finance: it is a process, not a global structure. It involves different forms of segmentation, and some contradictory features. This concerns the way in which the European Community is shaped as a capitalist region of the world, and the room for manoeuvre that workers' unions have today.

FINANCIAL INTERNATIONALIZATION: IMPORTANCE AND LIMITS

It is well known that international interdependence of countries, through trade, investments and finance, has considerably increased in the past few decades. For instance, in the USA, the share of exports in the output of manufactured goods rose from about 6 per cent in 1963 to nearly 20 per cent in 1993. The expansion of international finance has been much faster than that of trade, particularly since 1980. American cross-border gross transactions in bonds and equities have been multiplied by 50. A very large proportion of international financial transactions are unrelated to trade or to foreign direct investment. Gross short-term (less than one year) operations of international banking which are the core of the exchange markets of currencies, have the largest volume: daily foreign exchange turnover has increased from $15 billion in 1973 to $1.2 trillion in 1995.

Even though huge financial flows of mobile capital are daily circulating round the globe, a global single market of capital does not exist. There is no single world rate of interest and there are no single world prices for produced goods. 'One market, one price' is a theoretical fiction, whatever convergences of prices and rates of return may be. One factor of relative financial segmentation is monetary segmentation: financial assets are denominated in different currencies which are not 'perfect substitutes' for each other (nominal interest rate differentials do not cover exchange rate changes). Regimes of exchange rates between currencies, whether they are fixed or floating, take the place of a single world money, which does not exist. The abolition of exchange controls which started in the USA, in 1974, was the first and the most important measure of financial deregulation. It did not suppress differences between currencies. A first distinction must be made between currencies of the developed capitalist countries, decisive for international finance, and the others. Among developed capitalist countries, there are hierarchic differences too. The dollar, the D-mark and the yen are key currencies, and the dominant one, as an international unit of account and means of circulation, is the dollar. In the foreign exchange market it is the vehicle currency for transactions.

The 'efficiency' of this financial market is contested. The market volatility of the exchange rates, which is partly an effect of short-term finance mobility, is disconnected from what are called economic 'fundamentals', and often reflects destabilizing speculation. The dollar's variations have a worldwide influence. Strong speculative movements result in currency crises. Their consequences differ, depending on the place of the currencies in the world hierarchy.

Since 1979, there have been no dollar crises as such. The US policy of 'benign neglect' means that inconveniences of the dollar's rate of exchange instability affect other currencies' management. A notable exception of cooperation was a meeting of G5 in 1985, when American exports were handicapped by the strong appreciation of the dollar in relation to the D-mark and yen; it led to the Plaza agreements for depreciating the dollar. In the European Monetary System (EMS), secondary capitalist currencies, the pound sterling, the lira and the French franc, were attacked by speculation in 1992 and 1993. The EMS was then destroyed. But these crises were short, limited and managed by the national authorities themselves.

Of a different order are the consequences of crises of 'emerging' countries' currencies, many of them being linked to the dollar by fixed exchange rates. The Mexican peso crisis in 1994–95 and the South East Asian currencies crisis, which started in Thailand, in 1997, generated troubles in the concerned countries and in each region. In both cases, foreign financial funds, and some domestic funds, fled away. The intervention of the International Monetary Fund (IMF), together with the USA in the case of Mexico, and with Japan in the case of Asia, was required. Domestic financial systems and national rates of growth were affected.

Differences and hierarchies of currencies carry over from financial markets to some features of national financial systems. 'The global financial markets are not God-given. They are created by financial institutions as governments freed financial markets from control, since 1974' (Michie, 1995). Whatever the degree of international convergence of rates of return, financial assets are not close substitutes. The other side of the same coin is that national financial structures and availabilities matter.

Big institutional investors, like pension funds in the USA and the UK, first collect domestic savings. The greatest part of their investment, about 90 per cent, is made at home. International banks, chiefly American based, which dominate the foreign market exchange, need safe domestic systems of payments in their own countries. Deposit insurance involves governmental guarantees. Even in developed capitalist countries, financial openness and effects of international financial markets on the domestic ones do not mean that national roots of finance have disappeared. Financial internationalization does not suppress national segmentation. Monetary and financial policies matter.

The process of internationalization is not a purely economic one, driven by technological changes (development of global telecommunications networks) and by powerful market forces. It is supported by states in the developed capitalist countries. 'Competitive deregulation' is a political process unilaterally initiated by the USA in 1974 (abolition of exchange controls) and in 1975 (deregulation of the New York securities markets), to preserve the international pre-eminence of the dollar, and of American finance, during the crisis (the so-called 'stagflation') (see Helleiner, 1994). This neoliberal shift had a double meaning: it expressed the increase in international finance integration and the preservation of US financial hegemony. It paved the way for a new form of the 'hierarchic consensus' about the pre-eminence of the dollar and Wall Street, simultaneously with a hard competition between dominant currencies and financial centres.

Since the end of the 1970s, domestic monetary policies have been chiefly committed to escaping price inflation, which finance does not tolerate. Each country was supposed to put her own currency in order. Central bankers had to face the instability of the rates of exchange, and increasing risks of bank operations. The Basle Committee on Banking Supervision, established in 1974 by the central banks' governors of 10 developed capitalist countries,[1] published in 1988 a paper entitled 'International Convergence of Capital Measures and Capital Standards'. This document provided banks with a common risk-based standard of capital requirements,[2] but it only dealt with 'credit risks', not with 'market risks as the risks of loss through unfavourable movements in exchange rates, interest rates and securities prices' (Hayward, 1992). Anyhow, prudential supervision of international banks' capital ratio served as a weak substitute for international capital controls. It could not prevent financial instability and crises. Interventions of the IMF, consequent upon the crises, were required.

COMPETING VIEWS OF THE INTERNATIONALIZATION PROCESS

Some views of the globalization issue introduce different characteristics of the world economy: regionalization, differences of capitalist models, financial features of the accumulation of capital – all points which concern features of the European Community.

Regionalization

According to some economists, the emerging global economy will be regional. It is argued that 'the three economic superpowers, Japan, the United States and Europe, with their satellites, shape the global economy' (Sengenberger and Wilkinson, 1995). Most international trade takes place within three trade blocs: a North American one, a Western European one and an Asian one. Within the three regions, specific cross-national production networks are created by transnational corporations based on the three superpowers. This 'Triad' would be reflected by the international hierarchy of currencies seen above, and the competition of the dollar, D-mark and yen in the foreign exchange market.

As a matter of fact, the relationship between these currencies is not quite 'triadic', and it is changeable. In most Asian countries, and some European ones, currencies make reference to the dollar, which today dominates international financial transactions. Will the euro affect the predominance of the dollar? It will, according to some expectations pointing 'towards a bipolar system with Japan as a "junior" partner' (Bergsten, quoted in the *Financial Times*, 9 September 1997). Some Europeans, opposed to the American hegemony, now agree to the constitution of the euro, which would balance the international weight of the dollar. Recent discussions about the future of the euro/dollar have opposed supporters of a rather weak euro, favourable to European exports, to supporters of a rather strong one, in favour of domestic price stability and finance. Strange to say, these discussions do not explicitly take into consideration the danger of increasing financial instability resulting from competition between two big currency blocs. If the free market circulation of financial flows is maintained, the euro/dollar rate of exchange will be much more volatile than the D-mark/dollar one. Cooperation among central banks, if it is agreed, will not be sufficient to reduce that instability. In order to avoid a currencies war, the monetary relationships should be managed by new measures of regulation and control of the circulation of short-term financial flows of capital. Both American and European policies are today remote from this question.

Trading blocs also have some ambiguous features. They are both a step towards globalization and a defence against its domestic costs. The US trade policy reflects this ambiguity. It puts strong pressure upon regions and countries to achieve multilateral agreements for free and open trade and investment. At the same time, it promotes regional arrangements: NAFTA, including Canada and Mexico, and APEC, extended to Asian countries. This strategy of world trade liberalization through 'open regionalism' should result in US presence everywhere. It hurts the interests of other countries and of different groups within the USA too.

Even if economic internationalization was shaped by regions, the question of the world relationships between them should be considered further. Financial integration may be more important than the trade one, because finance has a relatively autonomous development. The competition between big currencies and the hegemony of one or two of them must also be taken in account.

The international management of the Asian crisis that started in June 1997 has to be considered once again (see above p. 50) This crisis is a regional one, but it calls into question the stability of world free-flowing capital, and the world management of financial slumps. Neoliberal explanations of the Asian crisis, ascertaining the absence of economic shocks in the region, refer to structural weaknesses common to the financial systems in the different countries stricken with the slump of their currencies and assets markets. The Asian crisis basically has Asian roots. As usual, IMF rescue packages were made in exchange for reforming domestic policies in a way that would open their financial systems to foreign investors.

And yet there was a turning point: when it became obvious that the financial turmoil could not be contained in a few emerging countries, and that it had reached South Korea (a member of the OECD: Organization for Economic Cooperation and Development), disturbed stock markets in rich countries and threatened corporate earnings of some multinationals, there was a shift in the US approach. Making use of the 'hierarchic consensus' seen above, the USA gave support to IMF agreements, rejected a Japanese proposal to create an Asian regional fund, and applied pressure to constrain international banks to reschedule their loans.

So the USA took the lead role in locating the Asian financial crisis within the Asian region. International interventions obviously go beyond 'market discipline' or prudential supervision of banks, and beyond regional turmoil. However, there is a new point at issue: how to manage the international financial instability induced by massive unexpected outflows or inflows of short-term capital? There is no answer from governments at the moment.

Differences of Capitalist Models

Some economists think that what is really at stake is the type of capitalism which should and could be promoted in different countries and regions. Capitalism has become the only world system, since the collapse of USSR and the uncertain future of China. However, there are different capitalist models, largely corresponding to differences between regions. The more liberal, market-oriented capitalism of the USA differs from the Japanese model, and from the German one. History, social relations, institutions and culture in Western Europe could pave the way for a political rejection of the Anglo-Saxon model, and for the quest for some 'social-democratic' oriented capitalism.

This distinction means that US capitalism is not the unavoidable fate of all countries and regions. It should not be 'equated with "modernity", the ultimate destination towards which other countries are said to be converging' (Levy, 1997). The present economic performance of the USA is not the beginning of a 'New Age' in that country: permanent growth without any more business cycles is a 'New Agers'' mirage. And the current American economic 'miracle' has been obtained at a very high price for workers and social relations. The US answer to the unemployment question does not fit Western European politics. Contestation of the Anglo-Saxon model of capitalism supposes that countries not only wish to resist, but are able to do so, and to pursue other objectives. From this point of view, 'liberalization' of trade and finance is no more a natural and irreversible process than globalization. It is a particular form and purpose of public intervention, rather than its elimination. Nation-states able to deregulate would also be able to reregulate. A new social compromise could be obtained. We come back to this question later.

Discussions about differences between models of capitalism are growing and they concern the future of the European Community. However important these differences are, *common features of capitalism today should be taken into account*. Two questions are especially relevant to the relationship between globalization and regions or models of capitalism: the 'financialization' of the capital accumulation process and the current balance of power between capital and labour.

Finance, Capital and Labour

The current financial internationalization is not a structure, but a process, chiefly set up by a restructuring of capital on a worldwide scale. International markets of finance encompass complex webs of national and international financial institutions. Generally speaking, capitalist finance accommodates the extension of productive capital. However, in some periods, its own development affects the process of capital accumulation and generates its 'financialization', in the words of Paul Sweezy (1997). This was the case between 1880 and 1913, when a coalition between financial interests, central banks and politicians was formed in the more developed capitalist countries of the time, and dominated the world financial markets. This previous trend of 'financialization' was reversed after 1914.

Nowadays, in a different situation, there is a new coalition between financial interests, central banks' monetary policies and governments in charge of economic policies. We do not know how and when this can go into reverse. A financial crisis, worse than the Asian one, is within the range of possibilities. 'The problem is that all financial markets, from currencies to shares, are subject to waves of excessive optimism followed by excessive pessimism' (*The Economist*, 17 September 1997). The wave of optimism and 'irrational exuberance' is still dominant today,[3] and it sustains the international 'financialization' process. But internationalization of financial opportunities is also that of risks and losses. When a currency and equity crisis erupts in one important financial place, as in Hong Kong in October 1997, and later in South Korea, it triggers a world slide in stock exchanges, already concerned about 'irrational exuberance'. Such a process of 'financialization', as it is validated by monetary and finance policies, includes some finance-linked standards of capital accumulation. They are connected together by the claim to freedom for national and international movements of private financial capital.

The first financial norm for economic policy, since 1980, is that of price stability of commodities within countries, or 'zero inflation'. This objective entails monetary politics of 'competitive disinflation', supervision of the stability of wages and pressures upon welfare state expenditure. High rates of return for financial assets' owners are required, and justify all free movements of capital, from short-term speculative operations to big deals for capital concentration. This affects strategies of 'real' investment, the management of firms and new practices of financial institutions and banks. 'Shareholders' are opposed to 'stakeholders', who, for instance, influence the current restructuring of German banks: they are now trying to reduce their extensive industrial stakes, and to earn more from fee-based investment banking. In general, owners of money, making more money without production, become more important than active people.

New ways of labour management are required in the quest for high and quick profitability. The main one is that of 'mobility' and 'flexibility' for workers. It means that the control of capital over jobs, wages and working conditions must be freed from national regulations, and from some international labour standards. Hard competition between corporations is put forward to justify high rates of return, between 15 per cent and 20 per cent, for share owners. Labour costs must be adjusted to this norm.

The effects of finance-linked standards upon workers are often concealed by the question of trade in products and services, which seem to owe their competitiveness to low labour standards. Unions in the capitalist developed countries sometimes call for a 'social clause' that would reduce the competitive advantage of developing countries. Some economists think that the growing inequality or unemployment in capitalist developed countries is a result of extensive trade with the 'South'. This is contested by most studies, which show that the increase of inequality and unemployment in capitalist countries has domestic roots. If international competition drives down labour standards, such as the minimum wage, rules on working hours, influence of trade unions and so on, it operates through the 'conservative revolution' initiated by Reagan and Thatcher in 1979/80 and more or less extended to all capitalist countries by coalitions of financial interests, central banks and governments. The costs of international competition have been shifted on to workers by national class policies everywhere.

After considerations of 'the comparative advantages' of free trade, it is now largely admitted that there are 'losers' in the capitalist countries. In the current competition, what to do with unskilled workers, who suffer low wages or widespread unemployment? To subsidize or educate them, public spending is needed, but this would weigh on public finance. This notion of 'losers' should itself be discussed. The working class is divided by some stratification, but it has a common fate. Recent events in western Europe show how relative it can be. When the French company Renault closed down its car plant in Vilvorde, Belgium, the losers, Belgian workers, were no more unskilled than workers in French plants. As a matter of fact, all workers are losers, because they are all more vulnerable to competition with one another, and to control of capital over jobs. Mass laying off is a practice of large international companies, called 'killers' of jobs in the USA, which destroy jobs when their financial rate of return is below the high ratings of investment performance.

Finance-linked standards are today the main consideration of capitalist interests. The 'financialization' of capital accumulation means that the balance of power between capital and labour has shifted, to the advantage of capital, in most countries. A decisive question is to appreciate the influence of finance-linked norms upon the behaviour and mind of social groups, and the working class itself. Leftist criticisms of the unproductive use of money by speculative finance, inspired by the Keynesian tradition, are well founded, but they are sometimes disconnected from an analysis of the meaning of financial internationalization, and of the endogenization of capitalist financial norms within capitalist practices and national class policies. Criticism of the convergence criteria imposed by the Maastricht Treaty on the adherents of the euro, and of the Stability Pact, is necessary. However it should be related to a discussion of the clause on freedom for national and international capital movements which is included in the Maastricht Treaty. How is it possible to promote a new 'social compromise' without facing class policies dominated by capitalist finance?

Consequences for labour of the free capital movements are perhaps less obvious than the effects of free trade. Some trade protectionism, including the relative depreciation of the national (or European) currency, may be a claim backed by a large fraction of business, besides workers and farmers,[4] but it may involve dangerous nationalism, xenophobia and racism, which increase the division of workers. A European Community acting as a fortress against foreign unskilled workers, at the same time as it is open to free flows of finance, would catch European workers in a trap.

A new regulation of finance should imply a political struggle against the dominant coalition which supports 'financialization'. Even if this struggle were a condition for the construction of a particular social model of European capitalism, better than the Anglo-Saxon one, it is not directly considered. What dominates is the fear of capital flight elsewhere, towards rival countries or regions, as if nation-states, or Europe itself, were powerless. Even moderate propositions for reducing currency speculation, like the Tobin tax on short-term exchange transactions, are not seriously taken into consideration. As a matter of fact, they would change the rules of the game in finance. Perhaps a worldwide financial crisis, starting with speculation on a central market, and including threats of deflation, would pave the way for some reregulation of finance. But without a new balance of power between capital and labour, this could also be dangerous for workers and other people.

Calls and struggles for a European Community different from the one established by the Maastricht Treaty and the Stability Pact are well founded. But it seems difficult to contest the Anglo-Saxon model, and to promote a more civilized European capitalism, without considering real obstacles, and real room for manoeuvre existing today. The internationalization process of capital accumulation, and its 'financialization', are not natural and irreversible data. They have internal limits and contradictions. They dominate economic policies through prevailing capitalist interests, and political and ideological agreements. All of these can be contested by unions searching for another Europe. International convergence of workers' struggles could oppose international 'financialization' of capital.

NOTES

1. The Committee's Secretariat is provided by the Bank for International Settlements, in Basle (Switzerland), whose role is very important for meetings and agreements between the main central banks' governors and staffs (Helleiner, 1994).
2. In the definition of banks' capital, core capital comprises equity and disclosed reserves for all banks. The Basle Agreement set a minimum ratio of capital to weighted risks assets of 8 per cent (Hayward, 1992).
3. Today: March 1998.
4. Some approaches of sectors within the capitalist countries make distinctions between two broad groups. The first includes financial private interests, finance managers, nationally based multinationals, competitive producers of traded goods and services; the other includes domestically bound producers of non-tradable goods and services. Interests of these two groups can conflict with monetary and exchange policies (Frieden, 1988). However, these analyses do not consider class policies and the common interests of capitalist groups *vis-à-vis* the workers.

REFERENCES

Brunhoff, S. de (1996), 'L'instabilité monétaire internationale', in F. Chesnais (ed.), *La mondialisation financière. Genèse, coûte et enjeux*, Paris: Syros.

Frieden, J.A. (1988), 'Capital politics: creditors and the international political economy', *Journal of Public Policy*, reprinted in J.A. Frieden and D.A. Lake (eds) (1995), *International Political Economy, Perspectives on Global Power and Wealth*, New York: St Martin's Press, pp. 282–98.

Hayward, P.C. (1992), 'Basle Committee on Banking Supervision', in P. Newman, M. Milgate and J. Eatwell (eds), *The New Palgrave Dictionary of Money and Finance*, vol. 1, London/Basingstoke: Macmillan, pp. 288–98.

Helleiner, E. (1994), *States and the Reemergence of Global Finance*, Ithaca, NY/ London: Cornell University Press.

Levy, J.D. (1997), 'Globalization, liberalization and national capitalisms', *Structural Change and Economic Dynamics*, a North Holland Elsevier Journal, **8**, Amsterdam: Elsevier Science.

Michie, J. (1995), 'Introduction', in J. Michie and J.G. Grieve (eds), *Managing the Global Economy*, Oxford: Oxford University Press.

Sengenberger, W. and F. Wilkinson (1995), 'Globalization and Labour Standards', in J. Michie and J.G. Grieve (eds), *Managing the Global Economy*, Oxford: Oxford University Press.

Sweezy, P.M. (1997), 'More (or less) on globalization', *Monthly Review*, September, **49** (4).

4. Britain under 'New Labour': a model for European restructuring?[1]

Hugo Radice

INTRODUCTION

The sweeping victory of 'New Labour' in the May 1997 elections was not marked by expectations of dramatic change in the political–economic institutions, practices and policies inherited from 'Thatcherism': the Labour leadership had carefully avoided, over several years, making the sort of promises that helped to return a Socialist government in France shortly after. Nevertheless, it is fair to say that many on the left and centre-left expected that *some* central aspects of the Thatcher model would go. There would clearly be no return to Keynesian fiscal activism or public ownership, but Labour had flirted with institutionalist critiques of Thatcherism, particularly with regard to the labour market (skills and training, minimum wage) and the capital market (corporate governance, financial short-termism) and this suggested a possible shift towards a 'social market', 'trust-based' or 'organized' variety of capitalism. Even some of the big business allies of the Labour leadership seemed to be sympathetic to this (for example, David Sainsbury and Chris Haskins).

Some 10 months later, however, there had been continuity more than change. The more visible changes – towards central bank independence, away from 'Euro-scepticism' – have been not only modest, but also not inconsistent with the inherited neoliberalism. Meanwhile, the government has renewed the privatization programme, has still not decided on its minimum wage policy, is stalling on the restoration of trade union rights, is pursuing US-style 'welfare-to-work' policies, maintaining the British nuclear 'deterrent', and so on. More generally, the government has trumpeted its belief that the 'flexibility' of modernized, globalized British capitalism makes it an appropriate model for continental European economies mired in high unemployment and slow growth.

The major exception to this has been the new government's acceptance of the Social Chapter, and its stated commitment to participate in future EU developments of labour and welfare measures. This has in principle met one of the main objectives of the British labour movement, which during the 1980s dropped its opposition to European integration, seeing Brussels instead (especially during the Delors presidency) as a potential source of support against the ravages of Thatcherism. However, the positive assessment by the unions of New Labour's engagement with its EU partner states has to be tempered by an understanding of the radical changes wrought in the past 20 years in the economic and managerial environment facing labour *throughout Europe*, not just in Britain.

This chapter explores the nature of the 'British model' and examines some of its causes and consequences. The general context of this appraisal is the continuing and connected debates on, first, the myths and realities of globalization and regionalization, and, second, the restructuring of work organization and the markets for labour and capital: that is, the direction of change, and possible convergence, of distinct national 'industrial orders' or 'business systems' (see, for example, Berger and Dore, 1996; Boyer and Drache, 1996; Hirst and Thompson, 1996; Lane, 1995; Radice, 1998; Smith and Elger, 1997). The next section summarizes some of the historically rooted features of the British model; the third section considers how far this model matches the current transnational ambitions of capital in general (that is, is globalization inherently 'Anglo-Saxon'?); the fourth section examines some aspects of the Anglo-Saxon model by comparison with alternative 'organized' models; and the chapter concludes with a summary prognosis for European labour.

THE BRITISH MODEL

A large literature developed from the 1960s on the historical 'peculiarities' (Fine and Harris, 1985) of British capitalism, mainly trying to explain the inexorable relative decline of Britain's economic performance in general, and its manufacturing sector in particular (the literature as a whole is summarized well in Coates and Hillard, 1995). On the right, the blame for decline was placed on the trade unions, the welfare state, or the 'anti-business' attitudes of the intelligentsia and the media; on the left, it was placed instead on the historical dominance of trade and finance over industry, the legacy of empire and post-imperial pretensions, or the amateurism of managerial elites both private and public.

In the 1980s, Thatcherism strove to break the syndrome of decline on the basis of a distinctive neoliberal critique, which placed the blame firmly on the strength of organized labour, and the excessive size and interventionism of the state. Extensive privatization, welfare cuts and anti-union laws were followed by a feverish boom in the late 1980s, centred on financial services and property development, and bringing with it a substantial redistribution of income and wealth from poor to rich (for details, see the essays in Michie, 1992). Those who rejected the neoliberal diagnosis and policies were not surprised when nemesis arrived, most notably in Britain's departure from the European Exchange Rate Mechanism (ERM) in 1992. Nevertheless, the relative rate of decline in several indicators of economic importance had halted or at least slowed by the mid-1990s.

In the meantime, a rather different critical literature arose which looked more deeply at the institutional foundations of the British political economy. Most notably, *The State We're In*, by *Guardian* journalist Will Hutton, became an unexpected best-seller in 1995: Hutton offered a powerful critique of Britain's institutions, centred on finance and industry but extending into many other areas also. But behind this lay a large and still growing body of academic work, on a range of topics:

1. A major programme of research at the National Institute of Economic and Social Research examined the differences in *productivity* between Britain and other European countries on a sectoral basis, and linked these differences to *training systems and the deployment of skills* (Prais, 1995).
2. On *innovation performance*, important weaknesses were revealed, such as the preponderance of defence-related work in industrial R&D and in the public finance of innovation, and the apparent inability to carry a strong research base forward into commercial development (for example, Walker, 1993).
3. Students of *labour markets and industrial relations* argued that the shift towards more decentralized, company- or plant-level bargaining, and 'numerical flexibility' through reliance on external labour markets, were perpetuating shopfloor antagonisms and a mutual lack of commitment between management and labour. Hence the apparent victory over labour in the Thatcher period could not shift British industry on to the higher productivity growth path expected from new technologies and new forms of work organization (for example, Visser and van Ruysseveldt, 1996).
4. The longstanding criticisms of the dominance of the City (the London-based centre of the financial services sector) over industry re-emerged in the more precise form of the *'short-termism' thesis*: this argues that the stock-market-based system of industrial finance, coupled with the dominance of private institutional investment funds (life assurance, pensions), compels businesses in general to pay attention to dividend payments and share price rises, rather than to long-term investments in innovation or training (for example, Dimsdale and Prevezer, 1994).
5. The overcentralized nature of the British state and the absence of strong regional institutions have been blamed for the persistence of *large re-*

gions of industrial decay and high unemployment, which have either missed out on the Thatcherite booms or experienced only the growth of low-skill, low-wage assembly work (for example, Hudson *et al.*, 1997).

Important though these arguments are, the focus on *national* institutions and practices has tended to draw attention away from one of the most important features of the British political economy, namely the extremely high *internationalization of capital*: although this is taken into account in many of the contributions to these debates (for example, on regional development or on innovation), it has received rather little attention in its own right (but see Fine and Harris, 1985; Radice, 1995). Levels of foreign investment, both inward and outward, are far higher in relation to the size of the economy when compared to the other three large European economies (see Barrell and Pain, 1997). As well as high levels of foreign *direct* investment, *portfolio* investment – again, both inward and outward – is also very much higher, while London dwarfs other European financial centres in the issuing and trading of global financial instruments of all kinds. Discussion of the consequences of this internationalization has focused on four issues in particular.

First, the general role of London as a financial centre is widely seen as having encouraged, for many decades, government policies aimed at supporting a high value of the pound, high interest rates and an advanced liberalization of capital markets in general and foreign capital movements in particular. These policies in turn have supposedly damaged the growth of both exports and investment, and hence the growth of output, productivity, employment and real wages.

Second, the importance of overseas assets and employment to British-based firms, and of foreign-owned assets and employment in the UK economy, has made successive British governments firmly committed to a liberal policy regime on foreign direct investments, both in the UK itself and in intergovernmental policy forums such as the OECD and the ILO. This has subjected British workforces and communities to forms of blackmail by mobile capital; reduced levels of corporation tax to among the lowest in Europe; and led to government expenditure on industrial support being devoted mainly to giving incentives to foreign investors.

Third, British businesses, especially in manufacturing, were seen as substituting investment abroad for investment at home. Before Thatcherism took hold, the argument was that British capital was escaping low profit and growth rates at home (or poor industrial relations in the anti-union version) by investing in more dynamic regions such as continental Europe or North America. More recently, such investment is seen as motivated by the search for cheaper labour, or for a superior technology or production environment, depending on the sector. However, the view that production abroad substitutes directly for exports, thus hitting output and jobs at home, is too simplistic, because it ignores the need in many sectors for firms to get behind tariff or non-tariff barriers, or to be 'embedded' in local networks, if they are to supply local markets at all (for example, witness the rapid growth in FDI in the USA by first Japan and then Germany).

Lastly, inward direct investors, whether from the USA (before 1970 and since 1990), continental Europe (since 1970) or Japan (since 1980), are widely criticized for creating mostly low-wage, low-skill employment, especially in so-called 'screwdriver' assembly plants.[2] The recent scale of these investments further reflects the desire of non-European investors in particular to use Britain as a low-cost platform for supplying Europe as a whole. While this view accords with the evidence in consumer electronics and many areas of engineering, other sectors such as pharmaceuticals and finance are, it has been argued, attracting 'high-quality' investments from abroad (though doubt has been cast on the UK success in pharmaceuticals by Froud *et al.*, 1997). Even in the automotive industry, the demise of the last British-owned mass assembler belies continuing strength in important component and sub-assembly areas (such as diesel engines), as well as automotive design. Nevertheless, what is undeniable is the transfer of *strategic control* of large parts of the British economy to foreign ownership.

This deep internationalization of the British economy was a major reason why capital so readily accepted the Thatcherite programme (Radice, 1986). Deregulation went furthest and fastest in financial services, but other sectors also welcomed their increased freedom to invest abroad (the last remaining controls on capital export were abolished in 1979), which enabled them to compete globally despite the apparently weak national economic performance. After 1979, North Sea oil revenues, a savage industrial recession and the accompanying high value of sterling encouraged a vast outflow of both portfolio and direct investments. But long after the disappearance of these short-term conditions, the financial sector has continued willingly to supply funds to successful British-based transnational corporations (TNCs) to finance takeovers and other investments abroad. On top of this, British disclosure rules and the general aura of the UK's financial success have also enabled them to tap foreign sources of finance. In a broader historical perspective, from around 1960, the *reinternationalization* (following a period of relative closure since 1931) of British capital steadily undermined the *economic* viability of the corporatist alternative presented by Labour and the centrist wing of the Tory party. After 20 years of this, British *politics* then quickly succumbed to the traditional, dominant, nineteenth-century ideologies of free markets (neoliberalism) and free trade (globalization).

At the same time, this deep internationalization is closely linked to the traditional dominance, economic and political, of the financial sector. Financial capital comes into its own in periods of economic crisis: it provides the means by which capitals can withdraw from unprofitable production, regroup and then transform themselves again into productive form. It also provides a haven in which capital can obtain its highest form, the nirvana of M–M', the circuit of money capital: making money out of money without having to extract surplus-value directly from production. Although Britain is no longer the 'rentier state' of the pre-1914 period when measured by the net income from foreign investments as a proportion of national income, the return on its net assets abroad, plus the transaction income from trading in financial instruments of all kinds, contributes a far more important share of total profits than in any other major European economy.

GLOBALIZATION, NEOLIBERALISM AND THE 'ANGLO-SAXON' MODEL

The conclusion from the analysis so far is that the 'British model' is now not simply one of flexible markets in the abstract (which means of course nothing more than the freedom of capital to accumulate by whatever means), but concretely one of untrammelled international mobility for capital, and of the dominance of financial interests and motives. This suggests that the British model may be, not only the ideal exemplar of financial orthodoxy and neoliberalism, but also a particularly suitable vehicle for the project of globalization.

The problem here lies first in disentangling the myths and ideologies of globalization from the realities. In centre and left-wing circles, both in Europe and elsewhere, there is a great deal of scepticism about globalization. This scepticism is associated in particular with institutionalism, regulation theory and various other schools of critical political economy (post-Fordist, post-Keynesian, neo-Schumpeterian and so on) (for example, Hirst and Thompson, 1996; Boyer and Drache, 1996; Ruigrok and van Tulder, 1995; Wade, 1996; Weiss, 1997). The common sceptical viewpoint is that globalization is most important as an *ideology* of big business: first, the extent and/ or depth of globalization has been exaggerated in order to present it as an inevitable and irreversible trend; and second, the reduction in the ability of nation-states to defend the interests of their citizens, when threatened by this trend, has also been exaggerated, in order to disarm potential opposition. These two propositions are accepted as regards the exaggeration for ideological and political effect; however, the sceptics tend to make the opposite mistake of underplaying the realities of globalization, and likewise of overstating the capacity of individual nation-states (or, sometimes, regional blocs) to impose priorities other than those of 'global' capital.

At the heart of this misunderstanding is the tendency of the sceptics to accept at face value an a priori and indeed *essential* opposition between capital and the nation-state. Ironically, the general form of this supposed opposition (market versus state) is at the heart of the neoliberal theory they claim to oppose. If the existing form of state is seen as intrinsically *capitalist*, representing the interests of capital in general, and the *nation*-state is seen as intrinsically part of a worldwide inter-state system (rather than an autonomous political agent) then it is precisely this opposition between 'capital' and the 'nation-state' which is revealed as an ideological veil. It is true that for a particular historical period – generally between about 1870 and 1970 – the working classes were able to make important gains within the political framework of the nation-state, but that was in the context of imperial rivalries exploding in world wars; the creation of mass trade unions, socialist parties and later the Soviet challenge; and, from 1929, cataclysmic economic depression which shook capitalism to its foundations. In the last 25 years or so, capitalist classes have quite unexpectedly recovered their confidence by reversing many of the post-war gains of labour. Not only have they 'restructured' workplaces, labour markets and so on, they have also re-established a global private financial system and restructured the nation-state system itself. The Keynesian ideal of a global regulatory system governing international trade, investment and finance has been reconstituted as a normative agency for enforcing the will of global capital markets – and this transformation has been, remember, *willingly accepted* by the vast majority of governments (any that disagreed are, almost without exception, no longer in power). They have, furthermore, turned the ancient humanist ideal of political internationalism into the exclusivist form of the regional trade bloc.

The sceptics argue that this is too pessimistic a conclusion; they feel that a renewed programme of 'reregulation' and reform is still feasible. This is entirely possible, but the sceptics do not offer any realistic road to change. In the light of the history of our nearly finished century, it is surely realistic to be pessimistic about the willingness of *capitalism* to reform *itself* beyond the most minimal measures. But by confining themselves to the political terrain of the nation-state, or at best the regional bloc, the sceptics are themselves being pessimistic *about labour*, and about labour movements in particular. The alternative to capitalist 'globalization' surely starts from the internationalization of labour, not the defence of the capitalist nation-state.

From this perspective, it is realistic to see the British, or more generally 'Anglo-Saxon', model as a serious economic and political threat to labour throughout Europe, and indeed throughout the world. The British state pioneered the liberalization of capital controls, the acceptance of IMF conditionality (in 1976), the mass privatization of public utilities and the dismantling of laws and regulations offsetting the inbuilt disadvantages of labour in labour markets and in the workplace. Thatcherism found its strongest ally in Reaganomics, and fostered the resurgence of free-market economics everywhere. The 'daughter' states of the 'white dominions', Australia and, still more, New Zealand, have in some respects taken Thatcherism further. Meanwhile, the Third World debt crisis which exploded in 1982 led in due course to the forced acceptance of neoliberalism throughout the underdeveloped world. The Anglo-Saxon model has dominated *politically* the restoration of capitalism in the Soviet bloc, even though compromises have been necessarily in practice. And now the latest 'regional crisis', in East and South-East Asia, is openly being exploited in an effort to force open the last bastions of state-led 'developmentalism'.

It should be stressed that none of this means that Anglo-Saxon capitalism is inevitable and irreversible. On the contrary, it is subject to very widespread resistance. The point to emphasize is that, 20 years ago, the Anglo-Saxon model seemed to be on the ropes, with the USA following Britain into stagflation and relative industrial and economic decline. Now, New Labour's version of the British model fully adopts the ideology of globalization, adding to it the even more vacuous ideology of 'modernization', which, despite the lip-service paid to training, seems to mean nothing more than achieving world market competitiveness by squeezing wage costs. The British model looks strong and self-confident, while the proponents of 'organized' or 'trust-based' industrial success are on the defensive (Streeck, 1997).

THE ANGLO-SAXON MODEL VERSUS AN 'ORGANIZED' ALTERNATIVE

It might well be objected that the Anglo-Saxon model's current success is merely conjunctural: that Britain's present relative boom arose only because her departure from the ERM triggered a premature end to the recession which persists elsewhere in Europe. Certainly, there is no shortage of commentators who continue to argue that important core features of the German or Japanese industrial orders (these are the two customary comparators in British debates) still represent fundamentally superior *principles* for capitalism (for example, Albert and Gonenc, 1996; Perkin, 1996). Before considering this point concretely in relation to European restructuring, we need to go a bit further into these principles.

In a classic contribution on work organization under capitalism, Friedman (1977) argued that two basic ways of establishing the control of capital over labour could be identified: *direct control*, typified by Taylorism, and *responsible autonomy*, typified by the then fashionable alternative of 'job enlargement', or earlier by the Hawthorn experiments. In Friedman's view, these could be seen as sequential alternatives, or subject to variation across sectors, or across levels within the hierarchy of skill and pay. In addition, he saw the form of control as closely related to the nature of labour markets and the evolution of labour's own organizations; and both the forms of labour control *and* their effectiveness as conditioned especially by the fundamental antagonism between labour and capital and the outcome of class struggles. This sort of approach was reflected in other writings in the new 'labour process' tradition, and in the various strands of the regulation school. The roots of this analysis lie in Marx's identification of the basic contradiction in the capitalist labour process: while the capitalist who buys labour power owns the potential for value creation, that potential still has to be extracted. Neither the length of the working day, nor the intensity of work, can be determined by appeal to any economic law; nor can the effective and timely conversion of raw materials and equipment into products saleable at a profit. Friedman's two types of control represent abstract strategies, while the capitalist must find concrete institutions and practices that can give an acceptable degree of control in the particular circumstances.

In the more recent debates, however, this point of origin has been lost, and instead we are asked to 'see' these abstract strategies as forming (obviously in connexion with other phenomena) the basis for different 'industrial orders'. In an extreme case, Lipietz (1997) sets out a chain of variant combinations of the two strategies, which are identified as distinct possible *national models*, ranging from the 'neo-Taylorism' of the USA (maximal direct control) to the 'Kalmarism' of Sweden (maximal responsible autonomy, or 'negotiated involvement'). The significance of this is the hypothesis that the latter is, first, preferable and, second, open to political choice.

But does capitalism offer such a straightforward choice; and if so, does it do so on a *national* basis? If the answer to these questions is a simple 'yes', then throughout Europe labour can indicate its clear preference for the model of negotiated involvement, especially if it continues to be associated with higher wages, better work conditions, more jobs, a superior welfare system and so on. But what if the answer is more complicated? Suppose that *some* workers are offered negotiated involvement, while others are subject to direct control? What if the dividing line between them runs, not neatly along national boundaries, but rather across and between regions, sectors, firms, individual plants, 'segmented' labour markets and, finally, workgroups? What if the price for Kalmarism in Sweden is neo-Taylorism in Portugal? And what if employers *in reality* offer subtle mixes of the two, as in the supermarket checkout, where workers benefit from the bar-code reader, but are thereby subject to stringent invisible policing of their pace of work? Realistic answers to these questions lead to the conclusion that labour movements need, now as ever, to question the *basic right to control*, not just its modalities, and to develop complex and multifaceted strategies which challenge division and exclusion.

Matters turn out to be just as complicated when we consider the question of corporate ownership, finance and control. Models of corporate governance exist primarily to regulate relations between individual owners of capital. For all the talk about 'stakeholder' models which 'incorporate' the interests of labour or the public at large, their basic aim is to secure a legal structure within which the capitalist labour process can take place, under conditions where the scale of production requires a collective or corporate form of capital. The vaunted German model of two-tier board with worker representation still leaves the final say in the hands of the owners: in the end, it is the traditional organizational strength of labour that matters, not having seats on the board.

It is true that the very existence of a legal framework at all gives the lie to the ideology of the free market, since only the state has historically been able to provide 'rules of the game' for the conduct of business. In certain respects and under certain historical conditions, the dominant owners of capital have had to make deals with the state, as in the case of patent systems or the principle of limited liability, which restrict the exercise of ownership rights. The embedding of employee rights, as in Germany, Austria and Sweden, occurred in specific historical circumstances when the political power of capitalists was at its weakest, through defeat in armed conflict or class struggle. Naturally, those who support employee rights argue that such 'stakeholder' forms of governance generate intrinsically superior economic performance, in the sense of long-term growth in productivity and living standards. In addition, it can be argued that a more 'stakeholder'-type system is likely to persist as a *consequence* of superior performance (in capitalist terms): so long as there are enough profits in aggregate to keep all capitalists content, they will cooperate and even extend the benefits of accumulation to employees. However, when this condition no longer holds, they seek to assert their individual ownership rights and to focus on improving performance through cutting wage costs.

The Anglo-Saxon model of corporate governance, on the other hand, evolved historically as a means of drawing into capitalist accumulation the monetary hoards of a large and varied middle class, either through direct share ownership (the USA) or via investment intermediaries (the UK), thereby allowing the banking system to concentrate on financing transactions rather than on accumulation. It substitutes stock market liquidity for the negotiated relations required between the much smaller number of owners typical of continental Europe; and it resolves the problematic relationship between industrial and banking capital also found in the latter. Despite being apparently prone to speculative disasters, the Anglo-Saxon system provides flexibility for capital, and a wider base of economic and political support for the capitalist class. The critique of 'short-termism' may appeal to the left, but it has yet to make serious political headway.

The clear conclusion from this is that corporate governance is, as much as work organization, a 'contested terrain'. From a capitalist standpoint, a market-based system of finance and control is both economically and politically preferable, although concessions may have to be made at times of acute political weakness.

EUROPE AT A CROSSROADS?

The argument above suggests that the two broad models of industrial order can only be judged from a class standpoint. What, then, can we say about the concrete prognosis for Europe? In order to simplify matters, let us take for granted that we are talking about two or more industrial orders in the broad sense, in which 'sub-systems' of industrial relations, labour markets, training systems, finance, state industrial policies and so on are all quite closely interlocked. Let us also assume that, broadly speaking, Europe remains capitalist, in the sense that it remains divided between a capitalist class and a working class, with interests that are fundamentally irreconcilable, but which nevertheless are in practice accommodated through the outcome of industrial and political struggles. In that case, there seem to be two general propositions which follow from the analysis so far: first, that in the present circumstances of deeper internationalization and, especially, transnational restructuring, there is a process of permeation or mutual erosion of national orders; and second, that in these same present circumstances, capitalists are seeking to shift Europe as a whole towards a more Anglo-Saxon model.

The cross-penetration of capital in Europe, especially since the Single Market, is an undeniable fact. While restructuring in some sectors might take place primarily on a national basis, accompanied by competition through exports, cross-border mergers and takeovers have grown enormously, and have added to the Europe-wide restructuring of production in existing transnational groups (including those based outside Europe). The present preoccupation with monetary union seems to have suspended further EU legislation in areas like company law and industrial relations for the time being. But even in the absence of such changes, cross-border capital flows and production integration entails the mutual accommodation of hitherto separate markets, institutions and practices. A *European* capitalism is emerging.

At the same time, in so far as there is a fusion between different industrial orders, it seems that New Labour's claim to offer a superior model of capitalism is credible from a capitalist standpoint. The privatization movement has spread from Britain right across Europe. Employers everywhere, backed by bodies like the IMF and the OECD, call for more flexible labour markets.[3] Independent shareholders are challenging cosy networks that maintain corporate control through cross-shareholdings and interlocking directorships.[4] Some academics, at least, suggest systematic shifts towards a more liberal model, for example in France (Schmidt, 1996) or Germany (Streeck, 1997), even if these claims are disputed by others (for example, on Germany, by Carlin and Soskice, 1997). Above all, however, the internationalization of capital – *not* just 'Europeanization', but including investments to and from other regions of the world economy – is deepening in the other larger European economies (and has long been apparent in smaller ones like the Netherlands and Sweden).

So 'which labour next?' In terms of a response to these trends, only three conclusions will be suggested. First, it is clearly *European* labour. Of course, it is in principle open to the left in any country to pursue a national road, to seek to block the processes of European integration in order to preserve past gains, or even to advance further the interests of labour; but the existing reality of integration makes this option highly doubtful except in very distasteful political company. Secondly, programmatically, we have nothing to lose by advocating reforms towards a more humane capitalism, but we have to recognize that they will not be readily conceded, without a struggle, to more than a thin layer and/ or in favoured core locations in Europe. If such reforms are to be permanent, and to provide a springboard for more radical change, they must be universal across Europe, and based upon the *highest* levels of employee and union rights, the *highest* levels of welfare, not the lowest. Thirdly, we have to integrate our own organizations and our own politics at the European level, if we are to have any chance of succeeding in this.

NOTES

1. For advice on the revision of this chapter, I am grateful to participants at the Bergamo conference, and to my colleagues Rumy Husan and Paul Marginson.
2. Although critics of poor UK productivity say much the same about UK-owned companies: see, for example, Prais (1995, ch. 3).
3. For example, BDI president Hans-Olaf Henkel, on a recent visit to England (as reported in *The Guardian*, 28 November 1997, p. 22).
4. See Jack (1997) for a detailed account of recent shake-ups in the French alliance system.

REFERENCES

Albert, M. and R. Gonenc (1996), 'The future of Rhenish capitalism', *The Political Quarterly*, **67**(2), 184–93.

Barrell, R. and N. Pain (1997), 'The growth of foreign direct investment in Europe', *National Institute Economic Review*, **160**, 63–75.

Berger, S. and R. Dore (eds) (1996), *National Diversity and Global Capitalism*, Ithaca, NY: Cornell University Press.

Boyer, R. and D. Drache (eds) (1996), *States against Markets: The Limits of Globalization*, London: Routledge.

Carlin, W. and D. Soskice (1997), 'Shocks to the system: the German political economy under stress', *National Institute Economic Review*, **159**, 57–96.

Coates, D. and J.V. Hillard (eds) (1995), *UK Economic Decline: The Key Texts*, London: Harvester Wheatsheaf.

Dimsdale, N. and M. Prevezer (eds) (1994), *Capital Markets and Corporate Governance*, Oxford: Oxford University Press.

Fine, B. and L. Harris (1985), *The Peculiarities of the British Economy*, London: Lawrence & Wishart.

Friedman, A. (1977), *Industry and Labour: Class Struggle at Work and Monopoly Capitalism*, London: Macmillan.

Froud, J., C. Haslam, S. Johal, K. Williams and R. Willis (1998), 'British pharmaceuticals: a cautionary tale?', *Economy and Society*, **27**(4), 554–84.

Hirst, P. and G. Thompson (1996), *Globalization in Question*, London: Polity Press.

Hudson, R., M. Dunford, D. Hamilton and R. Kotter (1997), 'Developing regional strategies for economic success', *European Urban and Regional Studies*, **4**(4), 365–73.

Hutton, W. (1995), *The State We're In*, London: Jonathan Cape.

Jack, A. (1997), 'New tricks for old dog', *Financial Times*, 26 June, p. 29.

Lane, C. (1995), *Industry and Society in Europe: Stability and Change in Britain, Germany and France*, Aldershot: Edward Elgar.

Lipietz, A. (1997), 'The post-Fordist world: labour relations, international hierarchy and global ecology', *Review of International Political Economy*, **4**(1), 1–41.

Michie, J. (ed.) (1992), *The Economic Legacy 1979–92*, London: Polity Press.

Perkin, H. (1996), 'The third revolution and stakeholder capitalism: convergence or collapse?', *The Political Quarterly*, **67**(2), 198–208.

Prais, S.J. (1995), *Productivity, Education and Training: An International Perspective*, Cambridge: Cambridge University Press.

Radice, H. (1986), 'Le thatcherisme et ses alternatives: quel est l'avenir du capitalisme britannique?', in L. Jalbert and L. Lepage (eds), *Néoconservatisme et restructuration de l'état*, Montréal: Presses Universitaires de Québéc.

Radice, H. (1995), 'Britain in the world economy: national decline, capitalist success?', in D. Coates and J.V. Hillard (eds), *UK Economic Decline: The Key Texts*, London: Harvester Wheatsheaf.

Radice, H. (1998), '"Globalization" and national differences', *Competition and Change*, **3**, 263–91.

Ruigrok, W. and R. van Tulder (1995), *The Logic of International Restructuring*, London: Routledge.

Schmidt, V.A. (1996), *From State to Market: The Transformation of French Business and Government*, Cambridge: Cambridge University Press.

Smith, C. and T. Elger (1997), 'International competition, inward investment and the restructuring of European work and industrial relations', *European Journal of Industrial Relations*, **3**(3), 279–304.

Streeck, W. (1997), 'German capitalism: does it exist? Can it survive?', *New Political Economy*, **2**(2), 237–56.

Visser, J. and J. van Ruysseveldt (1996), 'From pluralism to ... where? industrial relations in Great Britain', in J. van Ruysseveldt and J. Visser (eds), *Industrial Relations in Europe*, London: Sage.

Wade, R. (1996), 'Globalization and its limits: reports of the death of the national economy are greatly exaggerated', in S. Berger and R. Dore (eds), *National Diversity and Global Capitalism*, Ithaca, NY: Cornell University Press.

Walker, W. (1993), 'National innovation systems: Britain', in R.R. Nelson (ed.), *National Innovation Systems: A Comparative Analysis*, Oxford: Oxford University Press.

Weiss, L. (1997), 'Globalization and the myth of the powerless state', *New Left Review*, **225**, 3–27.

5.   The euro and Europe's labour

Guglielmo Carchedi

THE MYTH OF GLOBALIZATION

With 1999 upon us, writings on Economic and Monetary Union (EMU) and
the euro become increasingly abundant. This quantitative increase, however,
is hardly matched by their theoretical diversity: those analyses which are not
placed within a monetarist framework fall into an approach resting on the
globalization thesis. Analyses based on the labour theory of value, that is on
the production and distribution of value, even though potentially much more
fruitful, are few and far between. A first purpose of this chapter is to contribute to the development of such an alternative view.

In the monetarist approach the sudden eruption of monetary crises, the last
one having occurred in 1994–95, is ascribed to purely speculative capital
movements; the inability by some (at the time of writing, almost all) member
states to achieve the EMU convergence criteria seems to be caused only by
lack of fiscal discipline; and the introduction of the single currency, the euro,
is seen purely as a monetary operation. This chapter focuses, not on this
approach, but on the globalization thesis.

Usually, this thesis emphasizes three aspects. First is the further internationalization of capital within which the multinationals play a predominant
role. In this view, not only national capitals but even nation-states are no
match for global capital, which is often seen only in its financial form.
Second, there is the epochal victory of capitalism over so-called 'communism'. This makes it possible for capital to penetrate territories from which it
had been excluded from the Bolshevik revolution until 1989 and for democracy to be spread to all four corners of the world. It is, of course, a specific
type of democracy, which is functional for the development of capitalism,
that is referred to. Third, the new technologies will not only foster the further
capital internationalization but will also radically change our daily lives. The
two examples most commonly mentioned are the computer and information
technology. These technologies will put an end to human labour (and thus to
the working class) thus allowing men and women to become the arbiters of
their own destiny.

Such is the apologetic view. However, reality is different. To see this, it is not sufficient to stress the class content of the concept of globalization, that is the glorification of capital inherent in it. One should also analyse those real developments which are perceived by this concept, even though in a distorted way. To do this, one needs a different theoretical frame, one which allows us to see globalization as a partially new form of modern imperialism. The dominant role of the multinationals, the great mobility of huge masses of capital on the international financial markets, the fall of the Soviet Union, the constant introduction of new technologies: all these are real developments. However, the notion which unifies them in one single concept, globalization, is aggressively ideological. These aspects are seen as elements of a system which, having defeated its mortal enemy, 'communism', puts an end to history and opens the doors to a general cornucopia and global democracy. It is true, it is added with some embarrassment, that unemployment, poverty, wars, ecological disasters and so on have not disappeared, but these are residues of the past which will be wiped out by the triumphal march of global capitalism. In short, if capital were a person, this would be its rosiest dream.

Against this backdrop, let us briefly examine three specific claims made by the theorists of globalization. First, it is claimed that technological innovations (TI) will lead to the disappearance of the working class. Let us begin with some figures. While, in the early 1970s, there were 7000 multinationals, this figure had risen to 37 000 in the early 1990s. These 37 000 enterprises had 170 000 subsidiaries in the whole world. The largest 300 multinationals control one-quarter of the world's productive assets and almost half of foreign direct investments. Approximately 70 per cent of international trade is accounted for by the largest 500 multinationals. This huge concentration of economic power becomes even more visible in the financial sphere. These and other, similar figures are a vivid substantiation of Marx's theory of capital concentration and centralization. What does this mean for the working class? The 72 million workers employed by the multinationals are only 5 per cent of the world's labour force. Does this mean that, if we extrapolate this tendency, the working class is melting away? Certainly not. The reason is simply that there cannot be capitalism without a working class. Capitalism's essence is the production of value and surplus value and only labourers can produce (surplus) value. Without labourers there would be no capitalists; there would only be petty commodity producers (possibly operating at high technological levels). What these figures do mean is that, as the share of the world economy accounted for by the multinationals increases, difficulties of realization and poverty will increase too.

Second, it is claimed that TI will bring a general cornucopia and higher employment while increasing skills and work satisfaction. As far as the relation between TI on the one side and unemployment and lower wages on the other is concerned, analysis in terms of value and surplus value shows that the introduction of TI is the basic cause of both unemployment and decreasing real wages. It is impossible, within the limits of this chapter, to even summarize this thesis. The reader is referred to Carchedi (1991a; 1991b). This chapter will only briefly deal with the claim that TI brings about better jobs and working conditions.

There is no doubt that the application of TI has a profound effect on the composition and transformation of the working class. As I have argued through the years, one of the fundamental legacies left by Marx is that of developing his embryonic analysis of mental labour in order to identify new forms of labour as well as of what Marx called, in the third volume of *Capital*, 'non-labour'; that is, the work of control and surveillance. TI, however, while possibly leading to greater welfare for privileged strata of the working class, also leads to new forms of labour's subordination to capital. For example, the computer is a great step forward, not only in human productivity but also in labour's control by capital. But even more dangerous is the great stride made towards genetic engineering. This, on the one hand, alleviates human suffering but, on the other, is already creating new forms of life which reflect the capitalist division of labour and are functional for profit making. One aspect of capital's dream is that of moulding life itself in its own likeness.[1]

But new forms of labour's oppression should not hide the fact that the old forms are still alive and well. It is general knowledge that unemployment in the EU has reached 20 million. Perhaps less well known is the predicament which the mixture of TI and neoliberalist policies has brought to Europe's labour. According to a recent study by the European Foundation for the Improvement of Living and Working Conditions (Dublin) while levels of unemployment reach an average of 11.5 per cent, half of Europe's workers work for more that 40 hours a week and a quarter for more than 45 hours. For those lucky enough to have a job, rhythms of work are very high and working conditions appalling. Half cannot decide when to take their holidays and about 40 per cent have no influence either on when to take breaks during working time or on the tasks they have to perform. For almost 40 per cent, tasks are repetitive, for 45 per cent there is no task rotation at all, and for almost 60 per cent tasks are completely deskilled and consist of simple repetitive movements of the hand or of the arm. As many as 12 million workers are subjected to psychological violence, six million to physical violence and three million to sexual harassment. Work-related illnesses are on the rise and 30 per cent think that their work is a danger to their health. A quarter concede that they seek refuge from too high work rhythms in sick leave (European Foundation for the Improvement of Living and Working Conditions, 1997). There is nothing exciting for labour in globalized Europe.

Third, it is claimed that financial capital seems to have crushed the economic power of nation-states and central banks. It is common knowledge that, every day, 1200 billion dollars roam the international financial markets in a constant quest for speculative profits: a huge mass, whose movements not only cause the volatility of interest rates but also influence and sometimes dictate national economic policies. This is so, but these figures should be put in their proper perspective.

To begin with, while capital movements have basically a speculative nature, the source of this enormous mass of financial capital resides in the fact that that capital which cannot find a profitable outlet in the productive sphere tries its luck in financial/speculative operations. Seen from this angle, the magnitude of financial capital looking for speculative profits is an indication of the gravity of the present economic crisis. It is these figures, together with unemployment figures, rather than gross national product (GNP) figures, which are a reliable indicator of nations' economic health. It is these figures which reveal to us that the present economic crisis is far from having been overcome.

Moreover, the so-called 'globalization' of financial markets should be seen as a partially new form of appropriation of international surplus value. This is tied to seigniorage. Within limits, seigniorage means being able to print paper money with which real value (commodities) can be paid for without having to give back any real value. The nations which can exercise seigniorage are those whose money is the international money (the US dollar, but also, increasingly, the D-mark and the Japanese yen) because their economic power, and in the last analysis their level of productivity, is consistently greater than that of the other nations. It follows that the globalization of the financial markets, with the emergence of three rivals competing for the role of the only international currency (just like the US dollar after the Second World War), is a struggle among nations and their capitals for the appropriation of gigantic quantities of the world's surplus value as a reward for having reached a dominant technological position.[2]

EUROPEAN MONETARY UNION AND THE SINGLE CURRENCY

Having argued that these new aspects stressed by globalization theory indicate, in a distorted way, a new stage of imperialism, let us now focus on the effects of these new developments for a specific geopolitical area, Europe. The thesis submitted in what follows is that the European nations have to aggregate in an economic and monetary union in order to compete with the two other major blocs, the USA and Japan.[3] This, however, takes place under the leadership of Germany. This leadership is accepted because it allows for a common advantage, the extraction of greater surplus value by European capital. To understand this, an example will be discussed, that of the European Monetary System (EMS), the precursor of the Economic and Monetary Union (EMU).

The two basic features of the EMS are the Exchange Rate Mechanism, or ERM, and the European Currency Unit, or Ecu.[4] The Ecu is a composite currency in which all member states' currencies are represented in different quantities (weights). These are the bilateral central rates against the Ecu, or *central rates*, for short. Through this fixed value relative to the Ecu, national currencies have a fixed value relative to each other. These are the cross-bilateral central rates, or *cross rates*, for short. Up to 1992, the member states undertook to keep their currencies' fluctuations within relatively narrow limits, 2.25 per cent above and 2.25 per cent below the cross rates (Italy was allowed a ±6 per cent band but adopted the ±2.25 per cent band in 1990). These limits of fluctuations are the *bands* or *bilateral limits*. After the 1993 crisis, these bands were widened to ±15 per cent (except for Germany and the Netherlands, which retain the ±2.25 per cent band). To keep currencies within their bilateral limits, central banks and governments have to intervene. In the case of a weak currency, they resort to a rise in interest rates and support operations using a diversity of currencies, or a tightening of fiscal policy. They do the opposite in the case of a strong currency.

Consider the example of Germany (higher productivity) and Italy (lower productivity). Germany, given her higher productivity, is more competitive on foreign markets. Also greater productivity allows German labour's greater material welfare.[5] Germany's pursuance of higher profits, then, is relatively independent of high inflation. Moreover, inflation would dent price competitivity, thus requiring devaluation, something Germany is reluctant to use because, as we shall see shortly, this would check Germany's aim to make of the D-mark an international currency. Inflation, then, is enemy number one in Germany. Italy's situation is the opposite. Lower productivity levels create the conditions for inflationary policies as a means to reduce the level of real wages (that is, to increase the rate of surplus value and thus the rate of profit). To safeguard her international competitiveness, Italy has to resort to devaluation. But the less efficient country's possibility of resorting to competitive devaluation is limited by the relative fixity of the exchange rates within the ERM.

Suppose, for example, that the Italian government decides to resort to money creation to stimulate the economy, that is, profitability. This might generate inflationary pressures and call for a devaluation of the lira. However, the bilateral bands rule out large exchange rate fluctuations. Consequently, Italy, if she does not want to devalue by modifying her central rate, must either accept a deterioration of her balance of trade or reduce the rate of inflation. In this indirect way, through the ERM, Germany sets a limit to the Italian rate of inflation, thus restricting the (limited) effectiveness of this anti-cyclical measure in Italy. Or suppose that Germany lowers her interest rate in order to check pressures on the D-mark. Inasmuch as interest rate differentials play a role in financial capital movements, financial operators sell D-marks and buy lire. This tends to revalue the lira and devalue the D-mark. If this process threatens to send the lira through the upper limit of the band, Italy has to lower her interest rate in order to relieve the pressure on the lira. But this might have unwanted inflationary effects.[6]

In this way a seemingly neutral mechanism fosters specific economic policies and interests, those of the dominant country, Germany, and within it those of the German oligopolies. While Germany can compete basically through greater efficiency, technological laggards have to compete basically through higher rates of surplus value. This can be done in one of the following two ways. It can be done at the point of production, through longer working days and higher intensity of labour. The extraction of absolute surplus value increases, fostered by the dismantling of social security systems and the increased legal possibility of arbitrarily dismissing labourers, nowadays called 'labour flexibility'. Alternatively, higher rates of surplus value can be achieved through redistribution (inflation). The ERM forces technological laggards to renounce inflation and devaluation and to extract more absolute surplus value at the point of production rather than through redistribution mechanisms. This makes it possible for Germany, too, to raise its rate of absolute surplus value, as German entrepreneurs too demand more 'freedom' to deal with labour.

However, the law according to which technological leaders tend to revalue their currencies and technological laggards tend to devalue theirs is stronger than the conscious attempts to check it. In fact, since the EMS entered into force, the D-mark has only been appreciated (from 1979 to 1990, the D-mark has been revalued six times) and the Italian lira has only been devalued, six times (Swann, 1992, p. 211). As for inflation, if 1980 equals 100, consumer prices in Germany had risen to 121 by 1987 but to 214 in Italy. Moreover, if the weight of the ERM becomes intolerable for the weaker countries in terms of unemployment, loss of foreign markets and foreign currency, popular discontent, or simply speculative movements, only one solution is left: leaving the ERM. This is indeed what happened to Italy and the UK in September 1992.[7]

On the basis of this brief discussion of the EMS, we can now consider the (dis)advantages of the EMU/euro. According to official economic doctrine, the EMU is supposed to create a zone of monetary stability and this in its turn is supposed to contribute to the achievement of stability, equilibrium and a crisis-free economy. This, of course, bears no relation to reality, which obstinately continues to be instability, disequilibrium and a crisis-prone state. Also official economics suggest that the discipline imposed by the EMU will induce greater competitiveness through the introduction of TI. But what was said above shows that both the ERM and the EMU force laggard countries to extract more absolute surplus value at the point of production, something which, if anything, slows down the introduction of TI. If these countries introduce TI, they do so in spite of, and not thanks to, the EMS. On a less ideological plane, official ideology stresses the euro's common advantages, like better trade conditions deriving from savings on exchange rate costs and hedging, or the simplification which could be achieved in managing the Common Agricultural Policy. However, this is not the heart of the matter. Nor is it of decisive importance to know that the computer industry will gain from a greatly increased demand while the car industry will suffer from reduced demand.

The real reasons for the introduction of the EMU/euro is that it makes the extraction of higher rates of surplus value at the point of production even more compelling than under the EMS, given that the single currency will make it impossible to use different rates of inflation. This in its turn has five important consequences. First, German advanced capital's leading role (which translates at the level of the EMS as higher rates of surplus value at the point of production) is in the interests of all European advanced capital and not only of the German oligopolies. This is basically the reason why the other nations' capital accept that role. Second, in post-Second World War Europe, high rates of inflation have been a means to increase the rate of surplus value, and thus the rate of profit, in periods of heightened labour militancy. But inflation corrodes not only labour's income but also that of all other classes, including those which are traditional allies of capital, thus being a possible cause of generalized dissatisfaction with the national governments' economic policies. High rates of absolute surplus value at the point of production avoid this drawback.

Third, high rates of inflation in Europe might call for successive rounds of competitive devaluations and these would leave the relative competitive positions unaltered while weakening the international strength of the European currencies. Again this is not the case for high rates of absolute surplus value at the point of production. Fourth, while inflationary measures increase the average rate of profit by redistributing the value produced, higher rates of absolute surplus value at the point of production increase both the average rate of profit and the economic base (the production of value and of commodities). Fifth, contrary to inflationary measures, high rates of absolute surplus value at the point of production foster an increased direct control on labour within the labour process itself and the (ideological, political and organizational) weakening of labour's organizations. These are the common advantages for European capital and the common disadvantages for European labour. The euro, and thus German leadership, is accepted by the other European countries because the bill is paid by labour.[8] Thus the economic significance of the EMU and of the euro for labour cannot but be negative.[9]

It follows that the *German leadership hypothesis* should be seen, not as the dominance of one country over the others, but as the dominance of Europe's advanced capital by German advanced capital and of the rest of European societies by this advanced bloc. It also follows that, the more the EU countries are tied to 'Germany', the greater the expropriation of value from labour. This all occurs under a double deception. First, an anti-labour policy wanted by national governments (and by the multinationals) is disguised as an economic policy imposed by some distant bureaucracy, for which the member states are not responsible, and reflecting some socially neutral economic rationality. Second, an economic policy ultimately in the interests of (the technologically advanced) industrial capital appears as if it were imposed by financial capital. In reality, financial capital forces industrial capital to renounce the competitive instruments of the poor countries (inflation and devaluation), it calls industrial capital to task, and thus is functional for the greater creation of (surplus) value rather than simply for a more favourable redistribution of the (surplus) value created. Supranational financial capital (the European central bank – ECB) will enjoy a measure of relative autonomy in the interests of the expanded reproduction of most advanced European industrial capital. This is the meaning of the ECB's 'independence'.

Aside from the common advantages for European capital, there are *specific advantages* for different countries deriving from the EMU and the euro. For 'Germany' (that is, for Europe's advanced capital under German leadership), the EMU is important because it is supposed to be the first step to transforming the D-mark into the euro, and this into a world currency. At present, the D-mark is only a potential contender for the role of international money. Its economic basis is still too restricted. To become a truly international currency, it will have to become the currency used in the whole Community, in a market comparable to that of the USA, served by an efficient and technologically advanced production system. This will produce a volume of euro-denominated international transactions, so that the demand for the euro will be equal to or surpass that for the dollar. This, in its turn, will facilitate the placing of euro-dominated financial instruments on non-EMU markets, thus increasing the demand for the currency. Inasmuch as this process will be successful, the world's central banks and other institutional investors will adjust their portfolios from dollar-denominated to euro-denominated instruments, thus reinforcing this virtuous circle.

But this is not yet sufficient for the euro to become the new form taken by the D-mark. This will be the case only inasmuch as the euro will be managed according to an economic policy reflecting and fostering the interests of German (and thus Europe's) advanced capital (even though in a mediated and negotiated way), that is according to a relatively strict interpretation and application of the Maastricht convergence criteria (at least, as long as Germany retains its dominant position within the EU).[10] In fact, these criteria reflect economic policies functional for the interests of the dominant, technologically advanced, capital.[11] Within the EMU, the ERM will not disappear, but will tie the non-EMU members to the euro. The difference will be that the euro will replace the Ecu as the pivot of the central rates of non-euro currencies (European Council, 1996). This will tie the economic policy of the non-euro members to that of the euro area and thus of its dominant capitalist bloc. In this way, the introduction of the EMU and of the euro, a further step not only towards European integration but also towards a strengthening of German (and Europe's) capital-dominant position, will be paid for by labour both in the euro area and outside it.

As for the less competitive 'countries', that is the less competitive sections of Europe's capital, the disadvantage is that they renounce definitely inflation and devaluation as independent instruments of anti-conjunctural policy and international competition. This is offset by the above-mentioned common advantages, to which one more must be added. It has been mentioned that Germany's project is that of transforming the D-mark into the euro, thus profiting from seigniorage. In this process, the currencies of the technologically laggard countries will also be converted into the euro. This means that these countries, too, will be able to participate in the gains deriving from seigniorage, inasmuch as the euro does become a rival of the dollar.

But Europe's dominated capital has also specific advantages. Only three will be mentioned here. First, in a common market, given the free movement of goods, the effects of demand stimulation through inflation might be lost to other member states. Thus the disadvantages of renouncing inflation might be smaller than otherwise. Second, the EMU/euro deprives individual countries of the possibility of using competitive devaluation but, on the other hand, makes generalized competitive devaluations impossible. These would leave all countries concerned with an unchanged competitive position relative to each other, would create commercial and political tensions with Germany, and would ultimately endanger their membership in the European project. Third, a common currency by definition eliminates monetary crises and speculative movements against the weaker currencies. These crises can have a disruptive effect on the real economy as well.

Finally, *common advantages do not imply harmony of interests*. France, for example, is unable to match Germany's leading role in the formulation of common policies. She is thus interested in the single currency because, through it, she can influence the common monetary policy, including the euro's devaluations, if needed. This is why France advocates a flexible interpretation of the Maastricht criteria and of the Stability Pact which will follow the creation of the EMU. It is in this light that the French–German disagreement on the nomination of the European Central Bank's president and the creation of a Stability Council should be seen.

To conclude, while the concept of globalization celebrates the defeat of so-called 'communism', the end of an epoch in which capitalist development was inhibited by the 'evil empire', the concept of imperialism shows that, after this historic defeat of the international working class, we are on the verge of a new phase in which capital's contradictions emerge again, both in their time-honoured forms and in new, but perhaps even more dangerous, forms. While the notion of globalization stresses the speculative aspects of capital movements, the notion of imperialism perceives such movements both as one of the effects of a crisis which has not yet been overcome and as a gigantic redistribution of value and surplus value. While globalization perceives new technologies as the source of a new, generalized cornucopia, and as the great social equalizer, imperialism sees these technologies as one of the factors transforming and recomposing, but not erasing, the working class. While globalization theorists see the end of ideology, the theory of imperialism sees in these transformations and recomposition the objective basis of a new subjectivity, truly international and internationalist.

It is within this framework that the Bundesbank's insistence on the strict application of the Maastricht criteria should be seen. This is simply aimed at replacing the D-mark with the euro, that is, at making of the euro the tool for the enhanced predominance of Europe's advanced capital (under the leadership of Germany's advanced capital). The aim is that of making of the euro the new form through which the D-mark will become a true rival of the US dollar. But this project has not and will not remain unchallenged. On the one hand, the future form of the Community will continue to be shaped by intercapitalist rivalries (centring upon the relations among Germany, France and the UK) and on the power relations within member states. On the other hand, the consciousness that the process of economic and monetary integration is being paid for by the European working class is beginning to reach wide social strata. The impressive recent strikes in France, Germany, Greece and Spain may be harbingers of a new and more active role that Europe's labour will have in shaping labour's Europe.

NOTES

1. 'The first genetically engineered lamb, named Dolly...was born two weeks ago. She was cloned from a fetal cell that had a human gene... Cloning experts say the work is a milestone. Animals with human genes could be used, in theory, to produce hormones or other biological products to treat human disease. They could also be given human genetic diseases and used to test new treatments. And genetically altered animals might also produce organs that could be transplanted into humans with less chance of rejection than now exists... Genetic engineering of human beings is now really on the horizon' (G. Kolata, 'Dolly's creators take next step', *International Herald Tribune*, 26–27 July 1997). In June 1999, the American company Advanced Cell Technology did perform the first cloning of a human embryo and thus of a human being. One can only shiver at the idea of what kind of 'human beings' may emerge from profit-driven laboratories.
2. Not by chance was the EMS established in 1979, at a time of persistent weakness of the dollar (Gaveau, 1982, p. 35).
3. Actually, we witness a double process: on the one hand, the aggregation of nation-states in the EU as a step towards a United States of Europe, but on the other a tendency towards secessionism within the existing nation-states, as in the case of northern Italy and in Bavaria. This theme cannot be pursued here.
4. Up to now the Ecu is basically a unit of account and a major currency of denomination of Eurobond issues. However, the Ecu is increasingly being used for private transactions. Nevertheless, this is still a much more restricted role than that to be attributed to the euro, the successor of the Ecu.
5. This does not necessarily mean that Germany's rate of surplus value is lower than that of the other less advanced countries.
6. Incidentally, the above highlights the reason why exchange rates within the ERM cannot be stable: the member states' unequal development. But there is also a second reason. Investors, when moving out of dollar positions for fear of a fall in the dollar's value, seek a safe currency. They usually prefer to purchase the D-mark, which is in no danger of being devalued, or less than other European currencies. This extra demand for the D-mark affects the exchange rate between the D-mark and the other European currencies, putting the bilateral bands under strain and possibly forcing a realignment. In this way, a large influx of dollars threatens the working of the ERM, whose aim is to avoid realignments.
7. Italy was readmitted to the ERM in August 1996. The asymmetry in terms of value appropriation is obscured by terms such as 'symmetric adjustments', which refer to equal obligations to intervene by the central banks of both the weak and the strong currencies. But even in this limited meaning, adjustments are asymmetric because they are caused by a policy predominantly influenced by the strong country.
8. Within labour, some strata, such as women, children, foreign workers, racial and other minorities, are penalized more than others. This important point cannot be pursued here. See Gill (1997).
9. For a lucid analysis, complementary to the present one, of this and related points concerning Britain's membership of the ERM, see Bonefeld and Burnham (1996).
10. These are that deficit must not be greater than 3 per cent of GDP, debt must not be greater than 60 per cent of GDP, inflation cannot be higher than 1.5 per cent of the average of the inflation rates of the three countries with the lowest rates, long-term interest rates cannot be higher than 2 per cent of the rates of the three countries with the lowest rates, and the exchange rates must be within the ERM. While these criteria are meant to transform the future euro into the new form of the D-mark, it has been pointed out repeatedly that, quantitatively, they are arbitrary (why 3 per cent and not any other figure?) and irrational: Japan would not be allowed membership in the EMU because of its high level of debt.

These criteria are not limited to the accession to the EMU. They are also meant to continue to play a role after its inception. On 8 November 1995, the German minister of finance, Waigel, spelled out his proposal for a 'stability pact'. This was approved at the Dublin summit of 13 and 14 December 1996. Basically, after joining the EMU, member countries will have to aim at a budget deficit of 1 per cent in normal times and of no more than 3 per cent in difficult times. Countries failing these requirements will have to pay a deposit (of between 0.2 per cent and 0.5 per cent of GDP) which, if the deficit is not corrected within two years, will be turned into a fine. There are also escape clauses (*Europa van Morgen*, 1996).

11. This is the meaning of art. 3a(3) of the EC Treaty which lays down the EMU's guiding principles: stable prices, sound public finances and monetary conditions and a sustainable balance of payments.

BIBLIOGRAPHY

Altvater, E., B. Blanke and Chr. Neusüss (1971), 'Kapitalistischer Weltmarkt und Weltwährungskrise', *Probleme des Klassenkampfs*, **1**, 5–117.

Artis, M. and N. Lee (eds) (1994), *The Economics of the European Union*, Oxford: Oxford University Press.

Bladen-Hovell, R. (1994), 'The European Monetary System', in M. Artis and N. Lee (eds), *The Economics of the European Union*, Oxford: Oxford University Press, pp. 329–45.

Bonefeld, W. and P. Burnham (1996), 'Britain and the politics of the European exchange rate mechanism 1990–92', *Capital and Class*, Autumn (60), 5–38.

Bureau van de Europese Commissie in Nederland (1996), *Europa van Morgen*, 26e jaargang, no.20.

Busch, K., W. Schöller and W. Seelow (1971), *Weltmarkt und Weltwährungskrise*, Bremen.

Business Week, 9 January 1995; 16 January 1995; 30 January 1995; 13 February 1995; 6 March 1995; 28 March 1995.

Carchedi, G. (1984), 'The logic of prices as value', *Economy and Society*, **13**(4), 431–55.

Carchedi, G. (1991a), *Frontiers of Political Economy*, London: Verso.

Carchedi, G. (1991b), 'Technological innovations, international production prices and exchange rates', *Cambridge Journal of Economics*, **15**(1), March, 45–60.

Carchedi, G. (1995), 'Non-Equilibrium Market Prices', in A. Freeman and G. Carchedi (eds), *Marx and Non-Equilibrium Economics*, Aldershot, UK/Brookfield, US: Edward Elgar.

Carchedi, G. and W. De Haan (1995), 'The Transformation Procedure: A Non-Equilibrium Approach', in A. Freeman and G. Carchedi (eds), *Marx and Non-Equilibrium Economics*, Aldershot, UK/Brookfield, US: Edward Elgar.

Coakley, J. (1988), 'International dimensions of the stock market crash', *Capital and Class*, **34**, Spring, 16–21.

Deubner, Chr., U. Rehfeldt, F. Schlupp and G. Ziebura (1979), *Die Internationalisierung des Kapitals. Neue Theorien in der internationalen Diskussion*, Campus Verlag.

Europa van Morgen, **16**, 23 October 1996.

European Council (1996), *Conclusies van het voorzitterschap*, Annex 2 to Annex I, in *Europa van Morgen*.

European Foundation for the Improvement of Living and Working Conditions (1997), *Working Conditions in the European Union*, Dublin.

Evans, T. (1988), 'Dollar is likely to rise, fall or stay steady, experts agree', *Capital and Class*, **34**, Spring, 10–15.

Financial Times, 21 December 1994; 22 December 1994; 23 December 1994; 24/25 December 1994; 28 December 1994; 29 December 1994; 30 December 1994; 31 December 1994/1 January 1995; 9 March 1995; 1 November 1995; 22 January 1996.

Freeman, A. (1988), 'The crash', *Capital and Class*, **34**, Spring, 33–41.

Freeman, A. and G. Carchedi (eds) (1995), *Marx and Non-Equilibrium Economics*, Aldershot, UK/Brookfield, US: Edward Elgar.

Gaveau, G. (1982), 'Turmoil in the international monetary system', *World View*, London: Pluto Press.

Gill, S. (1997), 'The global political economy and the European Union: EMU and alternatives to neo-liberalism', unpublished paper.

Glyn, A. (1988), 'The crash and real capital accumulation', *Capital and Class*, **34**, Spring, 21–4.

Grahl, J. (1988), 'The stock market crash and the role of the dollar', *Capital and Class*, **34**, Spring, 24–32.

International Herald Tribune, 18/19 March 1995.

Robinson, J. (1962), *Economic Philosophy*, Harmondsworth: Penguin.

Senf, B. (1978), 'Politische Ökonomie des Kapitalismus', *Mehrwert*, 18.

Siegel, T. (1980), 'Wertgesetz und Weltmarkt. Eine Kritik am Theorem der modifizierten Wirkungsweise der Wertgesetzes auf dem Weltmarkt', *Mehrwert*, 21, July.

Siegel, T. (1984), 'Politics and economics in the capitalist world market', *International Journal of Sociology*, **XIV**(1).

Swann, D. (1992), *The Economics of the Common Market*, Harmondsworth: Penguin.

The Economist, 4 March 1995.

Whalen, C. (1997), 'Divided economy', *Financial Times*, 14 January.

6. The accumulation process in Japan and East Asia as compared with the role of Germany in European post-war growth[1]

Joseph Halevi

STAGNATION IN EUROPE

This chapter maintains that East Asia and Japan are now reaching the same situation as that prevailing in Europe which is characterized by prolonged stagnation. However, the historical process towards the state of stagnation has been very different. Hence this section will discuss the European case, while the remaining ones will outline the evolution of the East Asian economic zone.

The restrictive economic policies followed by the Federal Republic of Germany represent one of the most important causes of the European stalemate. The German stance has been made even more deflationary by the French authorities, whose degree of inflexibility is greater than that imputed to Germany (Parguez, 1998). Just the same, it must be pointed out that the Federal Republic acted for more than 20 years – from the late 1940s to the first significant revaluation of the D-mark in 1969 – as a growth pole for Europe's effective demand.

As an the case of Japan, the Korean War, financed by American public expenditure, gave a big impulse to the recovery in German production of capital goods. Furthermore, as the outbreak of the war led to a rise in raw material prices, the initial adverse effect on West Germany's balance of payments was cushioned by a large loan from the European Payments Union financed by the USA. The European recovery was helped by the USA through measures aimed at preventing balance of payments crises as well as by allowing Europe to protect its own industries. In this context, overall European growth came to depend crucially on West German accumulation. Throughout the 1950s, the Federal Republic expanded faster than the rest of Europe. This factor increased Germany's demand for imports, stimulating the modernization of many sectors in Europe's industry. The other European countries tended to expand exports to Germany more than to the rest of the world (Milward, 1992).

Although Bonn ran balance of trade surpluses with the rest of the continent, the low level of the rates of interest relative to the growth rates stimulated a quick transformation of the surpluses into commercial credits. The high German growth was the main factor for the creation of a Europe-wide inter-industry structure and for focusing this growth on Europe itself.

This process continued also during the 1960s when, with the full currency convertibility having been re-established in 1958, balance of payments concerns began to dominate economic policies. In this phase the stop–go policies periodically undertaken by the countries of the then European Common Market ended up eroding Bonn's surpluses. Under the fixed exchange rate regime prevailing at the time, a policy-induced recession in any one European country would slow down wages in relation to productivity. Since the exporting firms were largely of an oligopolistic nature, a faster increase in productivity than in wages enabled those firms to be price-competitive without endangering their desired mark-up (Sylos-Labini, 1974). German export surpluses with the rest of Europe were significantly reduced because Bonn remained on a high wage and high employment path for most of the 1960s.

The role of Germany within the Common Market, and later within the European Economic Community, was absolutely essential for the formation of a Europe-centred productive apparatus based on the dynamic of European effective demand and not, as in earlier periods, on the existence on the continent of multiple conflicting imperialisms. At the same time, such a role would not have been possible without the accommodating attitude of the USA which allowed its current account surpluses to be transformed into deficits, or without the regime of fixed monetary exchange rates in relation to the US dollar (Davidson, 1997). The stability of the exchange rates permitted European countries and Japan to expand exports on the basis of productivity increases rather than by means of cheapening the money price of exports.

The process of cumulative causation broke down after 1969. In the second half of the 1960s, Germany's authorities embarked on policies aimed at conquering export markets through the restructuring of industry induced by a deliberate revaluation of the D-mark in 1969. Such an orientation was later facilitated by the collapse of the fixed exchange rate system. The abrupt devaluation of the American dollar in 1971 imposed on German capital the necessity to compete internationally on the basis of foreign direct investment flows rather than on the basis of a perceived favourable exchange rate. Bonn's monetary authorities, in conjunction with the banking system, adamantly resisted the financing of foreign outflows by issuing liabilities against Germany itself. Restructuring had to be financed therefore by the current account surpluses with the rest of the world. Europe turned out to be the most secure area for the realization of export surpluses provided its main economies were anchored to Bonn by a series of quasi fixed exchange rates (Halevi, 1995).

The European Monetary System (EMS) did just that. It was brought about in 1979 by the action of the German social-democratic (SDP) government of Helmut Schmidt, being initially resisted by the Bundesbank. But it was the SPD which identified correctly the long-run interests of German corporations in building current account surpluses (Parboni, 1981). Throughout the 1980s, in spite of weakening European growth, Germany accumulated a current account surplus, reaching by 1990 4 per cent of GDP. These surpluses provided the financial means for the internationalization of German capital. In this framework the role of Europe appears in its full dimension if account is taken of the fact that Germany's current account position with the USA began to deteriorate after the Plaza accords of 1985 – which started the long devaluation of the US dollar – while the deficit with Japan kept expanding. Hence the high share of the current account surplus over GDP is a measure of the surplus pumped from Europe under conditions of stagnant growth. Such a surplus acted unambiguously in a deflationary direction and was made possible by the parities imposed by the EMS regime.

The EMS virtually fixed exchange rates, coming in a context of strong and non-uniform inflation rates, and compelled the weaker countries to finance the external deficit by attracting short-term capital via high interest rates. Such a situation applied to countries like Britain, Italy, Spain and France. Thus, along with traditional stagnationist factors represented by slow growth and large German surpluses, the European stage was set for the outbreak of financial instability in its weakest components, which should have included France. The fixed parity between the French franc and the D-mark was, however, the main pillar of the protection of Germany's export-oriented economy so that any threat on the franc's parity with the D-mark would have entailed an immediate support from the Bundesbank. The conditions for financial instability existed therefore prior to the absorption of the German Democratic Republic into West Germany.

After the absorption of the GDR in 1990, Bonn's authorities wanted to acquire a greater degree of freedom in Europe in order to tap the international capital markets to finance the external deficits arising from the cost of unification, the continuing expansion of foreign direct investment and the new activities in eastern Europe. In the short run these multiple objectives pushed Germany to privilege the international strength of the currency, thereby jettisoning in 1992 the EMS system. In the longer run, however, Bonn's policy-making bodies had to confront the conflict between the dollar and the yen without having a secure rear in the former fixed parities of the EMS. Perhaps this is the single most important economic factor which led Bonn to accept the Maastricht convergence criteria for the single European currency, although neither the government nor the Bundesbank wished to relinquish sovereignty over monetary policies.

Indeed, German stagnation in the period 1990–94 was characterized by a slow growth of exports up to the point where it called forth drastic cuts in domestic output and employment levels (Nardozzi, 1997). The poor German performance was due, not only to the devaluation of currencies like the lira, but also to the restructuring induced in countries such as France by the policy of high interest rates aimed at sustaining the parity with the D-mark. Thus, if after 1990 German unemployment was caused by slower exports not being counterbalanced by higher domestic demand, European countries like France experienced positive export performances at the expense of domestic demand growth. The gains in productivity generated by restructuring enhanced competitiveness and exports but, as such, did not generate jobs because of the deflationary scenario of fiscal and monetary policies.

The stagnation in export performance convinced Germany's authorities of the need to stem the negative impact of the devaluation of currencies like the Italian lira, given Italy's status as the second largest trading partner. Furthermore, a persistently undervalued lira would have eventually compelled France to abandon the parity with the D-mark, setting the stage for competitive devaluations. As a consequence, the German authorities used the Maastricht objectives to force a currency realignment closer to the D-mark. As of 1996, Germany's export position improved significantly, but the mechanism of upward realignment was based, in accordance with Maastricht convergence criteria, on very restrictive fiscal policies in all European countries. Europe moved from the high level of unemployment together with high interest rates of the 1980s to a still higher rate of unemployment with tight fiscal policies in the 1990s.

The solution to the stalemate is now being sought in increasing the rate of exports, a most remarkable neomercantilist attitude in a period of alleged European unification. An external outlet did come about from the second half of 1995 through the revaluation of the US dollar relative to the Japanese yen and the European currencies. Without the boost to exports provided by such a revaluation, Europe's rate of unemployment would have been even higher. The rise in the value of the American currency occurred chiefly in response to events in East Asia and Japan: it had little to do with European affairs. Thus the growth of European exports to the dollar area was stimulated by processes which depended upon the relations between East Asia, Japan and the USA. The next sections will therefore present a historical interpretation of the evolution of the economic ties between the USA, Japan and East Asia.

THE DOLLAR AND THE USA IN ASIA

During the discussions between the USA and Great Britain leading up to the Bretton Woods agreement, the American geopolitical orientation was predicated upon the strict cooperation between two partners, one senior (the USA) and one junior (Great Britain). In this framework, the pound sterling was supposed to act as a reserve currency sharing with the US dollar the task of creating international liquidity in a world of non-convertible currencies. Yet the British balance of payments crisis in 1946 and 1947 pushed Britain in the opposite direction, since it compelled London to declare its currency non-convertible on a par with those of the defeated/occupied nations such as Germany, France, Italy and Japan. As pointed out by Michael Schaller in his masterpiece on the American occupation of Japan, Britain's impotence in the face of the strategic objectives assigned to it by the USA determined a change in the American conception of world politics. The main intellectual actors in this change were James Forrestal and George Kennan (Schaller, 1985).

According to the Forrestal–Kennan view, the British failure required the restructuring of the world economy on the basis of one central power flanked by two regional centres. The USA would be the central power, with strong links to West Germany to the east and to Japan to the west. The Federal Republic was deemed to act as a regional economic power-house in Europe, while Japan was supposed to become the workshop of a non-existent Asian region.

As far as Europe was concerned, such a vision did not represent any particular problem, except for the practical question of how to iron out Franco-German differences, thereby enabling the rearmament of West Germany. For Washington the real problems were to arise in Asia since the American decision to isolate the People's Republic of China all but eliminated the possibility of forming a Japanese economic zone. Thus the Forrestal–Kennan idea of making Japan into the workshop of Asia was hanging in mid-air without a real hinterland to operate upon. In the end, that hinterland did come about, but in a way totally unforeseen by the two architects of the strategy. In the wake of the British crisis of 1947, the dollar remained the only international currency. Under the assumption of a persistent dollar shortage, the American authorities favoured the continuation of the traditional economic dependency of South-East Asia on the (sometimes former) colonial powers. The exports of raw materials to the world markets by colonies like Malaysia and Vietnam, or by independent nations like Indonesia, were supposed to create a dollar-based balance of payments surplus to be immediately lost to the European powers via the current account deficit of the exporting areas with the old continent (Rotter, 1987).

However, favouring the retention of the role of the colonial powers had two major shortcomings. The first was that, given the exclusion of China, those very areas were chosen by Washington to act also as the hinterland of Japan. As a consequence, the colonial economies of south-east Asia were given the impossible task of sustaining the dollar requirements of two large industrial centres. The second shortcoming lay in the specific role of France. In the eyes of Washington's policy makers, the presence of France in Vietnam had the dual function of contributing to the policy of containment towards China and other Third World movements, as well as securing the dependency status of the area. Yet, as long as France had its army tied down in Vietnam, the European side of the strategy could not be implemented in full since Paris would refuse any rearmament of West Germany.

Politically, as argued by Rotter (1987), the French defeat at Dien Bien Phu lifted one obstacle to the USA sealing both the European and the Asian strategies. Economically, the end of the dollar shortage, induced by the new form of institutional spending engendered by the Korean War, enabled Washington to untie south-east Asia from the old colonial powers. In relation to the European theatre, the departure of the French from Asia gave the green light to the rearmament of West Germany while firmly ensconcing it within the polity of western Europe and especially of the (soon to be) European Common Market. In Asia, US policy was based on the confrontation with Third World nationalist movements and with the need to provide a hinterland to Japan (Borden, 1984). In this context, American public expenditure and military intervention became the two interwoven instruments of the policy. But the policy could materialize only via a prior military intervention against Third World movements. Thus military intervention became the *long-term* policy and public expenditure its offshoot.

VIETNAM: AMERICA TAKES JAPAN TO ASIA

American confrontation with China and Third World movements did not create a hinterland for Japan, whose relations with South Korea and Taiwan were still of a colonial nature. South Korea and Taiwan exported to Japan mostly raw materials and staples, receiving industrial goods in return. Although relevant to Japanese trade, such a pattern contained no synergies. Importantly, therefore, until the Vietnam War there was no Japanese economic zone in Asia. The content of Tokyo's trade with South-East Asia was inconsistent with the import requirements of Japan's reindustrialization.

In this context the financing of Japanese imports of technology and of capital goods from the other capitalist countries – especially from the USA – occurred by overstepping Asia. In practice, this was due to the American decision to relieve Japan of a structural balance of payments constraint while allowing Tokyo's government agencies and the transformed *zaibatsus* (*keiretsus*) to undertake a domestic oriented *full-scale industrialization*. The insulation of Japan was obtained by extending the Korea-based special procurement programme, albeit at a diminishing rate. On the whole, American transfer payments lifted

Japan's import ceiling by more than 80 per cent in the years preceding the Vietnam War and covered Japan's current account deficit until the second half of the 1960s. With the USA guaranteeing the external environment, Japan's industrialization was freed from the historic structural balance of payments constraint. During the 1930s, with limited markets, the share of exports in GDP was around 18 per cent, but from the second half of the 1950s that share hovered between 9 per cent and 11 per cent (Itoh, 1990).

Full-scale industrialization gave priority to domestic investment while exports were sought on the basis of industrial targeting. Here too, however, the USA was of crucial importance. Before the signing of the 1952 San Francisco Treaty, which returned Japan to the status of a sovereign country, Washington approved the continuation of the wartime laws shutting out foreign investors. Likewise, it supported the use of foreign exchange regulations to stop imports of industrial consumption goods which, as the case of the car industry shows, permanently closed the Japanese market to foreign producers. The USA even went so far as to lobby other countries to accept Japan's lack of reciprocity. Such diplomatic activity occurred on the occasion of Tokyo's application to join both GATT and the OECD (Nester, 1990a; 1990b). The full-scale industrialization strategy and the asymmetrical institutional arrangements enjoyed by Tokyo explain today's oligopolistic position of Japanese companies in Asia. The possession in the home country of all the crucial technology-producing sectors made it possible to plan and select the stages in which Asian networks had to be set up. Likewise, the possession of a complete industrial structure allowed Japan to produce and export all the basic industrial inputs. A further and wider oligopolistic factor lies in that even firms which do not belong to Japanese networks, such as the Korean Chaebols, are vitally dependent on Japanese machinery in a way which is not symmetrical for Japan (Hatch and Yamamura, 1996).

The factor which brought Japan back into Asia was the Vietnam War and the consequent need of the USA to establish a system of alliances around its South-East Asian policies. The expansion of Japan into the region was the consequence of the public expenditure that Washington systematically poured into the area. American military-motivated expenditure generated demand directly as well as cushioning the countries of South-East Asia against chronic deficits. Yet US public expenditure would not have sufficed by itself to build a set of strong states from a productive point of view. American policy makers saw a further condition in the formation of technocratic states (South Korea, Taiwan) backed economically by Japan. This approach meant that the USA would give financial aid and open up its markets, while Japan would export technology and undertake FDI projects (Woo, 1991).

The phase in which American policy seemed to succeed was the 1961–67 period centred on events in South Korea and Indonesia. In the former case, the military regime, which initially aimed at a Japanese type of self-sustained industrialization, was pushed towards export-oriented policies and a heavy reliance on Japan in every institutional and technical aspect of the development process. In the early stages of industrialization up to 1970, the Vietnam War and direct US transfers rather than access to American markets sustained the exports of the nascent advanced sectors of Taiwanese and South Korean industries. These exports went overwhelmingly to South Vietnam, whose current account deficit was cleared by the USA.

The productive transformation of South Korea and Taiwan changed altogether the nature of trade flows between those countries, on the one hand, and Japan and the USA, on the other. Until the early 1960s, the bulk of South Korean and Taiwan exports went to Japan, while their imports came mostly from the USA. With Washington they tended to have a current account deficit, whereas with Tokyo they sometimes had current account surpluses. With the Vietnam War and the industrialization which ensued, the current account position of American Asia started to swing the other way. It became normal to have a deficit with Japan, while surpluses were sought by exporting to the USA. In this context, the USA became the main area for the exports of Japan and the rest of Asia.

STRUCTURAL AND MONETARY ASYMMETRIES

The Vietnam War transformed American Asia into American Japanese Asia (AJA). It remained so throughout the 1970s and it collapsed with the revaluation of the yen following the Plaza agreements in 1985. The fact that Japan acted as the capital goods sector of the region, but not as a buyer of the region's products, implied greater exchange rate and market dependency upon the USA.

The structural asymmetry between Japan and its periphery lies in that no other country has followed a full-scale industrialization strategy – not even South Korea. In fact, its growth depended crucially on building up the heavy-industry sectors, without a sufficiently vast corresponding network of local suppliers. The firms supplying Korean conglomerates are Japanese. The structural asymmetry implies that East and South-East Asian countries must be, unlike Japan, very open economies. At the same time, Japan is not a major buyer of their outputs. The share of their exports going to Japan is either stable or declining, whereas a period of systemic rises has yet to appear. It follows that Japan is not a dynamic factor in the creation of effective demand for the area as a whole. Japan acts as a force of technological transformation, the price of which is the oligopolistic position of Japanese corporations in the area. Consequently, Tokyo does not create a large enough effective demand to free the region from a structural balance of payments constraint. In other words, without the external markets represented by exports to the USA and Europe (although the latter absorbs a much smaller amount of East Asian exports) the structural deficit of the region with Japan would have required a negative adjustment process. Growth itself would have been stunted, regardless of the Japanese-induced modernization (Halevi and Kriesler, 1996).

Modernization was made possible by the relative certainty concerning the access to the external markets represented mainly by the USA. Initially, access to export markets was institutionally arranged by Washington. At a later stage, once American public expenditure dried up with the end of the Vietnam War, the export drive depended on the prevailing monetary conditions. During the first Reagan presidency, the rise in the value of the dollar helped both Japanese and East Asian exports, although the high interest rates policy of the Federal Reserve created serious debt-financing problems for South Korea. It was after the 1985 Plaza agreements, leading within a short lapse of time to a doubling in the value of the yen relative to the dollar, that a new asymmetry set in. The countries of East and South-East Asia increasingly pegged their currencies to the dollar, expecting a long-term revaluation of the yen. This policy was implemented in strict (and silent) coordination with Japanese monetary authorities as well as Japanese corporations. Although pegging the East Asian currencies to the dollar led to a real revaluation – because of the much lower rate of inflation in the USA – it was assumed that the productivity increases generated by Japanese FDI (or, as in the Korean case, by the acquisition of Japanese technology) would win in the end.

Hence the productivity increases induced by Japanese investment in the area were supposed to counter both the real revaluation against the US dollar and the sharp devaluation *vis-à-vis* the yen. The first phenomenon was easier to fend off, at least until 1995. The second aspect turned out to be uncontrollable. The devaluation of the East Asian currencies relative to the yen increased the unit cost of imports. The high growth rate of those economies increased the demand for Japanese imports. Since imports from Japan also went to sustain domestic oriented activities, import dependency on Japan increased more than the ability to find foreign markets. The other side of the coin was in fact the rapid rise in Japan's current account surplus with East and South-East Asia which became the largest source of Japan's external balances.

This state of affairs worked generally in favour of Japanese corporations: the lower growth rate in Japan, eventually reaching total stagnation, was compensated by the profits represented by the surplus with Asia and the rest of the world. From the Asian perspective, this situation would have been sustainable as long as enough pressure could have been brought to bear upon wage-earners. In other words, the sustainability of the external aspects of the East Asian growth process depended upon the ability to keep wage rises below those of productivity. Yet this is precisely what cannot be taken for granted in any long-term growth situation. The East Asian growth mechanism has, therefore, a major difficulty in accommodating systematic increases in wages.

In this aspect the East Asian case reproduces a trait common to all East Asian development, including Japan's. This trait has to do with the extreme rigidity against any wage increase equal to or above the prevailing rise in productivity. In Japan during most of the growth years, wages rose somewhat less than productivity (Itoh, 1990). From the late 1970s, wages became virtually stagnant. The purchasing power of the wage-earners expanded thanks to the revaluation of the yen, which enabled households to buy consumption goods reimported by Japanese multinationals (Steven, 1996). In East Asia, given the huge balance of payments deficits that those countries have with Japan, a deficit governing the whole spectrum of their export and financial activities, the pressure on wages is significantly stronger than in the case of Japan itself. The subordinate role of wages and of the demand they generate has been rendered more acute by the structural dependency upon Japan and by the inability of the latter to act as a strong source of regional demand. Thus exports of East Asia as a whole, inclusive of China, must rise chiefly outside the regional markets. In practice, this means exports to the USA.

THE CONVERGENCE OF ASIA AND EUROPE WITH THE USA

The long phase of the revaluation of the yen following the Plaza agreements may be considered a political turning point, as it defined Washington's desire to withdraw American institutional support for Japan and East Asian growth. At the same time, however, the absorption of the East and South-East Asian economies into the national American market continued and became more pronounced with the rapid emergence of the People's Republic of China, which swiftly integrated itself into a system initially conceived against it. The pegging of East Asian currencies to the dollar was made possible by the fact that Washington did not exercise pressures to deregulate too quickly the capital and foreign exchange markets of the area. These factors permitted a continuing expansion of East and South-East Asian exports, as well as a rise in intra-Asian trade. Given Japan's position as a major producer of capital goods for the whole region, Japanese corporations did not mind, up to a point, the monetary asymmetry based on a system of dollar-pegged currencies, on the one hand, and a revaluation of the yen, on the other. As long as Japanese corporations could reasonably expect an expansion of profit – through their net exports to Asia and their Asian-based production (both export and intra-Asia oriented) – at least equal to the expected losses induced by the revaluation of the yen, the adjustment to a lower value of the dollar appeared feasible.

Yet the deepening of the devaluation of the dollar during the period 1992–95 eliminated the possibility of finding a profitable strategy of adjustment. The sharp rise in the value of the yen destabilized the relationship between Japanese transplants in the USA and the value of their importation of goods from Japan. It also negatively affected the value of dollar-denominated financial assets, while the 'no growth' situation led to an internal crisis of the banking system. It is mostly for financial rather than for productive reasons that, in July 1995, American policy underwent a sudden reversal. Fearing a financial meltdown of Japan, the US authorities engineered, in agreement with the Bank of Japan and the Bundesbank, a long-term controlled devaluation of the Japanese currency. Had the devaluation of the dollar persisted or just stabilized over a longer period, segments of Japanese industry would have been relocated in East Asia and China, and eventually Japan itself would have become a major importer of regional industrial commodities.

The rapid reversal in the value of the dollar led instead to a revival of Japan's exports, very much at the expense of countries like South Korea. Furthermore, the yen devaluation slowed down the flow of foreign direct investment as industrial relocation became less profitable. It is clear, in this context, that this sort of decision reflected the well-informed expectation that American willingness to increase the value of the dollar to rescue Japan was a long-term strategy. In this way, the synergies which tied East Asia to Japan were broken and Tokyo started to compete for third markets against the area of its own hegemony. Therefore the pattern of the Japanese crisis emerges as comprising two components. In the phase of the revaluation of the yen, the links between home production and transplants in the USA were damaged, but capital goods exports to East Asia were stimulated and sustained Japan's current account surplus. In the phase of the devaluation of the yen, competition against the East Asian countries has been a prime structural factor in the overall financial crisis of the area.

In the process, Japan's capacity to generate domestic expansion without having to rely heavily on outside markets has become much weaker when it is much more needed. Large unused capacities in equipment and advanced consumption goods industries, tied to strong domestic oligopolistic structures, created a bias in which foreign markets are seen as the solution to the lack of profitable effective demand. Thus, during the revaluation of the yen, Japan's dynamics depended on East Asia's export drive and on American disposition to support it. Following the devaluation of the yen after 1995, Japan's dynamics have come to depend on the rise of direct exports to the other industrialized countries to the detriment of those of East Asia. The absence of automatic stabilizers both in Japan and in East Asia makes the dependency on foreign markets even more severe.

CONCLUSIONS

The reconstruction of the capitalist system after the Great Depression and the Second World War started with a strategic conception of the USA to structure the world around a central power flanked by two autonomous regional poles. This strategy did not materialize. American international public expenditure, especially on wars and armaments, sustained the recovery of both Japan and Germany. Furthermore, overall Asian capitalist accumulation started in earnest when the area got embroiled in a second and much more comprehensive American war in Vietnam. When the USA began, after the defeat in Vietnam, to withdraw its institutional and financial support, the continuation of the process of accumulation depended increasingly on the capacity to exploit contingent situations such as a more positive US disposition towards the smaller East Asian economies and – for political reasons – towards China. During the years of the revaluation of the yen, the willingness to absorb imports from the rest of Asia sustained the pegging of that region's currencies to the dollar and allowed Japan to build its own economic zone. Since then the zone has been severely shaken by the US decision aimed at helping Japan by revaluing the dollar against the yen. In both cases, dependency on the USA dominates any other element.

Europe does not appear to be as glued to the USA as Japan and East Asia are, yet the central role of Germany in the European Union does not invest it with any expansionary impulses. The restrictive attitude of European policy makers is not due to a constitutional design aimed at making all European countries converge in order to formally unify the continent. Rather, it is due to the fact that German authorities, banks and corporations, see Europe as their base for accumulating surpluses with which to finance the international drive of German capital. German priorities moulded, with France's surrender to them, Europe's contractionary fiscal stance.

Neither East Asia and Japan nor Germany and Europe are capable of internally generating dynamic demand. Both depend on net exports to the USA. Yet per capita productive capacity and per capita income differentials between Europe, Japan and the USA are negligible, whereas the combined absolute size of Japan and Europe is greater than that of the USA. America is therefore too small an economy to be the catalyst of external demand for those two poles. Yet Europe's and Japan's dependency on this external factor traps the bulk of the world economy in a state of long-term stagnation.

NOTE

1. An early draft of this chapter was read at the conference, 'Which Labour Next? Global Money, Capital Restructuring and the Changing Pattern of Production', Università di Bergamo, 3–5 December 1997.

REFERENCES

Borden, W. (1984), *The Pacific Alliance: United States Foreign Economic Policy and Japanese Trade Recovery: 1947–1955*, Madison, Wis.: The University of Wisconsin Press.

Davidson, P. (1997), 'The General Theory in an Open Economy Context', in G.C. Harcourt and P. Riach (eds), *A 'Second Edition' of The General Theory*, vol. 2, London: Routledge, pp. 103–30.

Halevi, J. (1995), 'The EMS and the Bundesbank in Europe', in P. Arestis and V. Chick (eds), *Finance, Development and Structural Change*, Aldershot, UK/ Brookfield, US: Edward Elgar, pp. 263–91.

Halevi, J. and P. Kriesler (1996), 'Asia, Japan and the internationalization of effective demand', *Economies et Sociétés*, **30** (2–3), 301–20.

Hatch, W. and K. Yamamura (1996), *Asia in Japan's Embrace: Building a Regional Production Alliance*, Cambridge/New York: Cambridge University Press.

Itoh, M. (1990), *The World Economic Crisis and Japanese Capitalism*, New York: St. Martin's Press.

Milward, A. (1992), *The European Rescue of the Nation-State*, London: Routledge.

Nardozzi, G. (1997), 'La disoccupazione europea ed il capitalismo tedesco', in P. Ciocca (ed.), *Disoccupazione di fine secolo*, Turin: Bollati Boringhieri, pp. 58–80.

Nester, W. (1990a), *The Foundation of Japanese Power: Continuities, Changes, Challenges*, London: Macmillan.

Nester, W. (1990b), *Japan's Growing Power over East Asia and the World Economy: Ends and Means*, London: Macmillan.

Parboni, R. (1981), *The Dollar and its Rivals*, London: Verso.

Parguez, A. (1998), 'The Roots of Austerity in France', in J. Halevi and J.M. Fontaine (eds), *Restoring Demand in the World Economy: Trade Finance and Technology*, Cheltenham, UK: Edward Elgar Publishing, pp. 182–96.

Rotter, A. (1987), *The Path to Vietnam: Origins of the American Commitment to Southeast Asia*, Ithaca, NY: Cornell University Press.

Schaller, M. (1985), *The American Occupation of Japan: The Origins of the Cold War in Asia*, New York: Oxford University Press.

Steven, R. (1996), *Japan and the New World Order: Global Investments, Trade and Finance*, London: Macmillan.

Sylos-Labini, P. (1974), *Trade Unions, Inflation and Productivity*, Farnborough, Hants: Saxon House.

Woo, J. (1991), *Race to the Swift: State and Finance in Korean Industrialization*, New York: Columbia University Press.

7. Historical notes on the rise and fall of Fordism and flexible accumulation in the United States

Michael Perelman

HISTORICAL INTRODUCTION

Although Fordism began in the motor industry, that industry was atypical among the major, future sites of the Fordist mode of organization. At the time when Ford began his famous Five Dollar Day, most large industries were highly cartelized. In contrast, the motor industry was still fragmented and highly competitive, although the number of car producers was already in decline.

Although a number of capitalists had already begun to practise what came to be known as 'welfare capitalism', Henry Ford's actions caught the attention of the world. Fordism originally arose out of the stubborn resistance of workers in the USA to the new form of industrial work. On the eve of Fordism, turnover and absenteeism at the Ford Motor Company were running at ruinously high levels. To make matters worse for Ford, the International Workers of the World was about to launch an organizing campaign. Ford's Five Dollar Day was a pre-emptive manoeuvre, intended to buy workers' compliance (Perelman, 1996, ch. 5).

Other major corporations adopted variants of Ford's system. Their approach became known as Welfare Capitalism. Although these welfare capitalists resisted unions, they expressed, and sometimes demonstrated, a modest concern for the well-being of their employees. Like Ford, the welfare capitalists also believed that (relatively) high wages would make workers more productive and less resistant to the demands of capital. In addition, they believed that the carrot of high wages and the stock of unemployment would induce workers to give up their old world traditions and accept the rule of capital as legitimate. They went to great lengths to 'Americanize' their workers by creating institutions that they felt were suitable to that goal, while undermining other institutions that they considered inimical to it. Gramsci captured this spirit, referring to the efforts to mould the worker's personality, such as prohibition and psychoanalysis (Gramsci, 1971, pp. 279–80).

Nobody should suffer under the illusion that some powerful humanitarian instinct drove either Ford or the welfare capitalists. On the contrary, welfare capitalism was merely an intelligent response to an upsurge in labour militancy. In truth, the Ford motor company was less Fordist than most of the other welfare capitalists. A relatively small share of the workers earned the famous $5.00 a day wage. In addition, Ford drove his workers so mercilessly that many workers rejected the bargain, preferring to work for more traditional employers. In the end, however, Ford found many workers who accepted his Faustian bargain (Perelman, 1996, ch. 5).

In the process, the nature of work in the USA changed dramatically. Once again, Gramsci saw what was afoot: 'A forced selection will ineluctably take place; a part of the old working class will be pitilessly eliminated from the world of labour, and perhaps from the world tout court' (Gramsci, 1971, p. 303). Gramsci knew full well that Fordism was only a temporary way station in the process of capital accumulation. In particular, he had accurately anticipated that competitive forces would eventually topple this new system, since the higher wages associated with Fordism depended, at least in part, upon the existence of a kind of monopoly rent associated with an absence of strong competitive pressures.

THE LETHAL PUNCH OF THE INVISIBLE HAND

Gramsci's understanding about the relationship between Fordism and competition is very important. Present-day economists understand precious little about the nature of competition. Until recently, conventional economic doctrine naively insisted that the more competition, the better the economy would be. Today, in light of the enormous success of the Japanese economy during the 1970s and 1980s, some economists are now claiming that a society might prosper by forgoing some of the benefits of competition in order to reap potentially greater fruits of cooperation: not social cooperation in general, but merely the cooperation between giant corporations.

A counter-argument could be made. Competition has two faces. Without competition, capitalist business becomes lax and inefficient, just as conventional economics suggests. At the same time, with too much competition, the economy falls into a depression. In fact, a depression is just an intensification of competition. According to the basic theorem of conventional economics, competitive pressure will naturally force firms to sell their wares at a price equal to the cost of producing one more item – what economists call 'the marginal cost'. This marginal cost pricing, according to the central doctrine of conventional economics, will ensure both efficiency and equity. Suppose you have a world in which prices do not equal marginal costs. The economists can demonstrate mathematically that, if you could somehow change the world so that prices would equal marginal costs, the economy could produce more utility – an economics term that is supposed to indicate happiness.

The language in the foregoing might sound hollow and unrealistic, even though the logic behind the claims of conventional economics is irrefutable. Unfortunately, the extravagant proposition that this simple rule of marginal cost pricing will lead to the best of all possible worlds rests upon a set of assumptions that have little relationship to the real world. Tear away the assumptions, and the theory withers. First and foremost, the theory assumes that the world is unchanging. In addition, the theory assumes that the economy is viable; that is, that the most efficient firms can always earn enough profit to survive. The first assumption is obviously wrong. The second requires some thought.

Consider the nature of modern technology. In almost any major manufacturing industry, the marginal cost is small, if not trivial. Take an extreme example, computer software. The marginal cost, the cost of producing another copy, of a program is virtually nothing. The condition of low marginal costs is perhaps even true for the majority of the most important service providers, such as those of the telecommunications industry. If a firm were to be paid its marginal cost and nothing more, it would earn nothing.

Now suppose that two companies have produced software products that are virtually identical. A customer goes to the first company, which quotes a price of $500. The company explains that it has spent millions of dollars in developing the program. The customer goes down the street to see the second company, which quotes a similar price. She says that she might as well buy it from the first company. The manager knows that, if the price falls much below $500, his company will not be able to recover the millions of dollars spent on creating the program. Nonetheless, he tells her that he wants her business, even though he will lose money on the deal, so he offers her a lower price. After all, to turn down $450 per program will not help to recoup the investment.

Now the customer can take the $450 bid back to the first company, which by the same logic might be willing to drop the price to $400. Each company knows that, so long as the price remains above the marginal cost – the cost of producing another copy of the program – it will earn something, even though the bulk of its original expenses will be lost.

This process illustrates the severe nature of the competitive process. Prices will fall toward marginal costs. The price of creating a computer program or the cost of purchasing plant and equipment – what economists call 'fixed costs' – will not figure in the final price of the good. Since prices will fall towards marginal costs regardless of the fixed costs, under vigorous competition firms will be unable to recover their fixed costs.

Let us shift our focus to manufacturing, to consider these fixed costs in a little more detail. Suppose we have an industry where all the firms are selling their output at a price equal to marginal cost, say $100. Our firm discovers a new technology that can actually eliminate half of the production costs. The new equipment that can accomplish this feat is expensive, but it reduces the need for a good share of the labour force. If the firm can cut its costs in half, then it can make an additional profit of $50 on each unit it sells. The marginal cost will be even less than the $50, which includes an allowance to cover the cost of the new equipment. Let us say that the new marginal cost is $25. In effect, much new technology converts marginal costs – in this case the labour that the new technology replaced – into fixed costs: the costs of the new technology.

So long as the price remains at $100, the firm makes a healthy profit, but if other firms pick up similar technology and drive prices down to $25 right away, the firm will be worse off than it was in the first place. It will only receive its marginal cost of $25 per unit, without gaining any return on the money that it has laid out on the investment. To make matters worse, the new technology has destroyed much of the value of the plant and equipment that it has replaced. Yet a firm that refuses to adopt the new technology will also be unable to compete since it will have marginal costs of $50 with a selling price of half that amount.

THE TWO FACES OF COMPETITION

My contention, that competitive markets without some sort of protection have a natural tendency to increase competition, leading to depressions, is heretical today. During the nineteenth century, this same idea was commonplace. In the wake of the prolonged depressions of the late nineteenth century, the leading economists in the USA founded the American Economic Association early in the twentieth century, primarily to make this understanding more general. They wanted to promote trusts, cartels, monopolies and other forms of industrial organization that would thwart competition to avoid depressions.

Once the immediate threat of a renewed depression passed by, in part because of the cartelization of the US economy, economists again became enamoured of laisser faire, until the Great Depression crushed their faith in markets once more. During the depression, economists turned to another mechanism to limit competition: expansionary fiscal policy, associated with the name of John Maynard Keynes. Few economists thought of Keynesianism as anti-competitive. Consider for a moment what deficit spending actually does. To the extent that added buying power relieves the pressure on suppliers, Keynesian policies must necessarily reduce the force of competition. To make this point does not mean that Keynesian policies were wrong-headed; however, the continued application of countercyclical policies will allow business to become lax and make the economy fragile.

In short, all the mainstream economists, both liberal and conservative, failed to see that capitalism is a contradictory system. The same mechanisms that protect the economy against competition also destroy the forces that impel business to become efficient. Yet these competitive forces take on a momentum of their own that can destroy the economy. No simple policy can get around this problem.

Today, our free market economists merely see the positive side of competition. They are oblivious to the threat of a depression. Business publications now naively proclaim that the new technologies have finally banished the depression from our future. Under the spell of this euphoria, our economic and political leaders have been enthusiastic in dismantling virtually every safety mechanism, except for two: military spending and intellectual property. I need not say much about military spending for the role of military Keynesianism is well known: its importance in propping up the economy and the risks it poses to humanity. We will return to the subject of intellectual property later.

THE ECONOMY OF HIGH WAGES

There is only one possibility of minimizing the destructive nature of markets within the existing framework of capitalism, one that the welfare capitalists commonly suggested with the expression, 'the economy of high wages'. Surprisingly, Gramsci overlooked this important element of the public persona of welfare capitalism.

According to the welfare capitalists, high wages were the key to economic health. High wages would not only domesticate the labour force; they would create an entirely different economic environment. For the welfare capitalists, high wages could even more or less eliminate class conflict. Although much of their talk was purely rhetorical, we can find some nuggets of great value within their rhetoric. Let us concentrate on one particular idea: in an economy of high wages, business would have a greater incentive to find better ways of production. In other words, we could look to high wages instead of low prices as a means to provide competitive pressure.

So long as labour has the means to force up wages (within some bounds), business will have to respond by finding means to enhance productivity, which will keep inflation in check. This kind of competition, where the pressure comes from higher wages rather than competition, avoids the risk of depression. At the time, the welfare capitalists seemed to understand the value of this kind of economic environment. Today the mantra of economic success is low wages. Merely invoking the economy of high wages will not suffice to make capitalism a perfect, or even a good, system. However, this strategy seems preferable to our current race to the bottom, competing by finding the lowest possible costs of labour: what has been called elsewhere 'the Haitian road to development'.

Gramsci saw Fordism as a temporary way station, before an outbreak of competition once again ravaged the economy. Presumably, he believed that the impending crisis would galvanize workers and thereby hasten the transition to socialism. Well, Fordism is gone and labour now is in the midst of a crisis. Socialism for the rich may be a reality, but the market forces are supposed to be good enough for the rest of us. How did this turn of events occur?

THE END OF FORDISM

When the depression first hit in 1929, Fordism appeared to have some resiliency. The welfare capitalists, true to their belief in the economy of high wages, held the wages of their most skilled workers relatively constant, although they cut back hours and laid off their less skilled workers. In late 1931, as the Great Depression worsened, the welfare capitalists abandoned their pretensions and began cutting wages severely. In the process, business became discredited. Even business leaders came to look to government to rescue the economic system from collapse (Perelman, 1996, ch. 7).

Although the New Deal never managed to lift the economy out of the depression, the more massive government presence during the Second World War did. After the war, economic conditions were ideal. The economies of all the potential rivals of the USA were in ruins. Interest rates were low. US consumers were flush with liquidity and hungry for consumer goods. For a couple of decades, a post-war boom lent credibility to the saying that a rising tide lifts all boats, but then the bloom wore off. During the immediate post-war period, Fordist practices revived, but with an immense change in emphasis. Decades of restrictive immigration meant that the majority of industrial workers were no longer foreign born. The concern with Americanization of the workforce was no longer relevant.

The legal status of the unions had also changed. Instead of buying off individual workers, large employers had to buy labour peace through the unions. Employers had to make sufficient concessions to the unions to give the unions sufficient credibility to prevent workers from taking militant action. To further reduce the potential for militancy, the unions purged much of their left wing. Once again, Fordist employers could afford to pay a premium on their wage. After all, in the immediate post-war period, the USA had an enormous competitive advantage *vis-à-vis* the rest of the world, but this practice could survive only under a narrow set of conditions, which began to disappear in the late 1960s and early 1970s. Although wages continued to be relatively high, the benevolent persona of welfare capitalism had long disappeared.

According to the theorists of welfare capitalism, unemployment should remain low. Relations between labour and capital should be somewhat amicable. Consequently, labour would not be unduly threatened by efforts to modernize production. The Fordism of the post-war period superficially resembled the ideals of welfare capitalism, but relations between business and its workforce were sour. Employers no longer considered high wages to be advantageous. Instead, they only reluctantly bowed to the growing power of labour, which compelled them to pay what they considered to be exorbitant wages. Indeed, business had done little to win the trust of its employees. Labour was not anxious to cooperate in the process of modernization, especially since comparable jobs were not always available at the time.

In once sense, wages were not high at all during the 'Golden Age'. According to the theorists of an economy of high wages, the cost of wages should be so steep that it would create an urgency to find ways to economize on labour. Such pressure seemed to be absent during the Golden Age. Business added considerable capacity, but it did little to modernize existing plant and equipment, since military Keynesianism effectively relieved the competitive pressures.

Few observers had recognized that, while military Keynesianism had staved off serious depressions, it had also held competitive forces at bay. After a while, modern economic capacity in Europe, Japan and even parts of mainland Asia stood ready to challenge the aging industrial plant of the USA, which was ill-prepared to meet the competition from abroad. As a result, profits suffered. As profits began to decline, business sought to improve its situation by becoming more aggressive, battling the left politically, culturally and on the shop floor, both through technical change and by attacking labour directly. Capital won a relatively free regime of flexible accumulation. Business successfully bolstered profits, winning relief from labour, taxes and regulation. In addition, new markets and new sources of cheap labour helped profits to recover.

THE TRIUMPH OF CAPITAL IN THE REGIME OF FLEXIBLE ACCUMULATION

In discussing the new regime of flexible accumulation, mention should also be made of the role of new technology, especially the computer. After all, most discussions of the cause of the new regime focus on the technological dimension. That perspective is rejected here. The fact is that the rise and fall of Fordism grew out of the social relationship of labour and capital. Technology was a secondary matter. For example, General Motors poured huge sums of money into robotizing its Hamtramck plant, under the delusion that technology alone would be sufficient to revolutionize production. The experiment was a total failure. In contrast, General Motors' participation in the New United Motor Manufacturing Inc. is generally considered a success, even though it used seemingly outdated technology (Keller, 1989, p. 208).

Although Fordism began as a response to the class power of workers, the key to the collapse of Fordism was, as Gramsci had predicted, an intensification of competitive conditions. Capital could enjoy the fruits of the new system that replaced Fordism only after it had waged intense social, cultural and political battles. In the USA, capital succeeded in reconstructing the entire legal and administrative terrain of labour–management relations. In the process, capital has managed to define the economic agenda. Capital has successfully created a vision of the world in which competition is both virtuous and efficient. In contrast, according to this perspective, every public institution, excepting the police and the military, supposedly is either wasteful or outright dangerous.

Capital has succeeded in changing the economic landscape so effectively that it has accomplished what economics teaches is impossible. According to economic theory, wages should reflect workers' productivity. When productivity expands, workers supposedly share in the social dividend. Instead, the top 5 per cent of households in the USA have captured virtually all of the fruits of economic growth, while wages have been stagnant or even declining. Recent economic changes have aided in this massive redistribution of income and wealth, but capital never could have managed to accomplish so much without effectively demonizing labour, as well as most disadvantaged groups. This cultural and political strategy has been so overwhelming that capital has remained effectively unchallenged for decades.

A 'divide and conquer' strategy is key to capital's success. Business offers to locate factories in the locale that promises the most benefits. In some cases, states offer hundreds of thousands of dollars for each job created. By foolishly depleting their funds in such competition, states have less to support valuable social programmes. In the process, states must look to the corporations to perform more and more social functions.

Business tells workers that it plans to close down one of a handful of plants. Rather than making unified demands to the company, workers vie with one another to show that their plant is the most efficient of the bunch.

Business creates illusory class differences within their workforce by creating two-tier wage structures, contracting out low-skilled workers or classifying them as temporaries. Business makes workers fear, not always irrationally, that certification of a union means that the workplace will shut down or relocate. The legal system condones flagrantly anti-union activity that would have been illegal only a few years ago. Ominously, international trade organizations now stand ready to dismantle many national reforms in the name of the sanctity of free trade. Building solidarity in this environment requires new tactics, along with large doses of courage, patience and creativity.

MONOPOLY RENTS AND INTELLECTUAL PROPERTY

In many parts of the economy, fiercely competitive conditions seem to validate business's anti-labour stance. How can any employer afford to pay something extra to labour when one misstep can spell the end of the company? Yet, in many other sectors, business enjoys a relative freedom from competitive pressures under an umbrella of intellectual property rights. If Gramsci was correct, and the lack of competition was a key to Fordism, here might be a place for labour to make some new inroads.

It seems that labour in the USA has largely ignored the subject of intellectual property. The creation of new intellectual property rights represents one of the more important methods whereby business has prospered at the expense of the rest of society. In the emerging industrial system, intellectual property is becoming more important than industrial property. Although intellectual property is not a direct concern on the shop floor, it does have an enormous effect on the relative powers of labour and capital (Perelman, 1998).

Under a regime of intellectual property, major branches of industry are shielded from competition of the usual type. Workers, in contrast, have become vulnerable to competition from every corner and find their rights are shrinking. So, while the government stands ready to protect business from competition in the name of intellectual property rights, workers must endure more competition because of the sanctity of market forces. Often the same companies that revel in the profits of their intellectual property profit from the most inhuman working conditions.

Even so, the regime of intellectual property does hold some promise. For most sellers of intellectual property goods – whether Nike, Disney or Microsoft – labour costs are an insignificant part of the final price of their product. Holding down labour costs adds relatively little to their profit margin. Instead, their ability to maintain their high margins is often associated with a type of good will. Reputation is very important for these companies. In the case of, say, Disney or Nike, they devote huge amounts of money to advertising, in the hope of making consumers feel good about their products.

Although labour in the USA has not directly addressed the question of intellectual property, some unions are beginning to challenge the reputation of such companies, knowing how damaging publicity about their superexploited workforce will be to that reputation. These campaigns are in their infancy. How much leverage they will ultimately give remains to be seen.

In addition, labour might challenge government to be less zealous in the protection of intellectual property in situations where business tramples on workers' rights. Given effective political action, the monopoly rents of intellectual capital might provide the basis for future improvements in labour's conditions, just as they did with Fordism. It is to be hoped that the benefits of these monopoly rents would not be restricted only to those workers who happened to find themselves in one of these monopolistic sectors.

COME THE DEPRESSION

Like Fordism, flexible accumulation is, at best, a temporary way station for capital. It is fraught with contradictions. After all, every economic formation in history has eventually fallen apart. This new system will do so as well.

Even though intellectual property rights may protect many industries from competition, eventually competitive forces will break out and throw the system into chaos. We are already beginning to reach a saturation point in effective demand. Labour would do well to prepare for major shifts in the current competitive structure. An upsurge in competition and, with it a depression are bound to occur some time in the future. When it happens, our world will be less prepared than it has ever been, now that most safety mechanisms have been dismantled.

Depressions represent both a threat and an opportunity for labour. The threat is obvious: depressions mean falling wages and unemployment. The opportunity is only slightly less obvious: a depression will discredit the prevailing neoliberal orthodoxy, opening the way for people to propose new alternatives – but only if we are well prepared before the opportunity falls in our lap. Before we face the next depression, we have to develop a clear vision of what we want to put in its place. In addition, we will have to have already laid the groundwork in public opinion. Here again we return to the theme of the continuing cultural conflict.

Within this context, successful labour tactics in the future clearly must take account of the destructive role of competitive forces, but they must also keep the social and cultural dimension in mind. Regrettably, capital has long understood this perspective far better than the leadership of organized labour in the USA.

CHARTING THE FUTURE

What then is the best strategy for labour? Changing the course of society will be more difficult than ever because of concentrated media control and the current form of political campaign finance. Obviously, we all know that labour must make alliances and communicate in ways that it has never done. Otherwise, capital's successful 'divide and conquer' tactics will continue to succeed.

In the USA, during the Great Depression, labour could win reforms with relative ease because few people were benefiting from the status quo. Much the same conditions exist today; once again disadvantaged groups and labour are bearing the brunt of the costs of competition. However, during the Great Depression, many middle and even upper class people also fell victim to the economy. The descent for many of these people is perceived as an individual tragedy rather than as part of a larger social process.

The creation of labour solidarity is not largely dependent on the addition of a large number of people from the middle and upper classes to our ranks, but their support could be convenient. There are some hopeful signs. The new market-oriented system is fast losing any credibility because of its excesses. Even business publications complain about high executive salaries. So far, this displeasure has mostly manifested itself in the political sphere, with the election of mildly reformist politicians who quickly adopt the cloak of neoliberalism. The actions of these politicians will discredit everyone who calls neoliberalism into question.

While we cannot ignore politics altogether, all of us need to work on developing an organizational infrastructure and to begin formulating a clear programme to eliminate all the toxic neoliberal excesses from our system and to make way for a new way of organizing our lives. We cannot recreate Fordism. Nor should we want to. The economy of high wages – an important part of early Fordism – is another matter. Although the call for an economy of high wages is a strategic retreat, it is possible that such an economy could serve as a way station on the path to a more rational organization of the economy, but it is by no means certain that an economy of high wages would work. Certainly, an economy of high wages could be no worse than what we have.

How would an economy of high wages work? Like Italy, the USA has a low-wage southern region. Our south remained an economic backwater until the time that federal legislation, such as minimum wage requirements, required management to be more efficient. Over time, some parts of the south have attained parity with the north, but much of the south still remains mired in poverty, a living legacy of a long history of low wages and slavery. How could we achieve an economy of high wages? Today we are in uncharted waters. Even history offers us little guidance in this matter.

The fact that the Great Depression brought an end to welfare capitalism does not prove that it could not work. After all, even during its heyday, the economy of high wages was never really put into effect. The population of welfare capitalists constituted only a minority of the capitalists, although this group included some of the most important capitalists of the day.

Let me close on a positive note. Typically, economists teach that many goals are worthwhile in themselves, but that the dictates of the market make them impractical. In contrast, the fight for high wages joins together the goals of social justice and economic efficiency. The one drawback of this strategy is that, by making the market more efficient, it may postpone the day when we will enjoy a better way of organizing our society.

REFERENCES

Gramsci, Antonio (1971), 'Americanism and Fordism', *Selections from the Prison Notebooks of Antonio Gramsci*, ed. and trans. Quintin Hoare and Geoffrey Novell Smith, New York: International Publishers.

Keller, Maryann (1989), *Rude Awakening: The Rise, Fall and Struggle for Recovery of General Motors*, New York: William Morris.

Perelman, Michael (1996), *The End of Economics*, London: Routledge.

Perelman, Michael (1998), *Class Struggles in the Information Age*, New York: St. Martin's Press.

8. Lean production in North America: myth and reality

Carl H.A. Dassbach

In the last 15 years, 'lean production' or the 'Japanese system of production' has been the object of considerable interest and discussion in the western industrialized nations. Proponents of this system claim that it results in a 'win–win' situation because both labour and management benefit. Management benefits from increased flexibility, improved quality and productivity and workers benefit from improved work and working conditions, enhanced skill levels and more meaningful work. This is certainly a compelling image for both labour, caught in the trap of tightly controlled repetitious work emptied of all meaningful content, and management, caught in the bind of low productivity, poor quality and inflexibility.

This chapter will argue that the claim that the Japanese system is a 'win–win' situation is, in fact, a myth which cannot stand up to close scrutiny. As experiences in North American transplants have shown, management wins and the workers lose because the quality of working life in a Japanese plant is not superior to a conventional or Fordist plant. If anything, the adoption of Japanese techniques leads to the *further* degradation of working life due to undermanning, faster work cycles, the elimination of any vestige of idle time and the elevation of stress levels.

THE ORIGINS OF THE MYTH OF THE JAPANESE SYSTEM

The myth of the Japanese system has its origin in attempts to explain Japan's advantage in world markets. During the late 1970s, explanations emphasized unique aspects of Japanese culture and business practices such as the role of the state, managerial attitudes, low wages and a more docile workforce. While all these explanations seemed plausible, none could be demonstrated with any certainty. In the early 1980s, attention turned to a new and relatively neglected factor: the Japanese system for organizing and managing production. Unlike other explanations, this one had some tangible evidence, namely the fact that Japanese automobile transplants in North America were able to produce vehicles, using a non-Japanese workforce, comparable in quality to those produced in Japan *and* despite being located in an industry long characterized by adversarial labour relations, excessive costs and poor quality (Treece and Hoerr, 1989; Rowand, 1983). The only explanation for this success was that transplants had duplicated most of the principles and practices of the Japanese system for organizing and managing production (Institute of Social Science, 1990; Florida and Kenney, 1991). As a result, this system came to be identified as the key factor in Japan's success and transplants were seen as evidence that these methods were not dependent on Japanese culture and could be transferred outside Japan.

It was on this foundation that academics and consultants, both at the forefront of myth creation for somewhat different publics, began their work. Starting from the apparent success of the transplants, these two groups generated an elaborate and well-articulated myth about the Japanese system and the nature of industrial work in Japan. Many (Wood, 1987; DiLorenzo, 1988; Lipietz, 1987; Cusumano, 1988; Krafcik, 1988, 1989; Hoerr, 1989; Brown and Reich, 1989; Yoshida, 1992; Adler, 1993) have contributed to this myth, but the efforts of two groups of authors stand out. In fact, they can be seen as the chief architects of the myth. One group, James Womack, Daniel T. Jones and Daniel Roos, are authors of *The Machine That Changed the World*. The other group, Richard Kenney and Martin Florida, have written two books and several articles on the Japanese system.

Womack *et al.*'s *The Machine That Changed the World* has been an extremely important text for disseminating the myth of the Japanese system to the wider public and corporate audience. The book's main contribution to the myth is its argument for the superiority of Japanese techniques; it devotes scant attention to the nature and quality of working life. This is Kenney and Florida's area of 'expertise'. Although their readership has largely been academics and specialists, their writings represent the single most important and consistent statement on the positive impact of Japanese techniques on the quality of working life. For this reason, and because of the fact that much of what Kenney and Florida write echoes the work of other people and finds itself echoed by others, their work will be used to outline the myth of work in a Japanese factory. In particular, this chapter will rely on their *magnum opus*, a 1993 book entitled *Beyond Mass Production*, which draws together a substantial number of articles and another book on the topic written during the previous decade.

Specifically, Kenney and Florida point to several unique features that explain the superiority of the Japanese system: team-based organization, the reunification of conception and execution on the shop floor, multiskilling, job rotation and cooperative relations between labour and management. Of all these features, team-based organization is generally seen as the most important, and they devote an extended discussion to the importance of teams as the 'core of the system'. Rather than summarize their claims, excerpts from their text are reproduced below. These are lengthy, but reproducing them is important, for two reasons. First, a summary could never do these passages justice because it would be difficult to lavish such unabashed praise on the Japanese system. Second, the language of these passages is revealing. The prose verges almost on awe and the system is invested with almost heroic qualities. These passages, in other words, clearly show Kenney and Florida constructing a myth.

> With teams, work roles overlap and tasks can be assigned to groups of workers and then reallocated internally by team members. ... The pace of production can be changed by adding or removing workers, and management and team members can experiment with different configurations for completing specified tasks. Teams also provide an internal source of motivation and of discipline for workers. Teams perform routine quality control, thereby undertaking much of the work that is performed by the quality-control department of fordist manufacturing. Teams are the basic mechanism for achieving the *functional integration* of tasks, which stands at the heart of the Japanese model. (Kenney and Florida, 1993, pp. 36–7, original emphasis)

> Team based organization of work provides the concrete organizational mechanism ... for moving decision making down to the shop floor and tapping the intelligence of factory workers. The team is the mechanism through which workers solve production problems and innovate for management... Workers use their intelligence and knowledge to devise cooperative strategies to overcome ... bottlenecks. The team is simultaneously the source of motivation, discipline and social control.
> The self-managing work team of contemporary Japanese capitalism devolves a variety of managerial responsibilities to the shop-floor. It thus facilitates the functional integration of tasks and overcomes the fine-grained specialized division of labor or fordist production organization. The team makes the extraction of intellectual (and manual) labor a quintessential, social, intersubjective and collective process. (Ibid., p. 39)

There are more passages but these are sufficient to capture the authors' main claims. First, as these passages repeatedly emphasize, teams in Japanese factories control their tasks and the nature of their work – workers perform overlapping tasks and tasks are allocated and reallocated within the team by the team members. Teams provide an atmosphere that fosters worker creativity and an avenue to exercise this creativity because teams, not managers, solve problems and implement solutions. Team-based organization permits management to move decision making to the shop floor and this reunifies conception and execution. Teams provide psychological support, motivation and discipline. Team members freely share the knowledge and short-cuts gained in the performance of their tasks with other workers through regular, voluntary participation in *kaizen* or continuous improvement activities. Teams are, in other words, tightly integrated, autonomous workgroups where members define how tasks will be performed, cooperate to complete these tasks, solve whatever problems arise and implement their solutions.

A second important feature of the Japanese system is job rotation. Unlike Fordist factories, where workers perform the same task all day, workers in Japanese factories rotate between different tasks within their teams, between teams and between departments. Rotation is also the basis for another important characteristic of the system: multiskilling. Because workers rotate between different tasks, they develop 'multiple skills' or become what Kenney and Florida (ibid., p. 39) call 'polyvalent'. Multiskilling means, in turn, that workers in Japanese plants are 'flexible'. Not only do they perform ancillary tasks, such as cleaning or simple machine maintenance, in addition to their regular tasks, but they can be easily deployed to different parts of the factory in response to contingencies.

Where labour relations in a Fordist factory are adversarial and antagonistic, labour relations in a Japanese factory are consensual and cooperative. Several mechanisms, according to Kenney and Florida, ensure open communications between labour and management. Lower- and middle-level managers are recruited directly from the shop floor, while upper-level managers spend part of their career on the shop floor. All employees belong to the same union, eat in the same cafeteria and park in the same car park. Managers constantly interact with workers on the shop floor and workers' ideas and suggestions are taken seriously by management. Lifetime employment for the core workforce means that peaceful relations with management is in the best interests of all parties. A system of bonuses for both managers and workers, which constitutes a substantial part of an individual's remuneration and which hinges on a company's performances, results in a strong collective interest in maximizing profits.

Just this brief summary is enough to show that the picture of work in a Japanese factory painted by Kenney and Florida stands in marked contrast to the repetitious, routinized and deskilled work in a Fordist factory. This is not to suggest that Kenney and Florida are indifferent to the negative aspects of work in Japan; they even devote a few sentences to discussing the intense pace, long hours and the problem of *karoshi*, or death by overwork, in Japan. But, on the whole, they dismiss these problems as minor and dismiss criticisms of the Japanese system as unsubstantiated or misplaced. Anyone reading their work cannot help but come to the conclusion that work in a Japanese factory is totally unlike work in a traditional Fordist plant and that all companies must rapidly implement the Japanese system.

THE REALITY OF THE JAPANESE SYSTEM

The reality of work in a Japanese factory stands in such marked contrast to Kenney and Florida's depiction that one cannot help but wonder how they came to their conclusions.[1] Whatever their reasons, Kenney and Florida go to great lengths to dismiss critical studies (Kamata, 1982; Dohse *et al.*, 1985; Burawoy, 1985; Parker and Slaughter, 1988) and, when they cannot avoid acknowledging difficulties in American transplants, they attribute these to 'unreconstructed American managers' and not the system itself (Kenney and Florida, 1993, pp. 103, 104, 267–9, 287–8, 289–91).

Well before Kenney and Florida's book, evidence was accumulating which indicated that work in a Japanese factory was not substantially different from that in a conventional Fordist factory and may, because of the stress resulting from undermanning and the intense rate of production, be even worse. Since publication of the book, additional studies have produced enough solid evidence[2] to demonstrate clearly the errors in Kenney and Florida's and similar discussions of Japanese factories. This does not, however, prevent the myth from continuing to circulate among academics,[3] consultants and companies trying to sell workers on a 'Japanese-style' work reorganization. In other words, the myth is still alive today.

One of the most striking differences between the myth and reality of work under the Japanese system is the role and function of teams. Teams in Japanese plants are not, as advocates maintain, autonomous, self-managing units which internally reallocate work tasks and harness the intelligence of workers to solve problems and implement solutions. In reality, team-based organization has an entirely different objective: enhancing control over work and workers. Teams enhance control in several ways. They formalize the informal workgroups of conventional plants, bring them under management's control (Rehder, 1990, p. 90) and significantly reduce the likelihood that these groups, which have historically been an important source of shopfloor resistance, will oppose management. At the same time, smaller workgroups with their own leaders result in a more finely graduated hierarchy and far closer supervision than traditional plants. Finally, teams provide an additional dimension of control, so-called 'lateral control' based on peer pressure which Rinehart *et al.* (1997, p. 89) claim 'may shape behavior more powerfully than hierarchical control'. Specifically, team members exert pressure on other team members to complete their tasks correctly and in the allotted time, so as not to place additional burdens on the team.

Given this reality of teams, team leaders cannot correspond to the image presented by proponents of Japanese production. Proponents would have us believe that team leaders act mainly as information 'transmitters' or 'expediters'. In reality, team leaders bear, as Lichtenstein (1988) observes, 'an uncanny resemblance to the old "straw bosses"' of the 1920s. The primary function of team leaders is 'control, surveillance and exploitation' (Garrahan and Stewart, 1992, p. 62). Team leaders supervise four to eight workers on the micro level. They directly oversee the work, act as relief and assist team members who are having difficulties completing their tasks. Consequently, team leaders must be not simply familiar with all of the team's tasks but adept enough at these tasks to demonstrate how they can be accomplished in the allotted time.

Team leaders in North American plants have found themselves divided between management and the workers: managers want team leaders to identify with the company and act as first-line supervisors, while workers want team leaders to identify with them and act in their best interests (Rinehart *et al.*, 1997, p. 94). In cases where this conflict has come to a head, team leaders have tended to side with workers and managers have responded in various ways. At Mazda, in Flat Rock, Michigan, team leaders were stripped of any power once the factory was running and salaried unit leaders took control of several teams and began making changes without informing workers (Fucini and Fucini, 1990). At the CAMI plant, the democratic selection of team leaders was discontinued and team leaders were selected by management (Rinehart *et al.*, 1997, pp. 93–8). Even at NUMMI, the Toyota–GM plant in California cited as the showcase 'lean' plant in the USA (Brown and Reich, 1989; Niland, 1989; Adler, 1993), conflicts about team leaders led to workers electing a slate of shopfloor representatives who campaigned on a platform of more aggressively protecting worker rights (Victor, 1989; Turner, 1989; Parker and Slaughter, 1988).

The internal operation of teams also differs markedly from that depicted in the myth. First, the ability of workers to reallocate tasks within the team or even to have a true input into the way tasks are to be performed is almost nil. In his definitive work on Toyota, *Toyota Production Systems*, Monden (1983, pp. 85–6) is quite clear on who determines work procedures and allocates tasks: foremen and not team leaders.

> *Standard operations* is aimed at production using a minimum number of workers.... A standardized order of the various operations to be performed by each worker, called the *standard operations routine*, is important in facilitating this goal. The components of the standard operation are determined mainly by the foreman (supervisor). The foreman determines the labor hours required to produce one unit at each machine and also the order of the various operations to be performed by each worker. (Original emphasis)

All Japanese companies use standard operations routine and discussions about transplants confirm that foremen or team leaders determine standard operations and assign tasks to workers (Parker and Slaughter, 1988; Kenney and Florida, 1993; Robertson *et al.*, 1992; Garrahan and Stewart, 1992).[4] According to Babson (1992, p. 7), 'team members [at Mazda in Flat Rock] can not alter their programmed Work Sheets without supervisory approval, and casual deviation from the programmed job sequence is strongly discouraged'. Standardization is also used to control non-working behaviour. All workers who have 'empty' time during a job cycle are instructed to remain absolutely motionless. This reveals the 'pores' in a worker's tasks so that these can be eliminated.

Similarly, the claimed autonomy of workers and teams looks much different from the shop floor. What Kenney and Florida identify as worker or team autonomy and participation in decision making is really 'pseudo-participation' that is rigidly and autocratically controlled by management. Individuals cannot innovate. Management and team leaders *decide* which work procedures can be modified and how they will be modified, and all changes must be cleared by *several layers of management* before they are implemented (Graham, 1993; Garrahan and Stewart, 1992; Robertson *et al.*, 1992). Moreover, transplants in North America have gone to great lengths to protect management's direct control over work. In the case of Mazda at Flat Rock, 'the Management Rights Clause in the collective bargaining agreement establishes the company's exclusive right to "direct and control ... the methods, process and means of handling work"' (Babson, 1992, p. 6).

The image of the multiskilled worker is another aspect of the myth which does not stand up to close scrutiny. While it is true that workers in Japanese plants perform multiple tasks, it is a gross exaggeration to call these workers '*multiskilled*'. Consider Monden's (1983, pp. 69–70) description of the work routine of what Kenney and Florida would surely call a 'multiskilled' worker:

> Toyota prepared a new workplace layout ... so that each worker could handle several different types of machines at the same time. In the gear manufacturing process, for example ... each worker attends to 16 machines ... which perform different types of operations: grinding, cutting, etc. The worker ... first picks up one unit of a gear brought from the preceding process and sets it onto the first machine. At the same time, he detaches another gear already processed by this machine and puts it on a chute to roll in front of the next machine. Then, while he is walking to the second machine, he pushes a button between the first and second machines to start the first machine. He performs similar operation on the second machine, and then he moves to the third machine pushing a button again to start the second machine, and so on, until he has worked on all sixteen machines and finally returned to the initial process.

In fact, there are very few *skills* involved in the multiple *tasks* which this worker or most 'multiskilled' workers in Japanese factories perform. Most critical observers would agree with Parker and Slaughter's (1988, p. 80) observation that 'Multi-skilling every worker means deskilling every job', or

> The essence of 'multi-skilling' is actually the *lack of resistance*, on the part of the union or individual worker, to management reassigning jobs whenever it wishes, for whatever reason.... Once hired, the worker does not benefit by learning more marketable skills. Instead, she learns how to carry out a large number of extremely 'job-specific' tasks. (Ibid., p. 25, original emphasis)

Kenney and Florida's claim that job rotation is a universal feature of the Japanese system is disproved by the experiences of the North American transplants. At best, there is evidence of rotation between cognate jobs at some transplants (Adler, 1993; Kenney and Florida, 1993; Brown and Reich, 1989) but rotation does *not* occur at all transplants. At Nissan's US plant, job rotation was abandoned after 14 months of operation and was only used to punish disgruntled workers by assigning them the most demanding jobs in the factory for months at a time (Junkerman, 1987). At Mazda, rotation was scrapped once the plant was at full production, even among skilled workers who had been specifically cross-trained (Fucini and Fucini, 1990; Babson, 1992). At the Mitsubishi plant in Illinois, rotation was largely abandoned after the United Auto Workers (UAW) replaced the original 'flexible' contract with a more traditional contract (Pinto, 1992). In the CAMI plant, rotation became increasingly problematic as both workers and managers objected to frequent rotation to different tasks (Rinehart *et al.*, 1997, pp. 56–9).

In point of fact, and despite the supposed centrality of these practices, self-managed teams, worker autonomy and job rotation are inconsistent with what many consider to be the most important feature of the Japanese system, JIT or 'just-in-time' production. JIT attempts to convert production to a continuous flow by eliminating intermediate or buffer inventories and manufacturing components as they are needed. In reality, JIT operates with buffer inventories far smaller than those found in a Fordist, or 'just-in-case', system. Because of these small buffer inventories, JIT is 'fragile'[5] or extremely vulnerable to disruptions, and requires a close coordination and synchronization of work operations. Hence the departures from precisely planned routines that would be expected in a situation of genuine self-managed teams and autonomous workers cannot be tolerated, since they would disrupt the system. Likewise, job rotation is inconsistent with JIT because of *kaizen*, or constant improvement, which is universal at all Japanese plants. *Kaizen* means that all tasks have been so thoroughly rationalized that only the most adept workers are capable of performing them at the rate demanded by fully operational JIT production, and rotating less than adept workers to these tasks would cause the system to stall.

Finally, there is the issue of so-called 'cooperative' labor–management relations in Japanese plants. In point of fact, Kenney and Florida have simply confused cooperation and worker participation with obedience and consent to authority. In a study of Japanese factories, Cole (1979, p. 201) captures the essence of the difference:

[The emphasis in Japanese plants is] on achieving the *consent* of workers for policies which *management wants to pursue as well as on guiding workers in the direction management wants them to move*. This is apparent in the rhetoric the company uses; the term *sanka* (participation) is not used, rather the focus is on *nattokusei* (consent) and *kobetsu shido* (individual guidance).... We have here a carefully controlled participation in which management often takes the lead informally or formally in initiating policies that workers are then guided to accept and pursue. (Original emphasis)

Most critical studies of North American transplants have come to essentially the same conclusion (Fucini and Fucini, 1990; Babson, 1992; Rinehart *et al.*, 1993; Pinto, 1992). For example, Graham (1993, p. 170) reports that at Subaru–Isuzu,

management controlled the parameters of what was in the realm of consideration and also when, how and where a job was altered.... Workers were seldom allowed to make even the most inconsequential decision on their own... [This] unequal relationship between management and workers made it nearly impossible to reach a consensus involving little more than token input from workers.

WORKER RESISTANCE TO LEAN PRODUCTION

Perhaps the best evidence that the Japanese system does not correspond to its myth is worker resistance in North American transplants. Initially, workers were, by all reports, enthusiastic about the system, but this waned as transplants achieved full production and workers discovered the reality of work in these factories (Graham, 1993; Rinehart *et al.*, 1993; Victor, 1989; Fucini and Fucini, 1990; Rinehart *et al.*, 1997). Except in cases of open strikes, few transplants will acknowledge these problems. In fact, most go to great lengths to erect a wall of secrecy between the company and the outside world by refusing interviews, forbidding researchers from entering the plant and punishing workers who discuss their work. Nonetheless, there is ample evidence of problems in North American transplants.

Even though some transplants consciously attempted to minimize potential problems with worker motivation by locating in rural or depressed areas and paying high wages, these problems remain. Further compounding these difficulties is the fact that North American workers are unwilling to accept the Japanese system of incentive and performance wages. As a result, transplants have resorted to promotions and special rewards as motivators, but managers admit that the usefulness of these strategies is limited (Maskery, 1990).

Another indication of problems in the transplants is the fact that some have abandoned the Japanese practice of no end-of-the-line inspection. At the North American operations of both Honda and Toyota, management implemented a system of final inspection and repair bays. Although company officials minimize this departure from Japanese practices by claiming either that the problems in most of the rejects 'wouldn't even be noticed by customers' or that North American plants assemble cars differently from Japanese plants, the fact remains that rejects are running in the vicinity of 10 to 11 per cent. According to Honda officials in Canada, this is 'high by company standards' (Chappell, 1991).

The most extreme cases of open worker resistance have occurred in the unionized plants. In September 1992, members of the Canadian Auto Workers union at CAMI went on strike after 98.9 per cent of the plant's 2100 workers voted to walk out. The strike was only settled with a new contract that was closer to a traditional contract. A similar, if less dramatic, situation occurred at the UAW-organized Mazda plant in Flat Rock, Michigan. First, in May 1989, representatives of New Directions, a faction of the UAW which opposed the cooperative agreement between the UAW and Mazda's management, won control of the local by displacing the incumbent leaders; 22 months later, in March of 1991, UAW workers at the same plant, now renamed AutoAlliance, Inc., replaced the original, cooperative agreement between the company and the UAW with a more traditional contract. At Diamond Star Motors, originally a joint venture between Mitsubishi and Chrysler, the UAW also replaced the original flexible contract with a more traditional contract (Fucini and Fucini, 1990; Pinto, 1992). Even at NUMMI, a dissident 'People's Caucus' emerged to challenge the leadership of the UAW local on issues such as line speed and grievance procedures (Victor, 1989; Turner, 1989; Parker and Slaughter, 1988).

Although non-unionized transplants such as Nissan, Honda, Toyota or Subaru–Isuzu have not had similar public displays of dissatisfaction, this is generally attributed to the lack of formal mechanisms for articulating dissatisfaction, rather than high degrees of worker satisfaction. Most likely, as workers get older and find it increasingly difficult to maintain the pace of production, they will unionize and implement grievance procedures and other formal mechanisms for articulating dissatisfaction. Privately, workers at many transplants confide that, given the line speed and the number of tasks they must perform, they doubt if they will be able to stay with the company for 20 years (Pinto, 1992). Reports indicate that workers at non-unionized transplants are also hesitant to voice complaints about working conditions or pull the cord which stops the production line out of fear of retaliation by team leaders and supervisors (Kraar, 1989; Kertesz, 1988). Similarly, workers at both Honda and Nissan are suspicious of, and reluctant to use, the available mechanisms for resolving disputes or adjudicating terminations, the so-called 'peer review panels', because these panels have generally favoured management. At Nissan, the panel has never overturned a management decision and, at Honda, 80 per cent of the decisions are in favour of management (Kertesz, 1988).

CONCLUSION

During the 1980s, concerns about the impact of lean production on the quality of working life were largely restricted to Japan and North America. During the 1990s, however, these techniques have been adopted by almost all car producers,[6] and lean production has now become a universal problem. In some cases, the implementation of lean techniques has not been accompanied by glowing descriptions, *à la* Kenney and Florida. Instead, it has been done by management fiat and presented to workers as an ultimatum: either accept these techniques or lose your jobs. In such cases the mythic elements are, of course, less important.

But, regardless of the actual 'bargaining process' by which companies have moved towards lean production, certain facts remain indisputable: (1) more and more companies have adopted these techniques; (2) these techniques significantly degrade the quality of work and working life when compared to Fordist practices;[7] (3) despite rhetoric about the growing importance of automatic systems of machinery, that working 'smarter not harder' is the most important factor in modern production and that labour costs are relatively unimportant in the highly mechanized manufacturing process, the massive shift to lean production serves to demonstrate again the true nature of capitalism. Profits depend on the extraction of surplus labour, and the continued heightening of the exploitation of the labouring classes is capitalism's characteristic feature and its eternal objective.

NOTES

1. One possible explanation may be that, despite having spent at least six months in Japan and speaking with managers, scientists and academics, Kenny and Florida did not, as far as one can tell, speak with *one* Japanese worker. In Kenney and Florida (1993), App. A: Overview of the Research, 'Research in Japan', pp. 326–7), they describe their research activities in Japan, but the discussion is contradictory. In the opening paragraphs, they say that they conducted more than 120 interviews with 'executives, R&D scientists, engineers and *workers*' (p. 326, emphasis added) and yet in the subsequent and more detailed description of their visits there is not one mention of workers. Even more telling is the fact that Kenney and Florida frequently use quotations from American workers in their discussion of Japanese transplants in the USA but do not use one statement by a Japanese worker in their discussion of the system in Japan.
2. Perhaps the strongest indictment of the Japanese system is found in Rinehart *et al.* (1997), a two-year study of workers at CAMI, a joint Suzuki–GM factory in Canada.
3. See, for example, Kochan *et al.* (1997) which, despite its title, *After Lean Production*, is

precisely about the superiority of these techniques, but under the rubric of 'high-involvement work practices'.
4. Still, Kenney and Florida (1993, p. 106) report that workers at Honda and Toyota's US plants have a 'significant input in the design of their jobs'. One wonders about the veracity of this statement, given both their previous observation (p. 105) that 'team leaders are the first line of supervision and play crucial roles in organization, design and allocation of work on a daily basis' and the fact that they cite interviews with manufacturing *executives* at Honda and Toyota, and not workers, as the source of this statement.
5. And Fordism or 'just-in-case' has been characterized as robust.
6. See Kochan *et al.* (1997) for a series of articles detailing the spread of lean techniques throughout Europe and other parts of the world.
7. This is not to suggest that working in a Fordist factory was a paradise, but all the available evidence shows that, despite the shortcomings and problems of Fordism, working conditions were superior to those of the Japanese system: manning levels were much higher, usually there was far more inactive time between task cycles, stress levels were lower and there were far fewer injuries.

REFERENCES

Adler, Paul S. (1993), 'Time-and-motion regained', *Harvard Business Review*, Jan.–Feb., 97–108.
Babson, Steve (1992), 'Lean or mean: the M.I.T. model and lean production at Mazda', draft, Wayne State University Labor Studies.
Brown, Clair and Michael Reich (1989), 'When does union–management cooperation work? A look at NUMMI and GM-Van Nuys', *California Management Review*, **31**(4), 26–44.
Burawoy, Michael (1985), *The Politics of Production*, London: Verso.
Chappell, Lindsay (1991), 'Transplants break from Japan's inspection-free methods', *Automotive News*, 3 June, p. 10.
Cole, Robert E. (1979), *Work, Mobility and Participation*, Berkeley: University of California Press.
Cusumano, Michael (1988), 'Manufacturing innovation and competitive advantage: reflections on the Japanese automobile industry', Report MITJSTP 88-07, The MIT Japan Program, Cambridge, Mass.
DiLorenzo, Thomas (1988), *Lessons from Abroad: Japanese Labor Relations and the US Automobile Industry*, St. Louis: Center for the Study of American Business.
Dohse, K., U. Jurgens and T. Malsch (1985), 'From "Fordism" to "Toyotism"? The social organization of the labour process in the Japanese automobile industry', *Politics and Society*, **14**(2), 115–46.
Florida, Richard and Martin Kenney (1991), 'Transplanted organizations: the transfer of Japanese industrial organization to the US', *American Sociological Review*, **56**, June, 381–98.
Fucini, Joseph J. and Suzy Fucini (1990), *Working for the Japanese: Inside Mazda's American Auto Plant*, New York: The Free Press.
Garrahan, Philip and Paul Stewart (1992), *The Nissan Enigma: Flexibility at Work in a Local Economy*, New York: Mansell Publishing.
Graham, Laurie (1993), 'Inside a Japanese transplant: a critical perspective', *Work and Occupations*, **20**(2), May, 147–73.
Hoerr, John (1989), 'The payoff from teamwork', *Business Week*, 10 July, pp. 56–62.
Institute of Social Science (1990), *Local Production of Japanese Automobile and*

Electronic Firms in the United States: The 'Application and Adaptation' of Japanese Style Management, Research Report 23, Tokyo: University of Tokyo.

Junkerman, John (1987), 'Nissan, Tennessee', *The Progressive*, **51**(6), June, 17–20.

Kamata, Satoshi (1982), *Japan in the Passing Lane: An Insider's Account of Life in a Japanese Auto Factory*, trans. Tatsuru Akimoto, New York: Pantheon Books.

Kenney, Martin and Richard Florida (1993), *Beyond Mass Production: The Japanese System and its Transfer to the U.S.*, New York: Oxford University Press.

Kertesz, Louise (1988), 'Transplant wages, benefits similar', *Automotive News*, 6 June, p. 1.

Kochan, Thomas A., Russel D. Lansbury and John Paul MacDuffie (eds) (1997), *After Lean Production: Evolving Work Practices in the World Auto Industry*, Ithaca, NY/London: ILR Press.

Krafcik, J.F. (1988), 'The triumph of the lean production system', *Sloan Management Review*, Fall, 41–52.

Krafcik, John F. (1989), 'A new diet for U.S. manufacturing', *Technology Review*, January, **92**(1), 28–36.

Kraar, Louis (1989), 'Japan's gung-ho U.S. car plants', *Fortune*, **119**(3), 98–108.

Lichtenstein, Nelson (1988), 'The Unions' Early Days: Shop Stewards and Seniority Rights', in M. Parker and J. Slaughter (eds), *Choosing Sides: Unions and the Team Concept*, Boston: South End Press, pp. 65–75.

Lipietz, Alain (1987), *Mirages and Miracles: The Crisis of Global Fordism*, trans. David Macey, London: Verso.

Maskery, M.A. (1990), 'Loyalty bid', *Automotive News*, 15 October, p. 1.

Monden, Yasuhiro (1983), *Toyota Production Systems*, Norcross, Ga.: Institute of Industrial Engineers.

Niland, Powell (1989), 'U.S.–Japanese joint venture: new United Motor Manufacturing, Inc. (NUMMI)', *Planning Review*, **17**(1), January–February.

Parker, Mike and Jane Slaughter (1988), *Choosing Sides: Unions and the Team Concept*, Boston: South End Press.

Pinto, Liz (1992), 'Japanese labor ideals don't fly', *Automotive News*, 9 November, p. 3.

Rehder, Robert J. (1990), 'Japanese transplants: after the honeymoon', *Business Horizons*, January–February, 87–98.

Rinehart, James, David Robertson and Chris Huxley (1997), *Just Another Car Factory: Lean Production and its Discontent*, Ithaca, NY/London: ILR Press.

Rinehart, James, David Robertson, Chris Huxley and the CAW Research Group on CAMI (1993), 'Worker commitment and labour–management relations under lean production at CAMI', paper presented at the annual meetings of the Canadian Association of Sociology and Anthropology, 5 June, Ottawa.

Robertson, David, James Rinehart, Chris Huxley and the CAW Research Group on CAMI (1992), 'Team concept and *Kaizen*: Japanese production management in a unionized Canadian auto plant', *Studies in Political Economy*, **39**, Autumn, 77–107.

Rowand, Roger (1983), 'GM teardown shows U.S. Honda quality equals Japanese', *Automotive News*, 30 May, p. 8.

Treece, James B. and John Hoerr (1989), 'Shaking up Detroit', *Business Week*, 14 August, pp. 74–80.

Turner, Lowell (1989), 'Three plants, three futures', *Technology Review*, January, **92**(1), 39–45.

Victor, Kirk (1989), 'Tensions over teamwork', *National Journal*, 20 May, 1228–31.

Womack, James P., Daniel T. Jones and Daniel Roos (1990), *The Machine That Changed the World*, New York: HarperCollins Publishers.
Wood, Stephen (1987), 'The deskilling debate, new technology and work organization', *Acta Sociologica*, **30**(1), 3–24.
Yoshida, Kosaku (1992), 'New economic principles in America – competition and cooperation', *The Columbia Journal of World Business*, **26**(4), 30–44.

9. Management-by-stress and skilled work: the US case

Mike Parker

As lean production sweeps the global economy, some unions, academics and politicians seek to make the best of the new system for workers. They focus on the claim of lean production's advocates that, under the new workplace regime, workers' skills will increase. Lean production is seen, at least potentially as 'high-wage/high-performance': high skill levels and intense worker involvement, combined with new technology and workplace reorganization, are to create high productivity that can sustain good wages and excellent working conditions.

Many analysts say that a highly skilled workforce is a necessary correlate of lean production. Higher skills then provide the basis for true partnership between management and workers, through their unions. Others see the possibility of choosing either a high-skill lean production strategy or a low-skill lean production strategy.

Our argument starts from the proposition that lean production is best described from the workers' vantage point as 'management-by-stress': management exercises tighter control over production by using devices such as 'Andon boards' (production status displays) and statistical process control (SPC) charts that make any problems in production immediately visible. Any unresolved deviation quickly generates large and visible consequences. (In the extreme, a single missing item under just-in-time almost immediately shuts down the entire operation.) This way of functioning is a more efficient and effective disciplinarian of the workforce than layers of monitoring supervisors (Parker and Slaughter, 1988; 1994).

In this system, the priority placed on 'flexibility' – instant worker adaptability to managers' shifting requirements – and an urgent, pressurized atmosphere largely shape the approach to skilled work. While the system may raise skills in some cases, it also retards the ability of skilled *union* workers to keep up with changes in technology, and it increases management's ability to shift key skills from union workers to management personnel and to outside vendors.

The issue of workers' skills is of crucial importance to unions, affecting both their size and power. But several complications make it difficult to identify trends: no common definition of skill exists; there is no standard to evaluate training and retraining programmes; a technology-driven *change* of skill and training requirements does not mean an *increase* in skill requirements; union involvement in institutionalized training programmes creates interests that disguise the reality on the shop floor; the distribution of skills within and outside the bargaining unit is a sensitive political question in unions; the technical content of the skills makes it difficult for those without the technical background to evaluate training and skill requirements.

This chapter identifies some critical areas for further discussion, based on the author's opportunity to view skilled work in manufacturing from a number of different vantages, including electrician, union activist, researcher, training designer and instructor, control programmer and engineer, and service manager. The organization and procedures of skilled work seem to be heavily influenced by national laws and customs, so a comparison of the US experience described here with that in other countries is welcomed.

WHY IS SKILL IMPORTANT?

Management's attitude towards skilled work is of central importance in understanding lean production, for three reasons. First, skilled work means better jobs. What has traditionally been called 'skilled work' has usually meant better jobs for workers. Not only do they pay more, but skilled jobs generally have all the properties that most observers would assign to 'good' jobs, which in turn contribute to higher self-esteem: higher wages, more control over the work, ability to vary the pace of work, more creativity, greater job security and marketability, opportunity to work in collaboration with others, more respect from management and more power in dealing with management. Ironically, while claiming to enrich jobs, improve the quality of work life and empower workers, lean production tends to destroy some of the best jobs there are.

Second, the ideology of lean production maintains that the system needs highly skilled workers to achieve high productivity. With such high productivity, workers can gain a share of the benefits in the form of high wages, good working conditions and job security. By achieving these for the members, the union becomes stronger. The situation is 'win–win' for management and labour. Indeed, some unions are so enamoured of this approach that they offer to teach management how to introduce such systems (International Association of Machinists and Aerospace Workers, 1997).

Third, skill is an important part of the economic power of unions. To the extent that skilled work is concentrated in a small segment of the workforce, that small segment has disproportionately large power. Skilled work has historically been critical to the labour movement, both for its direct economic power and also because the conditions of skilled work tend to generate leadership for the labour movement as a whole. In the 1930s, for example, skilled tradesmen (they were all male) made up a disproportionate number of the leaders of the campaigns for *industrial unionism*, the US term for industry-wide unions rather than separate, craft unions for different job classifications.

In addition, their position in the production system greatly magnified the leverage of skilled workers. A good example is the skilled car workers' strike of 1939. This little-known strike was preceded by perhaps the most famous event in the rise of the UAW, the Flint sit-down strikes of the winter of 1936–37, which forced General Motors to 'recognize' and bargain with the UAW. By the end of 1937, however, General Motors seemed to have the whip hand again, and for the next 18 months 'a bitterly divided union seemed unable to respond' (Lichtenstein, 1995, p. 104). During that period the union lost many of its contracts and many of its members; one reason was a collapsing economy. About one-fourth of the GM workforce was laid off and many more stopped paying union dues. There was a political backlash against unions and against the use of the sit-down strike. GM executives moved aggressively against the union on all fronts. Internal union factionalism was both the result and further cause of the union's weakness. By the beginning of 1939, the parent federation, the Congress of Industrial Organizations (CIO), had put the UAW into trusteeship and appointed its leaders. The CIO and its rival, the American Federation of Labor (AFL), were preparing separate conventions. Chrysler and General Motors both announced a suspension of collective bargaining in any plant where both factions operated.

In May 1939, as the UAW–CIO sought to rebuild and Walter Reuther took charge of the union's General Motors Department, estimates placed the number of dues-paying members at GM at between 6 and 8 per cent. GM was seeking a new government-sponsored election to decertify the union. The union needed a decisive system-wide victory against GM to ward off both the direct threats from management and the indirect threats from a company-encouraged break-away AFL union.

UAW leaders knew that any attempt at a general GM strike would meet certain failure. Instead, Reuther and others determined to use the leverage of the GM tool and die workers, who were solidly committed to the CIO. They were in a powerful position because the company was in the midst of tooling up for a major redesign of its product.

In July 1939, the UAW began the Tool and Die Strike. Fewer than 7000 unionists, around 3 per cent of the roughly 200 000 GM hourly workers, actually struck. They had important assistance: tool and die makers in job shops set the GM work aside. Most of the minority of GM skilled tradesmen who belonged to the AFL joined the strike, against the orders of AFL leaders. The strike began to affect production, as dull and unrepaired tooling fixtures piled up. When managers tried to stir up production workers against the trades, the UAW asked production workers to help identify skilled scabs, and to refuse to set dies and do maintenance. The union emphasized that only a victorious skilled trades strike would 'make GM talk turkey for production workers' (Babson, 1991, p. 222).

Indeed, the strike was a more decisive victory for production workers than it was on the trades' specific demands. Part of the settlement was that GM agreed to recognize the UAW as the exclusive bargaining representative for all workers in 41 of 59 GM plants. As Babson sums it up:

> without the successful tool and die strike of that year the UAW would have been a fundamentally different union. General Motors would not have been reclaimed to the CIO, and failure here would have diminished the UAW's recovery elsewhere. Defeat in 1939 would have made the preceding victories of 1937 less of a watershed and more akin to the spasmodic union advances of 1885 and 1919.... The victory of the tool and die strike enabled the union to win – on its own terms – a secure position in the auto industry's leading firm. (Ibid., p. 237)

WHAT IS SKILL?

For purposes of this discussion, skill has two components. The first, the technical component, is the combination of genetic and learned abilities to accomplish tasks. We will assume here that the skills under discussion are learned abilities. Second, the term has a social component, in that it is usually applied to those whose capabilities are greater than the average population. Thus, although driving a car requires substantial training, the ability to operate a passenger car is not usually regarded as a skill because the ability is so widespread. Early in the Industrial Revolution, jobs that required literacy were considered skilled. Universal public education now makes literacy a minimum requirement for 'unskilled' jobs.

Of course, enormous barriers exist in the labour market, and training is not readily available to all who want it. The result is that the common use of the term 'skill' is often a measure of how a set of abilities is rewarded in the market-place: the higher the pay, the more 'skilled' the job is regarded to be. This shows up in the distinction generally made between skill and experience. A worker can be trained to do a number of highly complex operations that require exceptional manual coordination and/or critical decision making, involving very expensive process and materials. Yet, if the combination of operations is specific to just one particular workplace, the worker is described as 'experienced'. On the other hand, a worker who is trained in a series of tasks which as a package have significant demand in the market-place is considered 'skilled' and is paid more than his or her 'experienced' counterpart.

The market is further distorted by various structural features, particularly sexism and racism. These cause jobs mainly held by women and minorities to be regarded as less skilled than jobs requiring similar amounts of training that are held by white males. Thus, for years, nurses and elementary school teachers were less well regarded and paid less than mechanics. Similarly, as dry-wall installation in the US south-west came to be a predominantly Latino workers' job, pay failed to keep up.

This dual nature of skill leads to two general approaches to increasing what is regarded as skill. One is for the worker to gain additional knowledge and analytic abilities and to become more proficient in a range of technical tasks. The other approach is to manipulate the barriers so as to improve the market position of skilled workers, by limiting entry into the trade. Training can be restricted and licensing and admissions barriers can be installed to prevent the hiring of those who have learned the trade on their own. Union contract requirements limiting specific tasks to specific trades provide a different market barrier. The barrier approach in turn can be pursued in different directions.

Skilled workers can make an alliance with management to maintain the barriers. What management gets from this arrangement is the skilled workers' political and social support for monopolistic practices and higher profits. This *conservative* approach can easily give social support to racist and sexist discrimination so long as these are convenient and effective barriers to entry. Historically, this strategy is associated with urban construction trades organized into a different union for each craft, allied with local political machines. This approach leads to identification with management goals and to a conservative political orientation.

An alternative path is an *alliance* with workers whom the market identifies as not skilled. What do the 'non-skilled' get out of helping skilled workers restrict entry? First, it is possible that the power skilled workers wield can be used to advance the interests of production workers. The Tool and Die Strike is an excellent example. Second, the organized relationship between non-skilled and skilled can provide the route by which non-skilled workers can move into skilled positions.

This, we suggest, is the genius of the CIO's strategy of 'industrial unionism' in the 1930s. It was not just that the new unions organized all production workers into one union facing a common boss. It was also that they found ways to unite skilled and production workers in the same union, building on the power of the skilled tradesmen and the consciousness of a class-wide movement which arises from the needs of production workers.

The alliance, though not without problems, has worked out well. The UAW leadership, historically conscious of maintaining this critical unity, adopted the policy of reducing the wage gap between production and skilled. The main tool turned out to be the standard wage increase derived from cost-of-living (inflation) adjustments, which maintained the absolute difference between skilled and unskilled while closing the percentage gap. The result was that the UAW achieved wages for its production members much higher than those of non-union workers and set the standards for other unionized production workers. The hourly wage of UAW skilled members lagged behind that of craft union construction workers, but industrial trades workers won more job security, better benefits and steadier work.

Of course, the conservative and solidarity paths described are neither automatic nor isolated from each other. Powerful streams of conservative craft consciousness exist among the skilled in industrial unions. Similarly, union identification and worker solidarity are frequently strong in unions organized by craft. Specific situations, leadership and traditions make a difference.

WHERE DOES THE POWER COME FROM?

While wages and the definition of skill may depend heavily on artificial market barriers, in the long run the power of skilled workers in the production process depends primarily on their technical skills. More important than their general technical abilities is the job-specific knowledge that results from the interaction of the technical skills and the specific machines and processes in that plant. Part of what gives workers power in a strike is the difficulty and expense management has in replacing them, either temporarily or permanently. As automation and capital equipment increase and tolerance requirements are made tighter, the leverage of the skilled worker responsible for set-up, adjustment and maintenance becomes greater, all else remaining equal. Until recently, if the UAW declared a strike, the major producers would not even consider trying to recruit a scab workforce. Even if they could recruit sufficient bodies with general skills, they would risk a lot by allowing them to work on expensive machines. When Caterpillar broke new ground by recruiting scabs – and using them productively – during UAW strikes in 1991–92 and 1994–95, the company effectively broke the bargaining power of the union.

Skilled workers also feel this power individually. The fact that a skilled worker has job knowledge required by management often gives him or her the choice to cooperate or not in specific instances, depending on the relationship with the specific boss. To the extent that skilled work requires mental activity, it is not so easy for the boss to monitor the worker's output. A worker standing in front of a machine with a cup of coffee could actually be working very hard.

Most skilled jobs, particularly repair work, require considerable mobility: to the work site, to the tool crib, to locate parts, to consult the vendor via phone or in person. Jobs require cooperation and frequent consultation between and across trades and with production workers. Are the two workers with the cups of coffee consulting or on break? Higher literacy levels in trades also facilitate written communication, which is a powerful tool for organizing large or dispersed groups.

These opportunities provided by the job or skill, added to the sense of power, the higher self-esteem and the degree of protection against management interference and punishment, all make it easier for skilled workers to be organizers. They help to explain the high proportion of organizers and leaders in industrial unions who come from the skilled trades. The union movement keeps rediscovering this lesson about organizers. The leader of a successful breakthrough drive to organize clerical workers at Harvard University makes this observation: 'What we found is that the more freedom and respect a person has on the job, the easier it is for her to get involved in the union. [We seek out for organizers] people who are the happiest at work and the most independent' (Hoerr, 1997, p. 156).

Sensitive to this power of skilled workers on the shop floor, lean production attacks it in several related ways: the bundling of skilled work, standardizing work and capturing knowledge, and the way training is conducted.

THE BUNDLING OF SKILLED WORK

If we think of skilled work as a bundle of specific skills, then lean production forces a change in the shape of the bundle. Traditionally, craft skills in the workplace have been bundled vertically. Figure 9.1 is meant as an example only; the hierarchical ranking of functions will vary depending on the particular skill and job. In some cases installation, for example, may require exceptional skill, while in others it will be only minimal. Also the relationship between trades is not two-dimensional but multidimensional; all trades have some overlap with several other trades.

Lean production's rearrangement of responsibilities illustrated in Figure 9.2 allows a significant amount of work to be moved away from those who traditionally have done it, well-paid skilled workers in the union. At the lower end, it shifts the lower-skill parts of the bundle traditionally done by skilled workers to production workers. As one of the leading authorities on total productive maintenance explains: 'The key innovation of TPM is that opera-

Time/experience

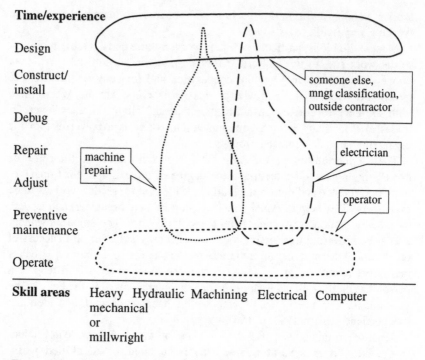

Design

Construct/
install

Debug

Repair

Adjust

Preventive
maintenance

Operate

someone else,
mngt classification,
outside contractor

machine
repair

electrician

operator

Skill areas   Heavy   Hydraulic Machining Electrical Computer
mechanical
or
millwright

Figure 9.1   Craft structure of skilled work in mass production

tors perform basic maintenance on their own equipment. They maintain their machines in good running order and develop the ability to detect potential problems before they generate breakdowns' (Nakajima, 1989, p. 2).

At the same time, the higher-skilled parts of the bundle are removed as well. Contracting out is increasing rapidly. And the technology allows some jobs such as machine troubleshooting and analysis, which previously had to be done on the shop floor, to be done now over networks in remote offices outside the bargaining unit.

The emphasis on 'cross-training' retrains skilled workers for a wider range of tasks. Although the horizontal training may seem to encompass the same total area of skills as the older vertical model, the horizontal formation has a number of negative consequences.

1.   The quantity of new skills taught is partly illusory. Knowledge about different trades has always been required in normal work. An electrician who is diagnosing problems in a Computer Numerical Control (CNC) milling machine must know a fair amount about its mechanical design and operation, as well as how the machine typically behaves, in

Time/experience

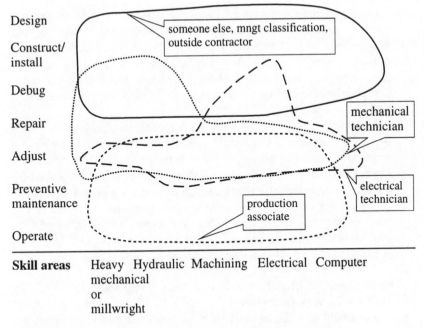

Design

Construct/
install

Debug

Repair

Adjust

Preventive
maintenance

Operate

someone else, mngt classification,
outside contractor

mechanical
technician

electrical
technician

production
associate

Skill areas   Heavy Hydraulic Machining Electrical Computer
mechanical
or
millwright

Figure 9.2   Lean structure of skilled work in mass production

order to work with the person repairing the machine and the operator.
This was true even when rigid lines existed between trades. The lines
did not prevent different trades from learning related areas covered by
other trades, or from working together as a team. Nor did it prevent
substantial work across lines on a voluntary basis. What the rules did
was keep the trades from performing major work in areas not their own
and provide a right of refusal in minor cases. The point of most cross-
training is not 'cross-understanding' but a way for the company to
require 'cross-working'.

2. Skills taught in this way are likely to be machine-specific and company-
   specific, adding little to the worker's value in the market. More importantly,
   the sense of craft in the job is reduced. It was craft pride, in part, that
   motivated workers to keep up with changing technology, and less craft
   pride means less incentive and ability to do so. Cross-training seeks to
   substitute pride in the company, usually unsuccessfully.

3. By moving in the direction of 'standardized work' and making skilled
   workers more interchangeable, the horizontal model changes the balance
   of power between management and workers on the shop floor and re-

duces the individual worker's protection in dealing with individual managers.

4. The horizontal arrangement may move substantial work out of the bargaining unit. In the USA, lean production is moving to limit in-plant maintenance workers to short-term jobs. This may be accomplished by outsourcing construction, installation and repair or diagnostic jobs that take more than four hours. It is the installation jobs and large repairs, particularly in combination, that use and develop the most skills in a trade.

5. Taking the more routine jobs from skilled work classifications and shifting them to operators benefits the operators in the sense of providing a more varied and less alienating job experience. But the advantages are limited. Remember that the operator's job is also being broadened for flexibility. Since the job has to be designed so that a new operator can be easily moved into place, the amount of maintenance the operator can learn or be entrusted with is limited. In addition, when skilled jobs are lost, chances for production workers to advance are also lost. The effect is to chop off the bottom of the career ladder.

The new bundling of skilled tasks also offers management the possibility of keeping or moving the critical skilled tasks out of the bargaining unit and into management classifications. This is most extensive in telecommunications, where the companies have long concentrated key skills in bloated management categories so that they can withstand strikes of many weeks with virtually no disruption of services. (The issue will not be framed the same way in countries, such as Japan, where all employees, including lower levels of supervision, are in the union, or in countries where there are stronger political and social limits on management prerogatives.)

The idea that the skilled trades must become 'multiskilled' seems deeply embedded in all lean production thinking, but here we see where the priorities lie, among the bundle of contradictory claims of lean production. Compare two possible arrangements for factory maintenance: a team of eight skilled workers each of whom is a specialist in his or her field (say electricians, machine repairers, millwrights and pipefitters) or a team of four people trained in general maintenance. The specialist arrangement raises a red flag for lean production, because often there will not be exactly the right work in the right proportions to keep all the specialists busy. Much better to have fewer skilled workers who can be assigned any job and always kept busy. This also helps maintain the atmosphere of urgency and pressure.

But lean production claims to have other goals. These include safety, quality, machine uptime and tracing problems to the root cause. If you examine each of these goals, the specialist model is preferable. Having a specialist in control of a task such as preventive maintenance means he or she is more likely to notice abnormal circumstances. The less a person knows about a particular trade, the more likely that he or she will 'jumper out' or otherwise defeat safety mechanisms or quality devices (lean production's 'foolproofing') to get production running again as quickly as possible, the less able such a person is to track a problem to its root cause and the less able such a person is to resist supervisor pressure to take short-cuts.

Of course, experts and specialists must still exist under lean production. Indeed, as technology advances, being expert in a field requires more, not less, specialization. But under the horizontal skill arrangement, increasingly the expertise is located in management classifications, or with outside contractors. In all the studies of work reorganization, we have seen none that seeks to prove the case for teams of generalists rather than specialists on the shop floor. For management, it is simply a given. We believe the reason management is so committed to multiskilling is the same reason that unions should be defending clear specialist lines: multiskilling greatly reduces the power of skilled workers in the production system.

STANDARDIZED WORK AND EXTRACTING KNOWLEDGE

Management attempts to apply these two well-known aspects of lean production to the trades. Documenting job knowledge through ISO 9000 or similar processes and writing standardized maintenance procedures may benefit the smooth running of the process and the quality of the product, but they also make it easier for management to use replacement workers during a strike, and hence greatly reduce the power of skilled workers. Documented maintenance records and standardized work quickly get turned into scab manuals. Job knowledge by its nature takes a considerable time to develop, but once given away cannot be retrieved. Never are workers or their union given job security or other sources of power in exchange.

TRAINING

While everyone pays lip service to training, almost no attention is paid to the reality of its content or to its implications for the power of skilled workers. The role of training for skilled work has changed substantially in just one generation. Previously, the apprenticeship model used in the USA was adequate. Young workers, presumably with recent high school (or perhaps college) as a background, were provided with an intensive combination of on-the-job and classroom training in their field at the beginning of their working careers. After that they maintained and advanced their skills through experience, on-the-job training, some vendor training and some extension courses. Those who wished could become masters in their craft. Technology changed, but sufficiently slowly for it to be possible to keep up through these means. To put it another way, with the apprenticeship model, the trades could maintain the required industrial skills and the power those skills provided.

But in the last generation advances in computers, automation and materials, as well as increased regulations and tighter tolerances, mean that the old model does not work. For most skilled workers it is difficult or impossible to keep up simply by on-the-job learning. Even if the apprenticeship training is adequate for the day (most is not), the technology base shifts so rapidly that tradespeople find themselves behind in a short time. For example, 15 years ago, an electrician who wanted to be at the cutting edge of his trade had to trace electrical circuits to the board level. This meant he had to understand the function of individual components in a highly complex arrangement and, using test and soldering equipment, locate defective components on a printed circuit board and replace them. Today this kind of work is rarely done in the plant. Today a skilled maintenance electrician has to be versatile with a computer and some number of programming languages and diagnostic programs. The 'half-life' of most computer programming skills is only a few years. To one degree or another it is the same in all trades. Drafting is out, computer-aided design is in. Gauging alignment on straightedges is out and laser interferometers are in.

The change in technology is so fast that it has caused a qualitative change in the ability of tradespeople to control their own training and therefore their relationship to the trade. The tools and software used by all trades become more elaborate and more expensive. Increasingly, skilled workers cannot afford to own their own, closing off another route for self-training. Unless they receive systematic and organized training, the current skilled workforce is automatically and rapidly deskilled by advances in technology.

As inadequate as on-the-job training is in keeping up with the march of technology, features of 'management-by-stress' make it an even less supportive environment for continuous learning: plants are not equipped with either the tools or the tasks conducive to learning. The removal of the construction, installation and major service portions of the work leaves little opportunity for training. The drive to utilize production capacity more fully means there is less time when skilled workers can use the machinery to investigate or learn. The 'leaning' of the workforce means that there is less learning time available. Even the new concepts of cleanliness and order (the five Ss) work against learning. One important method of on-the-job learning is experimenting with old or defective parts or equipment. Frequently, the first act of born-again managers is to clean up by throwing out parts that do not have an immediate use.

One result is that the economics of training are altered for management. If new generations of technology must be taught, it is more costly to train the current workforce than to recruit workers newly trained. The experienced worker requires much higher pay, both for training and afterwards. Besides, the experienced worker may not be as adept at the new skills. Much better to recruit new workers trained in their own time at public expense, where it is possible for management to select the ones with exactly the right skills and job attitude. Companies then add the job-specific training that binds them to the firm.

The older workers can be left to deal with the older technology that remains in use; with luck they will retire by the time all their usefulness is gone. This training strategy becomes even more attractive to management as unions agree to sharply reduced wages for new workers and to a longer period before reaching the full wage. It becomes still more attractive when the public subsidizes the costs of training.

Yet the need for some advanced training for those already working seems so obvious that unions, companies, government and various agencies all promote massive training programmes. What happens to these training efforts? Consider the experience of a 1994 training course to upgrade electronic skills for electricians in a newly remodelled car assembly plant. Electricians were to learn to troubleshoot the latest model programmable logic controller (PLC), a specialized industrial computer that controls the operations on a line. On the surface, everything was in place for a good training programme: the curriculum had been examined and approved by a joint company–union committee; the module had been used many times before with ample opportunity for improving it; the teacher had substantial experience with the particular PLC and with car plants. The class was scheduled for 80 hours (two weeks) at a well-equipped community college.

The class comprised 12 journeymen electricians with varying degrees of experience with PLCs. The instructor estimates that two of the 12 attended for less than 20 hours, and six others for less than 60 hours. Some used the class time to read newspapers, one worked on his private business and one played computer games. One thoroughly mastered the PLC, and one novice became reasonably proficient in simple programming. It would be correct to hold those electricians who did not master the material responsible for their own failure. But the subject goes deeper than that.

The company had refused a request to assign the electricians to jobs that involved PLCs beforehand, to stimulate interest and allow them to use the skills. The curriculum was generic, not based on plant examples or programmes. Thus for most of the electricians there was no connection between training and use. Most believed it unlikely that they would be assigned to work on PLCs in the near future. Up to that point, the company had carefully controlled which electricians got to do such work and they saw no reasonable chance that they would get a PLC assignment even if they asked. In some ways, not learning was a defence. One cited a previous experience of being sent to class and then not being able to work on the corresponding equipment for more than a year. By that time he had forgotten almost everything and looked foolish as his supervisor kept pointing out that he had been trained, hadn't he?

The lack of any reasonable connection with what they actually expected to do at work meant that, for most, the appropriate attitude was the same as for a hobby: namely, you spend as much time and attention as is enjoyable, then stop. It is noteworthy that the one electrician who did develop expertise brought to class programmes from machines he was assigned to in the plant, to work on and discuss with the instructor. Besides not being part of the curriculum, this behaviour violated company rules.

Second, there was little connection between the training plan and the workers' framework. The pedagogy was totally wrong for adult education. It treated the worker as an empty vessel to be filled with the appropriate layers of knowledge. No respect was paid to the learner's experience as the best starting point; the focus was on modules derived from a Taylorist 'task analysis'. (For discussion of a better approach at a different college, see Saganski, 1995.)

Why do the workers not object to the inadequate training? They feel powerless and see no connection to their work lives. Why does the union not object? The union representative who stops by each day to pick up the timesheet says nothing about the lack of participation. But the workers are not complaining and prefer the training time to their regular work assignment. Getting people paid time off can be good politically. Why does the company not object? The company needs to conduct training for political reasons and to fulfil contractual obligations. Consistent with its interest in horizontal rather than vertical bundling of skills, it is not interested in most workers getting advanced training. Indeed, the company uses the inadequacy of the workforce even after such 'training' as one of its chief arguments for moving skilled tasks out of the bargaining unit. Why do the instructors not object? Because the training work is well paid, and if class time is shortened the instructors get free time. Almost anything is acceptable as long as the company and the union are both happy.

THE BIGGER PICTURE

Unfortunately, all too much of current training follows the pattern described above. There are some exceptions when unions insert themselves consciously and actively in the programmes (Parker and Slaughter, 1994, pp. 271–86), but on the whole, companies pursuing lean production are not particularly interested in helping their union members to develop advanced technical skills. What they do want is a more flexible workforce, but management flexibility is decreased when worker skill translates into power and resistance to management. Management is most interested in training that can grease the process of work reorganization, and therefore much of the training money goes to the soft skills of work reorganization – problem solving, interpersonal communication, 'thinking outside the box' – and management's view of the demands of global competition. Another major portion is used to purchase the cooperation of unions by providing union-appointed jobs as programme administrators and facilitators.

It is not helpful, however, for unions to cling to old definitions of skill and old practices. Technology is changing. Unions need to be flexible. There is no future in internal union battles over the distribution of skills within the current bargaining unit. The task is to challenge for new areas of work.

The bottom line is that the 'win–win' vision – that management will promote higher skills for union workers because the lean system requires it – is not automatic. Quite the opposite: the only way workers can acquire the skills they need is for their union to fight for them. And that fight can succeed only if members are clear that higher skills will translate to better jobs and more power for the members.

REFERENCES

Babson, Steve (1991), *Building the Union: Skilled Workers and the Anglo-Gaelic Immigrants in the Rise of the UAW*, New Brunswick: Rutgers University Press.

Hoerr, John (1997), *We Can't Eat Prestige: The Women Who Organized Harvard*, Philadelphia: Temple University Press.

International Association of Machinists and Aerospace Workers (1997), *High Performance Work Organization Partnerships: HPWO Field Manual*, Upper Marlboro, Maryland: International Association of Machinists and Aerospace Workers.

Lichtenstein, Nelson (1995), *The Most Dangerous Man in Detroit: Walter Reuther and the Fate of American Labor*, New York: Basic Books.

Nakajima, Seiichi (1989), *TPM Development Program: Implementing Total Productive Maintenance*, Cambridge, Mass.: Productivity Press.

Parker, Mike and Jane Slaughter (1988), *Choosing Sides: Unions and the Team Concept*, Boston: South End Press.

Parker, Mike and Jane Slaughter (1994), *Working Smart: A Union Guide to Participation Programs and Reengineering*, Detroit: Labor Notes.

Saganski, Gary (1995), 'A Worker-Centered Approach to Education and Training', in Steve Babson (ed.), *Lean Work: Empowerment and Exploitation in the Global Auto Industry*, Detroit: Wayne State University Press, pp. 336–9.

10. Is technical change the cause of unemployment?

Antonella Stirati, Sergio Cesaratto and Franklin Serrano

INTRODUCTION

Since the mid-1970s, industrial countries and particularly European countries have experienced persistently high unemployment rates. These are often associated by public opinion and scholars with processes of technical change. In what follows we shall first discuss and critically assess the relation between technical innovation and unemployment which derives from different perspectives in economic theory. Subsequently, we shall use what we regard as the sounder theoretical approach to discuss the relation between technical change and unemployment in the experience of industrial countries in the post-Second World War period.

TECHNICAL INNOVATION AND UNEMPLOYMENT IN ECONOMIC THEORIES

The Marginalist or 'Mainstream' View

According to the marginalist approach, market economies, if left free to operate, that is, if prices are flexible and there are no obstacles to competition, always tend to the full employment of labour, and do so also when technical changes reduce the labour inputs required to produce a given output.

Such tendency to full employment is brought about by the substitutability between factors of production, which in turn relies on two mechanisms. The first, *direct* substitution, is the change in the proportion in which the factors of production are used in the production process. According to the theory, the additional employment of one unit of a productive factor (say, labour), given the amount of the other factors, has decreasing returns (the marginal product of labour is decreasing). Accordingly if, for example, there is a shift in labour

141

supply caused by immigration, or some other demographic phenomenon, and the price of labour falls as the additional labourers compete for employment, entrepreneurs will find it more profitable to use techniques that involve a higher proportion of labour inputs in combination with the other fully employed factors, up to the point at which the marginal product of labour equals the new wage level. If there are no constraints preventing the required fall in wages, this process will lead towards the full utilization of the additional labour supply, albeit at a lower real wage, and to a growth of national output.

The second, *indirect* substitution mechanism works through changes in consumers' optimal choice of their consumption baskets as the relative prices of factors and goods change. Again, let us suppose an increase in labour supply and fall in the real wage. According to the theory, this brings about a fall in the relative prices of the goods that are produced with labour-intensive techniques (techniques entailing a higher proportion of labour to the other inputs). This fall tends to alter consumers' demand in such a way that the (now supposedly cheaper) labour-intensive commodities will be demanded and produced in a higher proportion than they were before, thereby increasing the demand for labour in the economy. Thus, even if there is no factor substitution in production (that is, the 'production function' has fixed coefficients), the economy will tend to full employment.

In this analytical framework innovation has in one respect the same effect as an increase in the quantity of production factors, labour and capital:[1] as these tend to be always fully employed, such an increase will necessarily result in an increase in the level of production and income 'as soon as the liberated resources can be effectively transferred to new uses' (Hicks, 1932, p. 121).

However, while mainstream theory envisages an underlying tendency of market economies to full employment, in applied analyses it is generally admitted that not only temporary, but also persistent unemployment may result from innovation. Accordingly with the general approach outlined above, this must be the consequence of market imperfection and price rigidities, and particularly of institutional factors, such as unions, unemployment benefit, costly firing procedures and the like. These rigidities would tend to prevent the required adjustments both in the level and in the relative values of real wages and the necessary mobility of the labour force between sectors and occupations, with the consequence of preventing the working of the substitution mechanisms just described, and of rendering persistent (or longer lasting) the 'frictional' unemployment due to the changes in the composition of labour demand and the consequent mismatch between this and labour supply which will generally result from innovation and structural change.

The result of this approach therefore is that, while it is maintained that innovation and structural change will not cause long-run unemployment if markets work freely and competitively, in the actual situation of present-day industrial countries, and particularly in Europe, high and persistent unemployment is indeed caused by technical and structural change, but this is ultimately due to the existence of 'rigidities' in these economies which prevent the required adjustments. This is, for example, the diagnosis provided by the OECD's *Jobs Study* (a diagnosis, as we shall see, which is not quite confirmed by the data offered by this same study):

> After having considered the available evidence and the various theories which have been advanced to explain today's unemployment, the basic conclusion was reached that it is *an inability of OECD economies and societies to adapt rapidly and innovatively to a world of rapid structural change that is the principal cause of high and persistent unemployment.* (OECD, 1994, p. vii, emphasis added)

Quite obviously, this is the premise for pointing at an increased flexibility in the labour market as the remedy to unemployment.

Theoretical Criticisms of the Marginalist Approach

We shall see later that the interpretation of high unemployment provided by the mainstream approach is not fully consistent with the data concerning unemployment and the intensity of change in industrial economies in the post-war period. Here, however, we want to illustrate the theoretical reasons which suggest that a different approach should be taken to analyse the effects of innovation on employment and unemployment.

We believe these reasons have to be found in the works of Sraffa and other economists who in the 1960s contributed to the so-called 'capital controversy' (Harcourt, 1972; for more recent discussions, see Eatwell *et al.*, 1990; Kurz and Salvadori, 1005, ch. 14). Sraffa demonstrated that the substitution mechanisms envisaged by marginalist theory which are the basis for the supposed tendency to full employment of a competitive economy are logically flawed.

Put simply, this controversy pointed to the peculiar nature of 'capital', which is not an 'original' factor measurable in some conventional unit, as is the case for labour or land, but consists of a set of produced commodities measurable only in 'value'. This has important consequences for the reliability of the two neoclassical substitution mechanisms described above. The first substitution mechanism – *direct substitution* in production – predicts that when, for example, the wage rate falls, methods of production using more labour relative to the other inputs will become more profitable. Sraffa (1960) and other contributors to the capital controversy of the 1960s have shown that this is not the general case, and that, when there are a multiplicity of techniques and heterogeneous capital goods, the so-called 'reswitching of techniques' makes the neoclassical prediction unreliable. As distribution varies it may happen that a certain technique, using a certain amount of labour per unit of net output, is the most profitable (least costly) for low levels of the real wage rate as well as for high levels of it, while a different technique is the most profitable at 'intermediate' levels of the wage rate (Garegnani, 1970). This means that there is no a priori reason to assume that a fall in the real wage will lead to the adoption of techniques using more labour per unit of output rather than the opposite.

The second mechanism, *indirect substitution* through changes in consumption patterns, requires (a) that as, for example, the wage rate declines, the relative prices of the labour-intensive goods fall, and (b) that this is followed by a larger consumption of the relatively cheapest goods. Now the first step is put in doubt again by the conclusions of the capital theory controversy. It has been shown (Sraffa, 1960) that, as the wage rate varies from maximum to zero, the price of any commodity A may alternately fall and rise relative to the price of another commodity B, so that no a priori expectations as to the direction of the change, based on the 'factor intensity' in the production of the two commodities, are justified.

The Non-conventional View

An alternative approach to the marginalist one can be developed on the basis of the classical or 'surplus' approach to value and distribution integrated by Keynes's theory of effective demand with regard to the determination of output (Garegnani, 1978). This leads to what we call the long-run effective demand approach. We shall now outline its implications for the analysis of the relation between technical change and employment.

As a first step, we can enquire about the effects of innovation on employment with a given national real income. In order to fix ideas, we can write the following simple definitions and relations:

$$Y = X - vX = X(1 - v),$$

where Y is net product; X is total production, inclusive of the intermediate inputs which are used in production; vX is the share of total production which is used and consumed in the production process as intermediate inputs.

Given the amount of labour necessary for the production of each unit of output, l (which is the inverse of the average productivity of labour), employment in the economy is given by:

$$L = lX = lY/(1 - y).$$

Given net output Y, an innovation will lower either, and in general both, l and v, thus reducing total employment and creating persistent unemployment. Note that it is the absence of substitution mechanisms that explains the possibility of persistent unemployment in this framework and provides legitimacy for the (provisional) assumption of a given output. Hence, in contrast to mainstream views, innovation can determine a persistent fall in the employment *level* quite independently of any rigidities in prices and wages.

Now the next step appears to be that of enquiring what effects, if any, technical change may have on net social output Y. According to the mainstream view, the main explanation for economic growth lies in the saving propensity of the community in so far as a higher saving rate would allow the production of more investment goods that increase the capital stock. As is well known, in his major work, the *General Theory*, J.M. Keynes challenged this view by arguing that (a) productive capacity is generally not fully utilized, and (b) within the limit of the full utilization of the existing capital stock a larger amount of investment does not require a prior saving decision. To the contrary, a higher investment determines the higher utilization of capacity and higher income which generates a flow of savings equal to the additional investment (in other words, within the limits of the full utilization of existing capacity, investment is the source of savings and not vice versa).

The criticisms of the marginalist capital theory summarized above strengthen Keynes's positive theory of output as they provide the basis to deny the tendency of the economy towards the full utilization of labour and capacity envisaged by traditional theory. Hence there appears to be no obstacle to the statement that (a) even in the long period capacity may be underutilized, which leads to the proposition that (b) capacity will itself tend to adjust to demand so that a persistently low degree of utilization will tend to cause destruction of capacity, as the entrepreneurs will choose not to renew the capacity (plants, machinery and so on) that in each period is consumed in the production process. On the other hand, a persistently high degree of utilization will tend to stimulate capacity-creating investment.

In other words proposition (b) implies that capacity-creating investment is demand-induced. Accordingly, long-period productive capacity and, given the technology, long-period employment also depend on the long-period level of effective demand.

Our task, therefore, will be to enquire into the impact of technical change on the components of effective demand and their evolution through time. Now, again to help us to fix ideas, we can write:

$$Y = C + I + G + EX - M,$$

where C is consumption, I is gross investment, G is public expenditure, EX is exports and M is imports.

Next, it is useful for our purposes to classify the components of effective demand into autonomous and induced components, where autonomous in this context means that they are independent of the level of domestic output Y, while, in contrast, induced means that they are functions of Y. We can write:

$$C = Ca + cY$$

$$I = Ia + kdY^o + kgY^o = Ia + k(d + g)Y^o$$

$$M = mY$$

$$G = G$$

$$EX = EX$$

where

Ca is autonomous consumption, that is consumption financed by wealth or credit, and not by income derived from current production;

c is the community's propensity to consume out of current income;

Ia is autonomous investment, that is investment not aimed at the adjustment of capacity to demand, generally associated with innovation;

Y^o is the output associated with normal utilization of existing capacity (capacity output), which need not be equal to actual current production, if the demand expected when this capacity was planned does not in fact materialize;[2]

k is the desired proportion between the capital stock and the flow of output (K/Y) which depends on existing technologies and output composition;

d is the annual depreciation of the existing capital stock, so that in order to keep this stock unaltered there must be each year a gross investment equal to kdY;

g is the expected growth rate of demand with respect to installed capacity output Y^o between this period and the next (when the capacity created by investment will be used in production) – if expected effective demand is lower than capacity output, g will be negative, and gross investment (neglecting Ia) will be lower than required to preserve the existing capital stock;

m is the propensity to import;

public expenditure G and exports EX are given independently of Y.

Under the simplifying assumption that current output (Y) equals capacity output (Y^o), i.e., that it is at a level such as to allow the normal utilization of existing capacity, we can write:[3]

$$Y = (G + Ia + Ca + EX) / [1 - c + m - k(d+g)] \qquad (10.1)$$

In order to investigate the impact of innovation on the output level and on its growth over time we must look at its impact (a) on the level and growth of the autonomous components of expenditure, and particularly *Ca*, *Ia* and *EX* (*G* does not appear susceptible to direct influences from technical change) and (b) on the value of the parameters of the above equations and particularly *c*, *k*, *d* and *m*.

To begin with, technical innovation, in the form of *process* innovation, will tend to affect demand *negatively* in so far as, by displacing workers, it redistributes a given income from wage-earners to other social groups, thereby lowering the propensity to consume, *c*.

On the other hand, *product* innovation, by creating new needs or by rendering obsolete previous types of durables, will tend to have positive effects on consumption as it can both raise the propensity to consume out of contractual incomes and increase autonomous consumption, the latter being financed out of financial wealth and consumers' credit. Process innovation can also have this kind of effect when, by sharply decreasing the production costs of commodities, it makes them accessible to a much wider public.

For any single country, both process and product innovations tend to have positive effects on demand also through their positive effects on exports (a higher *EX*) and the reduction of the propensity to import (a lower *m*). If innovations are such as to allow a continuous enlargement of the international market share, this will entail higher rates of export growth than otherwise allowed by demand growth in the rest of the world. Such changes in export growth and the propensity to import may also have a further positive effect on demand by relaxing the balance of payment constraint, thus creating the possibility of more expansionary fiscal policies (increases in *G*).

The capital-output coefficient *k* depends on the technical conditions of production. By increasing it, capital-using innovations may increase gross investments and, *ceteris paribus*, increase the level of long-period effective demand. But innovation might well also reduce *k*, for example by reducing the cost of capital equipment, so that it is not possible to establish a priori the direction of this effect.

Finally, we come to two channels through which innovations can have positive effects on investments, and which are often emphasized by 'Schumpeterian' economists in support of the view that innovation would have a major role in increasing effective demand and fostering the accumulation process. First, innovation can lead to a higher depreciation rate *d*, with positive effects on gross investments. This may be due to the faster economic obsolescence of plants, that may follow both product and process innovations, which leads to their early replacement. This early scrapping can also take place between industries through the establishment of new industrial sectors (characterized by new products) accompanied by the decline of old sectors (Garegnani, 1962, p. 96).

Second, technical change may induce a level of gross investment higher than that otherwise justified by the *expected* patterns of effective demand because in the innovative sectors the expectation of a larger *market share* by a substantial number of competing innovating firms can lead to a positive level of the autonomous component of gross investment that thus results higher than that justified by the (initially given) expected rate of growth of effective demand. This may lead to an initial excess capacity. The vague idea proposed by the Schumpeterian economists is that this excess capacity may be at least partially justified by an *actual* rate of growth of demand higher than the expected precisely as a result of the higher level of autonomous investment on the demand side.

But can this 'technological' or 'Schumpeterian' process of creative de-struction sustain long-period growth of demand and employment? The first objective concerns the *persistency* of the effect of technological competition on gross investment. Let us start from the first channel. A process of wide-spread early replacement in a sector can be followed by subsequent periods of lower gross investment, unless further technical change is in view.[4] Con-cerning the second channel, although excess capacity can initially be partially matched by higher effective demand (itself a result of the higher autonomous gross investment), the process of adjustment of capacity cannot but lead to a fall of gross investment in the subsequent periods. The effects of technical change on gross investment seem therefore to lack the persistency and perva-siveness necessary to assure a long-period *growth* of effective demand and a stable level of employment, even as an average over very long periods of time (Kalecki, 1971, p. 151).

Summing Up

Technical change may have some positive effect on effective demand through various channels which may, to a greater or lesser extent, according to cir-cumstances, offset the negative impact it has on employment. However, there is no reason to expect that *in general* such positive effects on demand will be such as to prevent the creation of unemployment; nor can we expect such effects to be such as to lead to a sustained growth of the economy over long periods of time.

Hence the conclusions we draw from our theoretical discussion are the following.

● Technical change can cause persistent, structural unemployment, quite independently of 'rigidities' in the labour market.
● Such unemployment is caused by an insufficient *level* of employment compared with the given labour force and not just by problems con-

cerning the composition of the demand for labour relative to the supply.

- Employment growth through time is, by definition, given by $e = y - p$ (where e is the rate of employment growth, y is the rate of output growth and p is the rate of productivity growth). Unemployment will emerge whenever the growth of effective demand is not such as to compensate for the growth in labour productivity caused by technical and structural change. In addition, an additional growth of output and employment is necessary in the presence of a positive growth of the labour supply, due to demographic and social changes.
- The actual growth trend of output mainly depends on the growth trends of the autonomous components of effective demand (*EX, G, Ia, Ca*). Among these, *EX* appears to be the one most susceptible to undergo *continuous* growth caused by technical improvements. This, however, can always be true only for a sub-set of countries gaining international market share at the expense of others.

When the rate of employment growth is insufficient to prevent unemployment, economic theory does not provide any criteria to establish whether this is due to an 'exceedingly' slow growth of output or to an 'exceptional' pace of productivity growth. Such evaluations can be given only on the basis of cross-country and intertemporal comparisons, which we present in the next section.

INNOVATION AND UNEMPLOYMENT: WHAT CAN WE LEARN FROM THE POST-SECOND WORLD WAR EXPERIENCE?

Productivity, Growth and Employment Trends

Let us now look at the relationship between growth of output and productivity and unemployment in the post-Second World War period. This has often been divided into two phases: the 'Golden Age' lasting more or less until the beginning of the 1970s, characterized by high growth rates of GDP and productivity and very low unemployment rates, and a second phase characterized by lower GDP and productivity growth and high unemployment rates (see Table 10.1).

The first observation from this simple table is that productivity growth was not more intense in industrial countries in the 1980s and 1990s than it used to be during the previous decades; quite the contrary, productivity growth is, in the present phase, rather slow. The same conclusion can be reached by

Table 10.1 Output, unemployment and productivity, 1960–94

	Real gross domestic product (year to year percentage changes)				Real value added per person employed (year to year percentage changes)				Unemployment rate			
	60–73	73–79	79–89	89–94	60–73	73–79	79–89	89–94	60–73	74–79	80–89	90–94
United States	3.9	2.5	2.5	2.1	1.9	0.0	0.8	1.2	4.8	6.7	7.2	6.4
European Union (15)	4.7	2.5	2.3	1.3	4.4	2.3	1.8	0.7	2.3	4.6	9.2	9.6
OECD less USA	5.6	3.0	2.7	1.7	4.8	2.4	1.9	0.9	2.6	4.3	7.3	7.3

Source: OECD, *Historical Statistics.*

looking at the data on productivity growth for the manufacturing and the service sectors separately. In each we find the same trend of decline in productivity growth from the 1960s to the present for industrial countries (see OECD, *Historical Statistics*). In addition, other statistical indicators measuring the changes in the employment share of different industries show that structural change has been less intense in the recent phase. On these grounds, the OECD's *Jobs Study* concludes that 'virtually in all countries, turbulence in employment shares by sector during the 1980s either decreased or was stable compared to the 1970s. In the majority of countries for which data are available, industry shifts in employment during the 1980s were also much smaller than during the 1960s' (OECD, 1994, p. 16).

This evidence goes against the mainstream view that higher unemployment in the second phase of accumulation in the post-war period can be explained by an intensification of innovation and structural change coupled with a lack of flexibility in labour markets. Indeed, even the OECD is led to admit that 'despite considerable effort, it has been hard to identify changes in the basic structural determinants of the natural unemployment rate that are large enough to account for the observed trend increase in actual unemployment during the 1980s' (ibid., p. 67), where, by the 'structural determinants' of the natural unemployment rate is meant precisely the intensity of structural and technical change and the degree of labour market 'imperfection' and rigidity. The above evidence also casts doubt on the thesis advanced by some non-mainstream economists (Lunghini, 1997a; 1997b; Rifkin, 1995) that the present high unemployment is to be regarded as 'technological' unemployment.

The second observation that quite obviously emerges from Table 10.1 is a consistent correlation between high growth rates of GDP and productivity. Can this be regarded as mere coincidence? Economists of different conviction would agree that it is not. But which is the direction of causality? The mainstream point of view sees technical progress as a *cause* of GDP growth.[5] The 'Schumpeterian' view of technical change as the engine of growth through its effects on autonomous investment leads to a similar conclusion. In the previous section, however, we have criticized both positions. Another explanation of the association is that we find in the French 'regulation' school. Taking inspiration from Kaldor, they argue that a virtuous circle (or 'cumulative causation') was established, during the 'Golden Age', consisting of (a) a positive relationship *from* aggregate demand growth *to* productivity growth ('productivity regime'), accompanied by (b) a positive relationship *from* productivity growth *to* aggregate demand growth ('demand regime').

The 'productivity regime' would be explained by increasing returns, based on the so-called 'Fordist model'. We agree with the idea of a positive association between demand growth and productivity growth (albeit perhaps not so closely associated to 'Fordist' production only) and believe that this can be supported by a tradition in economic thought that goes back to Adam Smith (cf. Cesaratto, 1996). In contrast to the marginalist view, this tradition regards technical change as a *result* of economic growth. The Smithian approach links the competitive and innovative behaviour to the expectations concerning demand.[6] Similarly, Schmookler (1966) suggested that the existence of *indivisibilities* in the application of the new *process* technologies and the importance of the rate of growth of per capita income in inducing *product* innovations implied a reversal in the causation between demand growth and innovation with respect to that assumed in mainstream economics. Recent research, theoretical and applied, also confirms this direction of causality between economic cycles and innovative activities (Geroski and Walters, 1995).

The second step in the virtuous cumulative causation is associated, according to the 'regulation' approach, with the institutional set-up favouring the translation of higher productivity into higher wages and consumption, and/or into more competitive exports.[7] The so-called 'wage-led regime', that is the tendency of money and real wages to grow in step with productivity, has certainly had positive effects on the income level, but this cannot have been enough. By keeping at relatively high levels the marginal propensity to consume, a 'wage-led regime' magnifies the effects on the level of capacity generated by a given level of the autonomous expenditure. It cannot, however, explain how autonomous expenditure *growth* is generated. In this respect, a greater explanatory power can be attributed to the effect of technical change on exports, particularly in 'latecomer' European countries. In the post-Second World War period as a whole, and particularly during the 'Golden Age', these countries have been able to obtain very rapid gains in productivity through the process of technological catching up,[8] and these gains allowed them to increase their export share in international markets at the expense of the USA and other more technologically advanced European countries (Amsden, 1996). Such process, however, required acceptance on the part of the leading country (the USA) of a deterioration in its position in international markets.

We believe that two main forces were behind the high rate of growth of autonomous expenditure in the 1950s and 1960s: increasing government expenditure (including military spending, particularly in the USA, cf. Pivetti, 1992) and export growth.[9] The average annual rates of growth in exports in the OECD as a whole were 11.5 per cent, 7.9 per cent, 6 per cent and 4.1 per cent in the 1960s, 1970s, 1980s and in 1990–93, respectively. In the EU in the same periods, those rates were 11.4 per cent, 7.1 per cent, 5.6 per cent and 3.3 per cent. The corresponding growth rates of public expenditure in final consumption for the OECD countries were 4.9 per cent, 3 per cent, 2.6 per cent and 1 per cent; and, in the EU, 4.6 per cent, 3.9 per cent, 2 per cent and 1.6 per cent.

The association of high productivity growth with near full employment during the first post-Second World War decades shows that fast technical change is not necessarily linked to technological unemployment. But the figures above suggest that, without the *expansionary national and international set-up* that marked the post-war period, productivity growth would not have been so high, and unemployment would not have been so low.[10]

The main cause of rising unemployment in the last decades must be seen in the *slow growth of effective demand* (Eatwell, 1996). This in turn is associated with the changes in policy orientation in most industrial countries, from full-employment objectives towards anti-inflationary objectives, and with the changes in the international set-up, marked by increased rivalry among leading countries (USA, Germany, Japan). In the EU, the target of monetary stability has been the main consideration that has affected decisions concerning monetary unification, and has resulted in a highly deflationary stance of economic policies, which must be regarded as the main cause of the slow growth and high unemployment rates experienced in European countries.

Growth without Employment?

The positive effect of output growth on productivity growth that emerged from the data we have just discussed appears to play a role in the argument that output growth would no longer be able to create employment (for example, Lunghini, 1997a, p. 269; see also Petri, 1997, for a critical discussion). However, again the available data for the 1980s and 1990s do not appear to confirm this view. If we look at Table 10.2, we can see that, in almost all the countries considered, higher average annual growth rates of GDP in the 1980s than in the 1990s involved a better employment performance in the private, non-agricultural sector.[11]

Cross-country comparisons of GDP growth and employment performance in the 1980s show a certain diversity, which reflects diversity in productivity growth, partly accounted for by 'catching up' (see n. 8 above), so that employment tends to grow less, for any given GDP growth in the countries with lower productivity *levels*. In the 1990s, however, on account of lower productivity growth in general and of the much reduced differences now existing among the countries considered (so that the rates of productivity growth tend to be less diverse), a rather strong correlation emerges between employment growth and GDP growth. The scatter diagram (Figure 10.1) shows the correlation between the growth of GDP and employment (employees in the non-agricultural business sector) in 16 industrial countries. The high *linear* correlation is largely accounted for by three countries only (Sweden, Finland and Turkey), without which the linear correlation coefficient falls sharply (from 0.8 to 0.3). Correlation in general, however, independently of linearity

Table 10.2   Growth of GDP and non-agricultural employment in the business sector, average annual rates (per cent)

Countries	1979–89		1989–94	
	GDP	Employment	GDP	Employment
USA	2.5	1.07	2.1	1.06
Japan	4	2.48	2.1	2.33
France	2.2	0.31	1.2	–0.48
W. Germany	1.8	0.67	2	0.65
Italy	2.4	0.62	1	–0.70
Spain	2.8	–1.65	1.5	–0.08
UK	2.4	–0.11	0.8	–0.35
Sweden	2	0.91	–0.2	–2.70
Belgium	2	–0.006	1.6	–0.002
Canada	3.1	0.02	1.1	–0.001
Netherlands	1.9	0.009	2.3	0.012

Source: OECD, *National Accounts* and *Historical Statistics*.

assumption, is high: the Spearman rank correlation coefficient is 0.7 in the latter case and 0.8 in the former. Thus it could be said that the relation between employment and growth appears in fact to be stronger today than it was in the recent past.

There are also other reasons to believe that GDP growth could have significant favourable effects on employment. While in the 1960s and 1970s the structural changes associated with growth involved a large shift in employment from the agricultural sector, characterized by low productivity and slow productivity growth, towards manufacturing, where productivity was growing rapidly, today the sector that appears likely to gain occupational weight compared to the others is the service sector, where productivity growth tends, on the whole, to be slower. Indeed, there seems to be a general consensus on the role of the service sector as the main source of future jobs in industrial economies (for example, EU, 1993; OECD, 1994). In contrast, the manufacturing sector is not expected to supply much employment in the future, given (a) the absence of major product innovations whose stimulus to consumption patterns is comparable, say, to that of cars, or domestic appliances; and (b) because of the higher productivity growth in manufacturing and competition from new industrialized countries (NICs).[12] Nonetheless, manufacturing can still be an important source of jobs. For instance, in North America the manufacturing sector contributed in absolute terms to job crea-

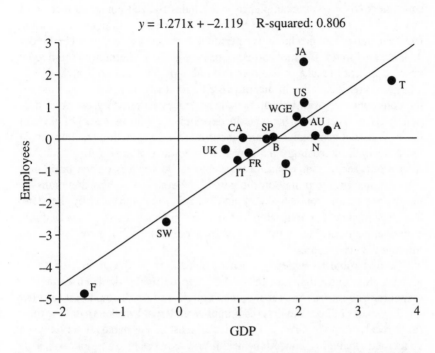

$y = 1.271x + -2.119$ R-squared: 0.806

Notes: A=Austria, AU=Australia, B=Belgium, CA=Canada, D=Denmark, F=Finland, FR=France, IT=Italy, JA=Japan, N=Netherlands, SP=Spain, SW=Sweden, T=Turkey, UK=United Kingdom, US=United States, WGE=West Germany.

Source: OECD, *National Accounts* and *Historical Statistics*.

Figure 10.1   Rate of growth of employees in the non-agricultural business sector and rate of growth of GDP, 1989–94

tion, whereas the opposite happened in Europe. Moreover, the development of many services (financial, transport and communication, and so on) depends on the trends of the manufacturing sector. On the other hand, many services may be the object of wide organizational and technological reshuffling. With these caveats, it is still reasonable to maintain that it is the service sector that will contribute most to job creation. Accordingly, the expectation is that, notwithstanding the fact that higher growth rates tend to stimulate productivity growth, a comparable GDP growth might well be accompanied by a better employment performance than in the 'Golden Age'.

The expansion of the service sector, and particularly of personal services, precisely because of limited possibilities of productivity growth, may encounter a limit, on the demand side, in the ability to pay of the potential consumers. To give an example, in many industrialized countries there will be a growing need for personal services from the elderly population. But the fact that most (low-productivity) personal services are costly might hinder their expansion (cf. Baumol and Bowen, 1965). Three alternatives seem to be open at present to make possible an expansion of demand in this area. One is a larger social inequality in income distribution that would allow one part of the community to afford cheap personal services supplied by the other section. This is what often happens in developing countries and, possibly, in those industrial economies where labour market deregulation has gone most far. A second, increasingly popular, road is to develop a so-called 'third' or 'non-profit' sector that would provide affordable services on the basis of a self-restrained wage policy on the part of the employees, *plus* donations by the private sector, voluntary work and tax relief and subsidies by the state. The third road is the public supply of services in which the state acts as direct employer and subsidizes the supply of services by income redistribution through the tax system.

The first route is evidently open to objections on the ground of social acceptability, and might not in the long run be really viable in advanced, democratic countries. The second one, it might be feared, could pull together the drawbacks of both the first (as it implies underpaid workers) and the third (as it receives public subsidies). As far as most of the personal services are concerned (including education, health and assistance to the elderly), it is indeed possible, as shown by the past positive experiences of many European countries, that the third system is the most efficient road.[13]

Employment without Growth?

In order to reduce unemployment, the only alternative to increasing employment by means of output growth appears to be that of redistributing existing employment and income. Reduction in working time is often regarded today as such an alternative. The foregoing shows that we disagree with some arguments often advanced in support of this policy (that is, that output growth would not generate employment). This, however, does not imply that such a policy could not be useful. On the basis of the approach developed in the first section of the chapter, we can say that, in principle, a reduction in working time with a given monthly wage would increase employment by two routes: first, by increasing the amount of labour (measured in 'heads', and not in hours) required to produce any given output; and second, by redistributing income away from profits to wage-earners, thus raising the average propensity to consume of the community, and hence increasing, other things being constant, the level of effective demand, output and employment. However, we believe it would be a mistake to think that such a policy could be an alternative, rather than a complement, to expansionary macroeconomic policies. There are two main reasons for this. The first is that such a measure can in principle have a relatively large effect on the *level* of employment, but cannot sustain a *growth* of employment over time (unless one thinks of a continuum of significant reductions in working time, which do not appear on the agenda). Yet, at least in some countries, such growth will be required to provide jobs for the generations entering the labour market and for the increasing proportion of women that can be expected to enter it.

Second, a significant impact on employment can be effected only by a sharp fall in working time (such as that from 40 to 35 hours a week) at a given wage, but this would imply a large increase in real hourly wages (of an order of magnitude of 12 to 13 per cent), which is bound to encounter very strong opposition from employers. Given the current weak bargaining position of workers and unions (itself largely due to the high rates of unemployment and stagnant employment growth) it seems rather unlikely that this result can be obtained. More moderate compromises, such as a *gradual* reduction in working time, would still be useful, but would not be able to generate the increase in the level of employment needed to significantly reduce unemployment.

Economic analysis and historical experience seem to suggest that reduction in *actual* working time (which may differ significantly from *legal* working time) can be made easier by higher growth rates of output. The increases in productivity that are usually associated with faster growth would allow working time reductions without reducing (or by reducing to a lesser extent) the rate of profit. In this form working time reduction would not per se create new jobs, but would magnify the positive effects of GDP growth on employment.

Summing Up

We have argued that, in the light of the post-Second World War experience, the high unemployment experienced in industrial countries and particularly in EU countries in the last decades cannot be regarded as 'technological' but must be related to the slow growth of effective demand due to changed macroeconomic policies and a changed international set-up and to an income distribution unfavourable to lower-income groups. Expansionary macroeconomic policies aimed at favouring GDP growth could very well improve the employment performance of industrial countries in general and European countries in particular. Specific policies aimed at rendering labour-intensive personal services accessible to their potential consumers might also be useful. Higher GDP growth would indeed promote higher employment growth: there are no 'structural' factors or 'economic laws' that would prevent expansionary macroeconomic policies from being effective. Of course, this does not mean that there are no obstacles to such policies, particularly for individual countries; such obstacles, however, are often themselves the result of policies and institutions (Screpanti, 1996; 1997). This seems to be particularly evident in the case of Europe, where the Maastricht Treaty actually prevents the use of fiscal and monetary policies as tools for economic policies aimed, for example, at reducing the differences among unemployment rates in different regions and countries. Yet the project of economic unification could follow a different route and even, under different regulations and institutions, be favourable to expansionary policies, as the European Union is less open to international trade than the individual economies which form it, and this would render the foreign constraint on expansionary policies less stringent (Pivetti, 1997).

On the other hand, there does not seem to be an alternative if the objective of a significant reduction in unemployment is to be pursued. Policies of redistribution of existing employment, albeit useful, do not appear sufficient. In addition, significant (as opposed to gradual) working time reductions (with a given monthly wage) are bound to encounter a very strong resistance, as they would entail a decline in the profit rate that does not appear consistent with the current state of the bargaining relations between the workers and the employers.

NOTES

1. In another respect, the outcome is different, as with innovation productivity increases, thus determining an increase in the returns of the production factors, or at least some of them.
2. Since no automatic tendency of aggregate demand to adjust to productive capacity is envisaged, the 'effective' level of aggregate demand will in general be different from the 'notional' or 'potential' level corresponding to the normal utilization of capacity.
3. For a fuller discussion of this approach, see Serrano (1995) and 'Technical change, employment and effective demand', by the present authors in *Review of Political Economy* (forthcoming).
4. If further technical progress is in view, this may induce the postponement of replacement investment until technology has 'stabilized', and also capital-saving innovations to compensate the shorter expected economic life of capital goods. In these cases technical progress would depress gross investment.
5. For a criticism of modern 'endogenous growth' theories, see Cesaratto (1998).
6. The increase of demand, besides, though in the beginning it may sometimes raise the price of goods, never fails to lower it in the long run. It encourages production, and thereby increases the competition of the producers, who, in order to undersell one another, have recourse to new division of labour and new improvements of art, which might never otherwise have been thought of (Smith, 1976 [1776], p. 748; see also Sylos-Labini, 1969).
7. See Petit (1995, p. 21): 'productivity and demand are linked ... by a set of agreements or institutional arrangements tying elements of production organisation to elements of the formation of demand'.
8. By 'catching up' is meant the fastest growth in productivity experienced since the Second World War (and before) by those industrial countries that had the lowest productivity

levels. These countries (including Italy, France, Spain and Japan) were able to rapidly introduce technical and organizational innovations already in use elsewhere; in addition, large gains in productivity were obtained because structural change involved rapid movements away from backward activities in all sectors towards more modern and productive ones.

9. Note that we talk of government expenditure and not of government budget deficits. Keynesian policies are often confused with big deficits. As shown in simple terms by the well-known 'Haavelmo theorem', an increase in government expenditure can have expansionary effects even with a balanced government budget.

10. Regulationists provide various explanations for the post-war 'accumulation regime' breaking down. The most characteristic, and least clear, refers to the 'breakdown of the Fordist model of production' when the so-called 'Kaldor–Verdoon law' ceased to operate (cf. Boyer, 1988, p. 240). Others have seen the cause of lower accumulation in the 'profit squeeze' caused by prolonged low unemployment rates and workers' high bargaining power in the 1960s (Marglin and Schor, 1990; for a criticism, see Petri, 1994). Interestingly enough, an econometric test run for nine OECD countries has concluded that, whereas the elasticity of productivity to output growth has not changed significantly in recent years, it is demand that has ceased to match productivity gains (Pini, 1994). The deflationary macro environment and the institutional set-up more favourable to profits would be the main explanation.

11. We have chosen to look at employees only, because self-employment may sometimes increase as a result of lack of alternatives, and therefore be, in practice, a form of employment and income redistribution rather than growth. We have also excluded the government sector, as it responds to social and political pressures independent of effective demand, and finally we have excluded the agricultural sector because is follows a negative trend that affects to a larger extent the latecomer countries that still have a large agricultural workforce, and this quite independently of GDP growth (see also Sylos-Labini, 1997).

12. According to some commentators (for example, Wood, 1994), European countries are 'exporting' jobs to the cheap-labour NICs. It is likely that Europe is losing *low-skilled manufacturing* jobs in favour of NICs. This could, however, be compensated by the increase of low-skilled jobs in the *service sector* (jobs that by their very nature are difficult to export and that are needed by the European population). And the reason why the service sector low-skilled jobs have grown so slowly seems to be precisely that effective demand in Europe has been growing too slowly.

13. Most of the successful job creation in European Free Trade Association (EFTA) countries in the 1980s consisted of government jobs. Far from being considered artificial job creation, the latter should be viewed as reflecting the long-run tendency towards the expansion of the service sector.

REFERENCES

Amsden, A.H. (1996), 'Convergence, Technological Competition and Transmission of Long-run Unemployment', in J. Eatwell (ed.), *Global Unemployment. Loss of Jobs in the '90s*, New York: M.E. Sharpe.

Baumol, W.J. and W.G. Bowen (1965), 'On the performing arts: the anatomy of their economic problems', *American Economic Review*, **55**, 495–502.

Boyer, R. (1988), 'New Technologies and Employment in the 1980s: From Science and Technology to Macroeconomic Modelling', in J.A. Kregel, E. Matzner and A. Roncaglia (eds), *Barriers to Full Employment*, New York: St. Martin's Press.

Cesaratto, S. (1996), 'Alternative Perspectives on Division of Labour, Structural Change and Economic Growth', in C. de Bresson (ed.), *Innovation and Interde-*

pendence: Input–Output Analyses of Innovation, Cheltenham, UK/Brookfield, US: Edward Elgar.

Cesaratto, S. (1998), 'New and Old Neoclassical Growth Theory: A Critical Assessment', in G. Mongiovi and F. Petri (eds), *Value Distribution and Capital. Essays in Honour of Pierangelo Garegnani*, London: Routledge.

Eatwell, J. (1996), 'Unemployment on a World Scale', in J. Eatwell (ed.), *Global Unemployment. Loss of Jobs in the '90s*, New York: M.E. Sharpe.

Eatwell, J.L., M. Milgate and P. Newman (1990), *Capital Theory*, London: Macmillan.

European Commission (1993), *Growth, Competitiveness, Employment: The Challenge and Ways Forward into the 21st Century*, December.

Garegnani, P. (1962), *Il Problema Della Domanda Effettiva Nello Sviluppo Economico Italiano*, Rome: SVIMEZ.

Garegnani, P. (1970), 'Heterogeneous capital, the production function and the theory of distribution', *Review of Economic Studies*, **37**, 407–36.

Garegnani, P. (1978), 'Notes on consumption, investment and effective demand', *Cambridge Journal of Economics*, vol. 2, reprinted in J. Eatwell and M. Milgate (eds) (1983), *Keynes's Economics and the Theory of Value and Distribution*, London: Duckworth.

Garegnani, P. (1992), 'Some notes for an analysis of accumulation', in J. Halevi, D. Laibman and E. Nell (eds), *Beyond the Steady State*, London: Macmillan.

Geroski, P. and C. Walters (1995), 'Innovative activity over the business cycles', *Economic Journal*, **105**.

Harcourt, G.C. (1972), *Some Cambridge Controversies in the Theory of Capital*, Cambridge: Cambridge University Press.

Hicks, J.R. (1932), *The Theory of Wages*, London: Macmillan (repr. with a 'Commentary', 1963).

Kalecki, M. (1971), *Selected Essays on the Dynamic of the Capitalist Economy*, Cambridge: Cambridge University Press.

Kurz, H.D. and N. Salvadori (1995), *Theory of Production. A Long-Period Analysis*, Cambridge: Cambridge University Press.

Lunghini, G. (1997a), 'Politiche eretiche per l'occupazione', in P. Ciocca (ed.), *La Disoccupazione di fine secolo*, Turin: Bollati Boringhieri.

Lunghini, G. (1997b), 'Il Problema della disoccupazione dopo Keynes: produzione di merci e bisogni sociali. Controrelazione a Paolo Sylos Labini', in L. Frey (ed.), *La disoccupazione nel lungo periodo – cause e conseguenze*, Collana della Società degli Economisti, Bologna: Il Mulino.

Marglin, S. and J. Schor (eds) (1990), *The Golden Age of Capitalism: Reinterpreting the Post-war Experience*, Oxford: Clarendon Press.

OECD (1994), *Jobs Study, Evidence and Explanations*, Paris: OECD.

Petit, P. (1995), 'Technology and employment: key questions in a context of high unemployment', *STI-Review*, **15**.

Petri, F. (1994), 'The Golden Age of Capitalism, investment, efficiency wages: a review article', *Economic Notes*, **23**, 217–36.

Petri, F. (1997), 'Commento ai saggi di Sylos Labini e Lunghini', in L. Frey (ed.), *La disoccupazione nel lungo periodo – cause e conseguenze*, Collana della Società degli Economisti, Bologna: Il Mulino.

Pini, P. (1994), 'Dinamica della produttività, della domanda e dell'occupazione industriale in nove paesi OCSE: evidenza empirica per un modello di crescita cumulativa', in L. Frey (ed.), *La disoccupazione nel lungo periodo – cause e conseguenze*, Collana della Società degli Economisti, Bologna: Il Mulino.

Pivetti, M. (1992), 'Military spending as a burden on growth: an "underconsumptionist" critique', *Cambridge Journal of Economics*, **16**, 373–84.

Pivetti, M. (1997), 'A proposito di Maastricht: cos'è e a chi giova l'entrata in Europa', *Giano*, January–April.

Rifkin, J. (1995), *The End of Work*, Tarcher Putname.

Schmookler, J. (1966), *Invention and Economic Growth*, Cambridge, Mass.: Harvard University Press.

Screpanti, E. (1996), 'Una politica per l'occupazione: keynesiana o comunista?', *Atti della conferenza di programma del partito della Rifondazione comunista.*

Screpanti, E. (1997), 'La mitologia del post-Fordismo e la soggezione ideologica della sinistra: quali fondamenti per la politica dell'occupazione?', *Marxismo oggi*, January–April.

Serrano, F. (1995), 'Long period effective demand and the Sraffian supermultiplier', *Contributions to Political Economy*, **14**, 67–90.

Smith, A. [1776] (1976), *An Enquiry into the Nature and Causes of the Wealth of Nations*, edited by R.H. Campbell, A.S. Skinner and W.B. Todd, vol. II, Oxford: Oxford University Press.

Sraffa, P. (1960), *Production of Commodities by Means of Commodities. Prelude to a Critique of Economic Theory*, Cambridge: Cambridge University Press.

Sylos-Labini, P. (1969), *Oligopoly and Technical Progress*, revised edition, Cambridge, MA: Harvard University Press.

Sylos-Labini, P. (1997), 'Il problema della disoccupazione dopo Keynes', in L. Frey (ed.), *La disoccupazione nel lungo periodo – cause e conseguenze*, Collana della Società degli Economisti, Bologna: Il Mulino.

Wood, A. (1994), *North–South Trade, Employment and Inequality. Changing Fortunes in a Skill-Driven World*, Oxford: Clarendon Press.

11. Intensive and extensive investment, employment and working time in the European Union

Vittorio Valli

DIFFERENT TRENDS IN LABOUR INPUT

From the time of the first great energy crisis of 1973 up to now, several countries in the European Union have failed to increase labour input; that is, the total amount of hours worked. In the same period, most East Asian countries, some Latin American ones, Canada and the USA have substantially increased their labour input. As Table 11.1 shows, in the period 1973–92, according to the estimates made by Maddison, total labour input increased by more than 50 per cent in Mexico, Venezuela, South Korea, Peru, China, Chile, Taiwan, Colombia and Brazil; by more than 25 per cent in Canada, the USA and Australia; and by more than 10 per cent in Argentina and Japan, while it was almost stagnant or decreased in the countries of the European Union, with the exception of Portugal.

Although for the period 1973–96 the different set of data for annual hours worked per employed person collected by the OECD for a smaller group of countries gives a somewhat different picture (see Table 11.2), the general trends are consistent with Maddison's figures.[1] Therefore, being unable to increase at an adequate rate the total labour input and thus experiencing an increase in unemployment, most EU countries tried to sharply decrease the annual working hours per capita in order to sustain employment. However, the trend in the reduction of working hours was subject, on the labour demand side, to the growing constraint of international competitiveness and, during recent years, to the increasing pressure, from the labour supply side, of the stagnation in real wages and in employment. Indeed, in the late 1980s and in the 1990s, in some EU countries, the decrease in contractual working hours was accompanied by an increase in effective annual hours worked per capita. The reduction of working time can, therefore, remain a very useful tool for employment policy, but its utilization is increasingly difficult and has

Table 11.1   *Changes in labour input in selected countries, 1973–92 (per cent)*

Countries	Total worked hours	Total employment	Annual hours per employed person
Mexico	75.7	75.6	0.1
Venezuela	72.8	81.8	–9.0
South Korea	72.1	65.0	4.4
China	62.9	62.5	0.3
Chile	62.5	58.4	2.6
Peru	60.0	69.0	–5.3
Taiwan	57.6	62.0	–2.7
Colombia	57.5	73.0	–9.0
Brazil	56.4	76.4	–11.4
Canada	29.0	39.2	–7.4
USA	27.0	37.2	–7.5
Australia	26.5	32.5	–4.5
Portugal	17.4	31.1	–10.5
Argentina	12.9	23.4	–8.5
Japan	12.4	22.3	–8.1
USSR	5.1	10.6	–5.1
Italy	4.4	13.0	–7.6
Sweden	4.3	6.2	–3.6
Denmark	2.6	9.2	–6.0
Norway	1.8	19.6	–14.9
Netherlands	0.8	29.2	–22.0
Austria	–0.5	12.2	–11.4
Greece	–3.3	12.4	–14.0
Finland	–3.6	0.2	–3.8
Germany	–7.0	7.3	–13.4
France	–8.4	5.2	–12.9
Switzerland	–9.5	6.2	–14.8
United Kingdom	–10.3	1.6	–11.7
Ireland	–10.8	5.4	–15.4
Spain	–13.8	–3.0	–11.1
Belgium	–14.3	1.4	–15.6

Source: Adapted from Maddison (1995, pp. 246–8).

Table 11.2   *Average annual hours actually worked per person in employment, 1973 and 1996*

Country	1973	1996	% change
Australia		1 867	
Canada	1 867	1 732	−7.2
Finland		1 790	
France	1 904	1 645	−13.6
Germany		1 568	
Italy*	1 842	1 682	−8.7
Japan*	2 201	1 898	−13.8
Mexico		1 955	
Netherlands*	1 724	1 372	−20.4
Norway	1 712	1 410	−17.6
Portugal		2 009	
Spain		1 810	
Sweden	1 557	1 554	−0.2
United Kingdom	1 929	1 732	−10.2
United States	1 924	1 951	1.4

Note: *   Italy: dependent employment (1973 and 1994); Japan: 1994 instead of 1996; Netherlands: dependent employment.

Source: OECD (1997a, p. 179).

to be applied in a subtle and adaptable way in order to have durable positive effects on employment.

INTENSIVE AND EXTENSIVE INVESTMENT AND THE LABOUR INPUT

The analysis of the trend in total labour input is, therefore, crucial in order to explain, together with differences in labour policies and institutions, the trends both in employment and in effective working hours per capita.

One of the main theses of this chapter is the following: the countries which in the long run rapidly increased extensive capital accumulation, without increasing intensive capital too quickly, were able to increase total labour input. Therefore they were able to raise employment and at the same time to reduce or to increase, according to their collective choices, the per capita hours worked. On the other hand, the countries, such as most EU economies, which increased intensive investment much faster than extensive investment, could rapidly increase productivity, but not labour input, and therefore were more willing to reduce working time per capita in order to sustain employment.

The distinction between extensive and intensive capital accumulation is here considered with regard to the impact on employment. Intensive investment tends to increase labour productivity and thus to reduce employment for any given level of product; extensive investment tends to increase employment and is usually associated with an increase in the stock of capital and in the productive basis of an economy. Within the European Union, several countries, in particular latecomer countries such as Italy, but also, to some extent, some first-comer countries such as Belgium and France,[2] were induced to increase intensive investment much faster than extensive investment in order to foster the process of catching up in productivity with the higher level of the USA.

It is very difficult to give a precise empirical measure of the two distinct forms of capital accumulation. Rough proxies can be provided by the trends in 'fixed gross capital in equipment' for intensive investment and in 'fixed gross capital in structures' or in 'structures excluding dwellings' for extensive investment. An increase in equipment based upon a net increase of the stock of capital, but also, to some extent, the simple replacement of old machinery with new, generally brings about an increase in labour productivity, while an increase in non-residential structures usually fosters an increase in production and in employment. The increase in dwellings tends to have important positive effects on employment through its direct effects on the employment of the building sector and its indirect effects on several other productive branches.

Table 11.3 gives us an idea of the two forms of capital accumulation in some industrialized countries in the period 1980–93. Since the data on *flows* (fixed capital formation) can be strongly influenced by cyclical effects, we have preferred to use the data on the evolution of fixed capital stocks. Table 11.3, combined with the information given by Tables 11.1 and 11.2, suggests that labour input has increased more in countries such as Japan and Canada, where capital accumulation has been much faster than the average of industrialized countries, or in countries, such as Australia and the USA, which have experienced a consistent rise in capital in non-residential structures and, at the same time, have not increased productivity very rapidly through a much faster rise in the stock of capital in equipment than in non-residential structures. Indeed, changes in the composition of the capital stock appear to be sometimes as important in their effects on employment as the overall trend of the capital stock.

Table 11.3   *Gross stock of fixed capital in selected countries, 1993, values at constant prices (1980=100)*

Countries	Total	Structures	Structures excluding dwellings	Equipment	Structures excluding dwellings in % of equipment (changes)
Australia	149.4	149.3	143.6	149.5	96.1
Canada*	155.7		143.0	194.9	73.3
USA	139.5	136.9	141.3	147.0	96.1
Japan	235.0				
Belgium	138.4	131.8	131.0	172.4	76.0
Denmark*	123.0	119.5	122.8	140.2	87.6
Finland	146.9	148.4	144.2	140.9	102.3
France	142.4	133.6		152.3	87.6
West Germany	139.6	139.6	122.1	139.6	87.5
Italy	147.7	139.7		179.8	
Sweden	140.8	138.9	148.6	150.3	77.7
UK*	129.1	129.2	131.1	129.0	98.9

Note: *   UK: private sector only; Canada: total excluding dwellings; Denmark 1992.

Source: OECD (1996b).

INTERNATIONALIZATION AND CATCHING UP IN PRODUCTIVITY

Why have European countries, and in particular, most latecomer EU countries, employed much more intensive than extensive capital accumulation? One of the main reasons is the attempt to foster their process of catching up in productivity with the level of the USA under the powerful stimulus of the growing internationalization process. At the beginning of the 1970s, the level of labour productivity of the USA, measured both by GDP per person employed and by GDP per hour worked, was much higher than the level of EU countries.

As we can see in Table 11.4, in 1973 labour productivity in EU first-comer countries, such as France, the Netherlands, Belgium, Germany and the UK, was between 67 per cent and 82 per cent of the level of the USA, while latecomer countries such as Italy, Spain, Finland, Greece, Ireland and Portugal had a

Table 11.4   Labour productivity in selected countries, 1973–92 (USA=100)

Countries	GDP per person employed 1973	GDP per person employed 1992	GDP per hours worked 1973	GDP per hours worked 1992
USA	100.00	100.00	100.00	100.00
Canada	84.24	90.67	81.41	87.01
Netherlands	82.18	83.34	81.11	98.97
France	77.64	98.78	75.78	101.79
Belgium	76.35	97.88	70.49	98.11
Germany	74.06	93.12	70.96	95.02
Australia	71.27	79.56	71.94	87.18
Sweden	69.85	75.72	76.84	79.42
Denmark	68.53	77.24	67.97	74.95
Austria	66.99	82.51	65.12	83.20
UK	66.33	77.31	67.89	82.41
Italy	61.96	79.22	66.44	84.50
Spain	57.61	83.56	46.31	69.48
Finland	56.50	72.65	57.23	70.27
Japan	56.17	81.15	47.55	68.80
Greece	53.17	63.22	45.93	57.87
Ireland	49.91	79.85	42.90	71.68
Portugal	46.23	51.68	42.05	48.32
Taiwan	26.22	59.81	17.61	38.01
South Korea	21.35	51.36	13.73	29.14
China	7.12	13.28	5.59	9.59

Source: Adapted from Maddison (1995, pp. 249–50).

product per person employed between 62 per cent and 46 per cent of the US level. At the beginning of the 1990s, the gap had been considerably reduced by all countries. The process of catching up was very fast in latecomer EU countries such as Italy, Ireland, Finland and Spain, slower in Greece and Portugal and relatively fast also in most EU first-comer countries, as Table 11.4 (based upon Maddison estimates) clearly shows.

Table 11.5, which is based upon EU data for 1973–96, confirms the rapid process of catching up of productivity of all EU countries, and in particular of latecomer EU countries *vis-à-vis* the USA. In 1973–96, the average percentage annual rate of growth of labour productivity (measured by GDP at constant prices per employed person) of the whole group of 15 EU countries was 1.37 points higher than in the USA, while for the latecomer EU countries it was

*Table 11.5   Convergence or divergence of productivity and employment in
EU countries relative to the USA, 1973–96*

	Real productivity	Employment
Latecomer		
EU countries	*1.87*	*–1.49*
Ireland	2.80	–1.02
Portugal	2.35	–1.86
Finland	2.06	–1.30
Spain	1.88	–1.02
Italy	1.44	–1.30
Greece	0.67	–0.83
First-comer		
EU countries	*1.04*	*–1.31*
Germany	1.40	–1.64
Belgium	1.36	–1.73
France	1.30	–1.54
United Kingdom	1.18	–1.62
Netherlands	1.04	–1.23
Austria	0.95	–1.04
Denmark	0.94	–1.51
Sweden	0.73	–1.59
Luxembourg	0.49	–0.18
EU15 (simple average)	*1.37*	*–1.38*

Note: Convergence on or divergence from the USA is measured by the difference between the annual average compound rates of change of the indicators in each country or group of countries and the ones of the USA.

Source: Eurostat: elaboration by Marilena Locatelli. The table comes from a background paper of Coripe-Iuse (1997), *Turin European Report* (Turin: Camera di commercio di Torino).

1.87 points higher than in the USA. However, the table shows that a rapid convergence in productivity was often accompanied by a poor performance in employment, with the partial exception of Ireland, where the catching up process for productivity was particularly rapid, partly because of the massive flows of direct investment from abroad, and it has been accompanied in recent years by some recovery in employment stimulated by high rates of growth of GDP.

The catching up process for productivity was even more rapid in East Asia, where the high rate of capital accumulation and of extensive investment made it possible to obtain at the same time a rapid increase of productivity and an even more rapid increase of GDP, so that labour input and employment could rise over time at a substantial rate.

In the EU, the catching up process was faster as regards product per hours worked than as regards product per employed person. This is because the reduction in annual worked hours per employed person was considerably greater in several EU countries, such as the Netherlands, France, Germany, Belgium, Austria and the UK, than in the USA (see Table 11.1). It is likely that the stagnation in total employment that has affected most European countries since 1973 induced them to reduce the working time per employed person in order to try to sustain employment. This policy was pursued with particular intensity in the Netherlands, mainly through a great increase in various forms of part-time work. In fact, the percentage of part-timers out of total employment more than doubled from 1979 to 1995, rising from 16.6 per cent to 37.4 per cent. In other countries, the policy was pursued with a combination of a widening of part-time work and a reduction of the working hours for full-time workers. However, the effect on employment was insufficient, with the partial exception of the Netherlands. Indeed, the labour force increased considerably in most EU countries, while employment rose only a little or even decreased, so that unemployment increased very sharply in the 1973–96 period.

The catching up process in productivity has therefore been a central factor in explaining the EU performance as regards labour input and employment and the choices regarding the different forms of capital accumulation. Figure 11.1 summarizes some of the basic interrelations involved in the process.

In the 1970s and 1980s, the growing process of internationalization and the relevant cuts in external tariffs due to GATT (General Agreement on Tariffs

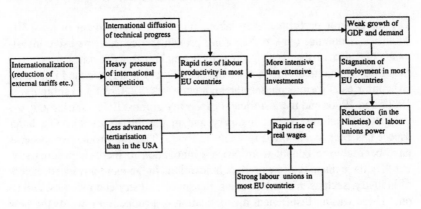

Source: Coripe-Iuse, *Turin European Report*, 1997, p. 11.

Figure 11.1   Some determinants of catching up in productivity in the EU

and Trade) rounds (the Kennedy round, the Nixon round, and so on) obliged the countries with a relatively low level of labour productivity, such as most European countries, to rapidly increase productivity in order to be competitive with the USA, which showed higher average levels of productivity, and with the emerging East Asian countries, which registered a high rate of growth in capital accumulation and productivity. The catching up was facilitated by the fact that the tertiary sector, where productivity tends to grow less, was smaller in Europe than in the USA.

Since productivity grew rapidly, the European firms could concede relatively high increases in wages to their employees, but this tended to stimulate continuous recourse to intensive investment and to forms of restructuring and rationalization of productive processes. In addition, several EU countries had strong labour unions which, until the beginning of the 1990s, agreed to stimulate rapid wage rises, which often induced enterprises to raise productivity through intensive investment, replacement of labour with capital, and so on.

The consequent semi-stagnation in labour input and employment, however, caused a rapid increase in unemployment, which, in the long run, contributed to reducing the contractual power of trade unions. This was reflected in the trend of real unit labour costs in the period 1973–96. While real compensation per employee increased much faster in the EU than in the USA, real unit labour costs (that is, the ratio of real compensation per employee to real labour productivity) decreased in the EU, both in absolute terms and relative to the USA, and this decline was particularly pronounced in the 1990s.

THE DIVERSIFICATION OF PRODUCTION

The rather poor performance in labour input and employment of most EU countries is due not only to the strong propensity to make intensive investment, but also to the weak propensity to make extensive investment. The major determinants of this fact are the deflationary policy pursued in several EU countries in various phases, the high real rates of interest prevailing in the 1980s and 1990s and the insufficient capability of most EU countries to make product innovations both in industry and in the tertiary sector. The latter aspect has been overlooked in many analyses. The EU productive systems have been able to benefit from process innovation to increase productivity, but they have made too few product innovations in the more advanced sectors of industry, such as microelectronics, the space industry and avionics, and so on.[3] There was an insufficient diversification of production towards the new frontiers of technology, which is often the key to the acquisition of new markets. Moreover, several EU countries have become net importers in some advanced branches of the tertiary sector. Having been unable adequately to diversify their production of goods and services in sectors where the demand grows rapidly and economies of scale continue to be important, the EU economies have been unable to increase aggregate demand rapidly without encountering inflationary pressures. The poor performance in this regard mainly reflects the severe shortfall in R&D, the retention of some monopolistic positions, rigidities and barriers in the product and labour markets, and the rather poor performance in the education and training of the labour force.

As regards R&D, it is sufficient to remember that the expenditure in R&D as a percentage of GDP has been much lower in most EU countries than in the USA and Japan (see Table 11.6), that patents, a possible outcome of research, have been comparatively much less numerous, and that the RCA (revealed comparative advantage) indicator of the OECD declined in Germany and in six EU countries in the period 1970–90, revealing a weak performance in high technology.[4] The lack of competition in sectors such as public utilities, banking and insurance, has been gradually reduced as an effect of the great unified market of 1993 and the action of the EEC Commission and of antitrust

Table 11.6   *Some indicators regarding research and development, education and employment*

Countries	R&D expenditure as % of GDP (1995)	Education* USA=100 (1973)	Education* USA=100 (1992)	Employment as % of population (1995)
USA	2.6	100	100	47.5
Japan	3.0	83	82	51.6
France	2.3	80	88	37.8
UK	2.1	80	78	43.7
Germany	2.3	79	67	43.9
Sweden	3.0	72	79	45.4
Italy	1.1	52	62	35.0
Spain	0.8	43	64	30.7
Portugal	0.6	32	50	38.8
Taiwan		50	77	
South Korea		47	75	45.5

Note: *   Equivalent years of primary education for person aged 15–64, where primary education is weighted 1, secondary 1.4 and higher 2.

Sources: OECD (1996b; 1997b), Maddison (1995), ILO (1998).

authorities, although the entire process will take much more time, while some
rigidities in product and labour markets have been partially removed.

The major problem, however, is associated with the education and training
of the labour force. The quality of the labour force depends essentially on two
factors: schooling and processes of 'learning by doing'. On the basis of
quantitative indicators, as regards school and university education, most EU
countries have a much worse situation than the USA, as is shown in Table
11.6. The gap has even widened in the period 1973–92 for Germany and the
UK, while it has diminished for Sweden, France and for latecomer countries
such as Italy, Spain and Portugal. In the same period, however, East Asian
countries such as Taiwan and East Korea have reduced the gap much more
rapidly, overtaking the EU average level, while Japan has maintained its
relative advantage. The scanty information about the *quality* of education
shows, however, that this is generally better in East Asia and in some EU
countries than in the USA, except for post-graduate studies.

But the greatest discrepancy is in 'learning by doing' processes. Since the
rate of employment (the percentage of population employed) is much lower in
most EU countries than in the USA and in East Asia, the number of people who
may benefit from forms of on-the-job training is comparatively lower in Europe. Moreover, the gap regarding high-tech activities means that fewer people
have access to on-the-job training in technologically advanced activities.

There is therefore a sort of vicious circle for Europe, and especially its
latecomer countries, and a sort of virtuous circle for the USA and some East
Asian countries. The employment weakness of the former worsens its human
capital and its prospects for the future, while the opposite is true for the USA
and for East Asia.

TOWARDS A MODULAR SYSTEM OF WORKING TIME

In order to solve the problem of unemployment it is above all necessary to
raise the total number of hours worked through extensive investment. However, it can be important also to share it in a less unequal way in order to try
to increase employment and the quality of life.

In a given phase of her or his life cycle, a person may be willing to have
more free time to take care of children or of parents in old age, to learn a new
profession, or for other personal reasons. The present situation, with a sharp
dichotomy between full-time and part-time jobs, drastically reduces the range
of choices. If one wants to have job security and a career, one must choose a
full-time occupation and stick to it.

It would be much better to build a modular system of working time, where
a person may choose to work less (and be paid less) in one phase of his life,

and then to go on to full-time and full wages.[5] If accompanied by incentives to offset the higher transaction and training costs of enterprises, this system could reduce the average working time to well below the level of 35 hours a week, without reducing the competitiveness of EU productive systems. It could be completed by a set of incentives for 'entrance schemes' with reduced working time for young workers and by other schemes aimed at a gradual reduction of working time for older employees. These schemes might increase employment in a substantial way. Moreover, they could facilitate the access of more people to experiences of 'learning by doing'. They could therefore help to build a better future.

NOTES

1. The data on annual working hours are of rather poor quality. The estimates by Maddison for annual hours worked per capita are in some cases different from the OECD data. They sometimes regard dependent workers only, sometimes all employed persons. There are also some differences in the estimates of total employment between Maddison and OECD since, for some countries, such as Italy, Maddison tried to take into account also the workers unofficially employed in the 'submerged' labour market. (See Maddison, 1995; OECD, 1996a; 1997a.)
2. The distinction between first-comer and latecomer countries in the process of industrialization and economic growth is due to authors such as Gerschenkron (1962) and Fuà (1980).
3. Vivarelli (1995, pp. 162–7), for example, has shown that the impact on total working time and employment of product innovation has been much higher in the USA than in Italy.
4. See Englander and Gurney (1994, p. 83). RCA is the ratio of each sector's share in a country's manufacturing exports divided by its share in manufacturing output. The USA has maintained its leadership in high technology, while Japan has increased its RCA ratio, and Germany and the EC6 have seen a decline in their ratios, thus widening their technological shortfall.
5. See Valli (1988; 1996a).

REFERENCES

Coripe-Iuse (1997), *Turin European Report 1997*, Turin: Camera di commercio di Torino.

Englander, A. Steven and Andrew Gurney (1994), 'Medium-term determinants of OECD productivity', *OECD Economic Studies*, no. 22, pp. 50–110.

Fuà, Giorgio (1980), *Problemi dello sviluppo tardivo in Europa*, Bologna: Il Mulino.

Gerschenkron, Alexander (1962), *Economic Backwardness in Historical Perspective*, Cambridge, Mass.: Harvard University Press.

ILO (1998), *World Labour Report: 1997–98*, Geneva: ILO.

Maddison, Angus (1995), *Monitoring the World Economy*, Paris: OECD.

OECD (1996a), *Employment Outlook*, Paris: OECD.

OECD (1996b), *Flows and Stocks of Fixed Capital*, Paris: OECD.

OECD (1997a), *Employment Outlook*, Paris: OECD.

OECD (1997b), *Main Science and Technology Indicators*, no. 1, Paris: OECD.

Vaccarino, Gian Luigi and De Vincenti Claudio (1997), 'Orari di lavoro, salari e disoccupazione: un'analisi macroeconomica', *Rivista di politica economica*, May, 3–38.

Valli, Vittorio (ed.) (1988), *Tempo di lavoro ed occupazione*, Rome: Nuova Italia Scientifica.

Valli, Vittorio (1996a), 'Tempi di lavoro e tempi della vita: un sistema modulare di orari di lavoro per rilanciare l'occupazione e la qualità della via.', in M. Canzi *et al.* (eds), *Proposte eretiche per l'occupazione*, Turin: Rosenberg & Sellier, pp. 163–94.

Vivarelli, Marco (1995), *The Economics of Technology and Employment*, Aldershot, UK/Brookfield, US: Edward Elgar.

12. The transformation of the Italian labour market: a process of segmentation

Giovanna Altieri

INTRODUCTION

When we examine labour market transformations under way in developed countries, normally we tend to grasp the uniform and common aspects because we are struck by the similarities, albeit in profoundly different institutional contexts. In all developed countries, the employment systems appear to be under great stress, the common trait being the curtailing of the careers of breadwinners and the considerable increase in atypical employment relations, with the consequent reduction of job security and employment standards. Regardless of whether the changes under way affect the growth of employment levels, as in Europe, or the extraordinary increase in the number of jobs, insufficient to support a family economically, as in the USA, or the growth of low-security jobs in subsidiary companies and lesser services, compared with the weight of the main branches of the stable and high-productivity economy, as in Japan, it has been observed that the results are always the same.[1] The job divide between high-productivity careers and support activities no longer functions as the engine of economic growth and, above all, as a form of redistribution sufficient to offset the increasing social imbalance, at least as regards the guarantee of a minimum standard of living.

This leads us to stress globalization, to focus on the limits of national governments, faced with dynamics that appear increasingly under the control of supernational entities. These issues are undoubtedly real, and both the economists and governments of industrialized countries are called on to deal with them. The margins of uncertainty are broad; nevertheless, these macroprocess-based approaches perhaps somehow underestimate the importance of the national and local environments, as regards both the interpretation of the events under way and the process management decision-making level.

MAIN CHARACTERISTICS OF THE ITALIAN MODEL

According to Solow,[2] the labour market, more than other markets, must be considered a real 'social institution'; for example, one must of necessity take account of its non-economic components too. When we speak of flexibility or of the American, Japanese or European models, we are not comparing homogeneous economic systems based on a scale of greater or lesser efficiency, but 'social institutions', social agreements inspired by different values and principles.

By implementing specific strategies, each welfare system (and even systems without welfare) provides a specific system of interdependencies within the community. The laws governing working hours, like trade union policies on this issue, are further factors that contribute to defining the traits of 'typical' employment models, in an economic and social context; for example, the number of working hours, who works, how the job must be done. Employment policies, therefore, are not unrelated to other political decisions, ranging from social to economic policy issues; likewise, we cannot speak of employment models without taking account of the prevailing social models and values.

International comparisons are always hard to interpret, so this chapter will try to focus on the way the Italian employment system has adapted to changed and changing economic conditions. It is a well-known fact that unemployment in Italy is polarized and heavily concentrated in a few social groups (the young, women and people living in the southern regions of the country). To understand the employment situation in a country, it is necessary to refer not only to unemployment rates, but also to employment rates; therefore, to understand the characteristics of unemployment in Italy, it is necessary to take account of the employment models. Employment in Italy is very unbalanced. There are four characteristic features of this imbalance:

1. the 'selective' nature of unemployment in Italy, for example the fact that it tends to affect certain social groups more than others;
2. the welfare system, which tends to protect only certain groups of workers, excluding others;
3. the structural heterogeneity of the labour market, from the point of view of its geographical distribution, for example the north/south divide, which produces different opportunities and constraints in the different contexts;
4. the increasing segmentation of the labour market, resulting from the implementation of labour flexibility policies.

We focus here, in particular, on the fourth characteristic, to highlight how it is impossible to solve the persisting problem of unemployment in Italy simply by deregulating and increasing the flexibility of the labour market.

In reality, the flexibility/rigidity polarity is not adequately representative of the Italian situation. Increasing flexibility and atypical employment relationships have been a widespread and pervasive process, resulting in the marked segmentation of the labour market. The characteristics of the process are a consequence of the Italian regulatory system and, generally speaking, of the employment model. If, therefore, rigidity is not a trait of the Italian labour market, the relationship between the flexibilization of the labour market and new forms of employment appears very uncertain. In any case, it is necessary to find a new mix between labour and benefits consistent with the various employment relationship patterns that characterize the present situation.

FLEXIBILIZATION AND SEGMENTATION OF THE ITALIAN LABOUR MARKET: TRENDS AND EFFECTS

Faced with a constantly falling labour demand, the Italian employment system has become more and more flexible, combining the new regulations with regard to the so-called 'atypical' employment contracts (in 1997, of hirings in a sample of 36 Italian provinces, 49.5 per cent, compared with 42 per cent in 1996, were fixed-term and 8.7 per cent part-time employment contracts) with alternative flexibility measures, such as the decentralization of production, parasubordinate employment relationships, and irregular and undeclared employment. These measures have resulted in the fragmentation of the juridical status of employees, varying degrees of job protection and security, down to the total lack of any contractual or legal rights for workers who find themselves 'obliged' to work for the grey economy. There are two typical aspects of this situation. First, in the process of segmentation, the weaker positions, in terms of income, health and safety at work and working conditions, have mainly involved several well-defined social groups, such as the young and women, with very differentiated effects and results within these groups, as will be described shortly, where the discriminating factors seem to be living standards and educational qualifications.

Second, in Italy, the increase in insecure and atypical forms of employment (such as non-full-time positions regulated by open-ended contracts) has mainly affected the self-employed. That is, while in other European countries the increase in insecure labour has mainly affected employees, in Italy this has occurred mostly in the self-employed sector.

According to official statistical data (the source being the quarterly ISTAT survey on the labour force), 60 per cent of employed women work in standard positions; for example, they work full-time in a stable position; the corresponding number of men in the same position is only a few points higher, at 64 per cent. This difference is determined by the different weight of part-time work, which involves 12 per cent of women employees, but only 2.5 per cent of males, besides fixed-term contracts, involving 9 per cent of women, but only 6 per cent of men. As regards subordinate or self-employment, working hours and job security, there do not appear to be any significant gender-based differences. However, if we examine the working hours in greater detail, there are significant differences between men and women in all positions, and according to the sector of activity.

Taking 'part-time' to mean fewer than 25 working hours per week, we see that women employees in this condition amount to about 21 per cent. Male employees in this position are only 5 per cent. In the service sector, 25 per cent of women employees are engaged on a part-time basis, compared with only 7 per cent of males, and the largest gap between the working hours of male and female employees is among the blue-collar workers in the service sector. Moreover, if we examine professional positions, we find that female managers double in number, while female professionals and entrepreneurs increase by one-quarter and blue-collar female workers in the service sector by two-thirds. The last group is the one that has grown most, in absolute terms, with over 500 000 additional positions filled by female workers.[3]

These data explode the widespread myth that the growth of female employment has mainly involved white-collar positions. The truth is that the service sector has supplied almost 900 000 additional jobs, about half of which are unqualified positions and, in any case, positions requiring manual labour. This accumulation of blue-collar female employment in the service sector is one of the critical aspects of the processes under way.

In the first place, it must be pointed out that, while in the manufacturing sector industrial automation processes are transforming manual labour, at least in part, by replacing men with machines and upgrading the workers' tasks, the main characteristic of labour in the service sector is that it remains essentially manual in nature. A further matter is job security. Employees engaged in low-quality jobs in the service sector are subject to the stability (or instability) of the enterprise. This entails the difficulty of gaining experience, the risk of recurrent unemployment, low and uncertain incomes and reduced pension expectations. These workers have unstable careers, the result of disorderly moves from one enterprise or sector to another, rather than a progressive career within one enterprise. These problems affect workers with low qualifications engaged in certain areas of the services sector, and especially women.

As mentioned above, women are taken on mainly in part-time positions. If we examine in greater detail the distribution of working hours in Italy, regarding both male and female employees, we see that the majority of positions are full-time, with 36 or 40 working hours per week, established by contract, while part-time positions are very few. In other words, enterprises tend to respond to seasonal adjustments or contingent fluctuations by asking their employees to work overtime, or by resorting to various forms of external labour: subcontracting to small enterprises, outworking, temporary/irregular employment. Moreover, in Italy there is no direct relationship between the family situation and part-time and/or discontinuous employment.

Another feature of the Italian situation is that it is not so much the work-load within the family that determines whether a woman works full- or part-time, but the type of position available on the labour market. That is, if the position is satisfactory from the point of view of job security and salary, or if the woman manages to gain access to those sectors that impose fewer constraints on women with family workloads (such as the civil service), the position will generally be full-time. For other women, the solution is self-employment. This does not necessarily mean shorter working hours, but it does give the opportunity to organize one's own working time. Alternatively, women are employed in discontinuous and/or irregular jobs. One might wonder, amongst other things, if self-employment in Italy has boosted female em-ployment, as has been the case in other countries. From this point of view, comparing the distribution of female employment in Italy and Europe in the various non-standard forms of employment (considering full-time employ-ment as the standard), we see that, while in Europe part-time employment accounts for 65 per cent of the atypical employment of women, in Italy it accounts for only 24 per cent. On the other hand, the majority of atypical female employment, 51 per cent, is represented by full-time non-subordinate employment.

A large share of non-subordinate employment consists of self-employment (60 per cent of non-subordinate employment) and 52 per cent of female self-employment is concentrated in trade, while another 13 per cent is in the service sector: that multiform reserve of which little is known, but which includes a large share of non-qualified labour. Thus, more than in subordinate employment, women are segregated in feminized sectors, with hardly any career opportunities. The educational qualifications of these self-employed women confirm this theory: 80 per cent have minimum qualifications (com-pulsory education), while the average in subordinate forms of employment amongst women is 59 per cent.

In Italy, therefore, the domestic markets are very rigid with respect to working hours. Therefore female employment tends to be concentrated in either full-time employment in secure positions or, and increasingly in a more composite area, in that grey part of the economy which has its own rules and which does not observe the typical employment contracts.

From one point of view, the very low incidence of part-time work in Italy has given Italian women fewer employment opportunities, but it has also limited the segregation of female workers, as compared with other countries.

Can we, therefore, conclude that, for Italian women, the labour market has had a relatively 'equalizing' effect, compared with other countries?[4]

The theory that seems to best represent the model of female employment in Italy is that of the segmentation of the female labour market. During the last 15–20 years a large number of women have gained access to the central labour market (in all sectors and areas of activity); this has been especially true for women with medium to high educational qualifications, and equality of access to the labour markets is widespread amongst the young men and women of the centre–north of the country. The segregation within male trades/professions and female trades/professions, however, is still character-istic of workers with medium to low educational qualifications. This means that women in higher social positions are more equal to men compared with other countries, while inequality among women is increasing. In other words, social stratification among women plays a strongly selective role in Italy.

To understand the specific position of young people in the world of work in Italy, and to evaluate how they are affected job-wise by the new discontinuous forms of employment, we must examine the economic, social and institu-tional dynamics at play, which, on the one hand, tend to increase negative selectivity in this social group, and, on the other, promote segmentation. As regards young people, families still play a crucial role, as is confirmed by the fact that 59 per cent of unmarried young people aged between 18 and 34 still live at home with their families (compared to 52 per cent in 1990). In a general context of scarce job opportunities, the employment status of young people in Italy is heavily subject to social and environmental factors. One of the most influential variables is educational qualifications. Indeed, higher education plays a key role in favouring employment sooner or later, while the holders of lower qualifications – who in the majority of cases also belong to a lower social class – must make do with unstable forms of employment or remain unemployed.

Furthermore, as part of a general trend that lengthens the time required to find a relatively stable job, there is an ever-increasing gap between young people with good educational qualifications and substantial family resources, living in economically dynamic local environments, and young people living in more disadvantaged areas, where the only alternatives to unemployment are unqualified job opportunities.

In greater detail, in Italy we may observe three types of jobs open to the young, in the transition towards employment.[5]

1. The first type includes jobs that, though insecure, may be the first stage in a career process, in that they contribute to the construction of a job security system (especially regarding the acquisition of skills/qualifications). These job opportunities mainly concern males living in the north of the country.

2. Then there is a second type of job, typical of more privileged groups, offering even more opportunities for finding a stable and permanent job. It consists of temporary jobs, chosen precisely because they do not require much commitment and do not trigger deprofessionalization processes, since they have no connection with job security models (for example, young men who work as mail couriers before leaving for their compulsory military service or university students who do these jobs during the summer holidays).

3. A third profile of workers is encountered most frequently on the labour market in the south of the country, although it is present also in other geographical areas. It features all the traits of a downward slide, consisting of a number of low-income jobs that require a large number of working hours and entail manual labour and/or deprofessionalization. People are forced to accept these types of work to maintain a minimum standard of living. This is the world of the unstable and insecure, where there is no hope of a 'normal' working career, where people such as building construction workers, waiters, port workers and salespersons, with no alternatives, pass from one unqualified job to another. These jobs are carried out mainly by young people with low or no educational qualifications or older people with medium educational qualifications and no family to support them or no acquaintances capable of giving them better expectations. These jobs trigger deprofessionalization processes, both because they do not lead to the construction of a model of job security and because they contribute to the sliding down the social ladder of young people with secondary school leaving certificates.

In the areas of employment protected by bargaining, where there is a prevalence of male employees, flexibility has been achieved through various mechanisms and has taken on two positive dimensions: compensation and negotiation. It would appear, however, that negotiation has hardly modified a model of employment largely based on the reduction of the number of employees (partly through protection mechanisms for those who leave) and on the extension of working hours. Newly hired employees, therefore, have few opportunities of employment and are also burdened with the new fixed-term contracts.

Whereas in other countries the trend is towards the loss of job stability and security, in Italy there has been a segmentation of the labour market, with different jobs/positions for the young, women and adult males. The last group, neither too young nor too old, continue to be the privileged beneficiaries of the standard forms of employment. The flexibility strategies that affect adult male employees are essentially either flexibility with regard to the termination of the employment relationship – protected by such income protection measures as the Wages Guarantee Fund, the so-called 'mobility lists' and early retirement – or negotiated variations of working hours. In any case, the measures adopted have no connection with underemployment.

On the contrary, atypical/marginal employment relationships are reserved for the newly hired and may be considered a sort of intermediate stage towards permanent employment, in the case of male employees and of women with medium to high educational qualifications in the more developed areas of the country. But they remain an area of segregation for the majority of women.

The categories described above have suffered most from the negative effects of trends in the labour market on unemployment and on the lack of continuity and stability in work. From the beginning of the 1990s, we must add unskilled male workers and workers who have been made redundant, and who are having increasing difficulties in finding re-employment, though they have hitherto been protected by the institutions.

CONCLUSION

Obviously, one must not underestimate the employment problems of the scores of adult male workers who have lost their jobs, or abolish a job security system which was an achievement of the trade unions. However, the following must be taken into account. First, the characteristics of unemployment and the distribution of employment in Italy are the expression of a gap between the generations and the sexes, which cannot be bridged unless the labour market is radically reformed and unless new regulations are passed to rebalance the system of opportunities and rights, thus opposing the segmentation of the labour market currently under way. Second, regarding the structural nature of the changes currently under way in the production models, we read the following in the latest interim report by a group of experts appointed by the EU,[6] on the future of employment perspectives:

> while the Fordist model was grounded on the stable organisation of groups of workers, the new models are based on the opposite idea of the co-ordination of mobile individuals. This leads to the necessity (and difficulty) of outlining a professional status capable of integrating the individualisation and mobility of professional careers. If individual mobility is to be the key characteristic of tomorrow's world of labour, the impact and scope of labour law, which in the past was to guarantee job stability and security and, therefore, to guarantee employees a real professional standing, should now concern how to adapt the law, rather than sacrifice it to change.

If this process is not supported by decisive political actions focusing on labour demand, the new rules and prospective regulations run the risk of leaving the problem of Italian unemployment unresolved. Only in a labour market with a wealth of opportunities will it be possible to develop a culture of 'employability', to which many labour market researchers make reference today, as opposed to the mirage of a secure job or to a job for the job's sake, regardless of the employment conditions, which are the prevailing conditions in the south of Italy. But the problem does not affect Italy alone.

Accornero (1997) asks himself the following question,[7]

> Is the crisis of the welfare state of an endogenous or exogenous nature? Is it due to the fact that governments have made promises and undertaken obligations such as to create expectations beyond the limits of current incomes or viable taxation, or is it due to the fact that in Europe development is almost at a standstill, while the population is growing less steadily and people are living longer, thus negatively affecting the relationship between the active and the retired populations?

This is the key issue that, regardless of the various models of labour market regulation and social security in the various countries, affects all European countries, and Italy above all. Rather than continuing to debate the issue of employment flexibility as a policy for creating new jobs and a tool capable of safeguarding the relationship between labour and social security, which has constituted the key element of social cohesion in European countries, we should address the issue of whether and how the European countries can devise new development strategies.

A lot of work has already been done in this direction; some, for example, highlights the importance and the strong employment potential of innovation strategies, combined with new work organization models; and, likewise, the need to stress the profoundly local nature of economic development, which inevitably entails the reorganization of the tools to support the production system and to manage the labour market at the local level.

Lastly, mention should be made of three matters that ought to be followed up as a blueprint for labour policies:

- deregulation per se does not solve the problem of the segmentation of the labour market; on the contrary, it may worsen it;
- even though the struggle against unemployment in Italy, owing to its concentration in the southern regions, strongly depends on the structural development policies in that area, it is in any case necessary to invest resources to create new jobs, starting from the qualitative planning of the employment that is being created;
- the problem of segmentation must be addressed by reuniting the labour market, which will be possible only if we focus on the models of employment and a job security system for all workers.

NOTES

1. See Mingione (1998).
2. See Solow (1990).
3. See Bianco (1996).
4. See, in this connection, Reynieri (1996); Bettio and Villa (1995).
5. See IARD-Ue (1996).
6. See the interim report, 'The transformation of work and the future of labour law in Europe' (1997).
7. Accornero (1997).

REFERENCES

Accornero, A. (1997), *Era il Secolo del Lavoro*, Bologna: Il Mulino.
Bettio, F. and P. Villa (1995), 'Changing patterns of work and working time for men and women in Italy', working paper, UMIST.
Bianco, M.L. (1996), 'La Partecipazione delle Donne al Mercato del Lavoro', in *La Mobilità della Società Italiana*, Rome: Confindustria, SIPI.
IARD-Ue (1996), *General Introduction Report: Youth Unemployment and Unofficial Economy in Southern Europe*, (ed.), E. Mingione; and the national reports: M. Karamesini and D. Vaiou (eds), *Youth Unemployment and Unofficial Economy in Greece*; M.T. Amaro Ganhao (ed.), *Youth Unemployment and Unofficial Economy in Portugal*; M. Nogera y Guell (ed.), *Youth Unemployment and Unofficial Economy in Spain*; G. Orientale Caputo (ed.), *Youth Unemployment and Unofficial Economy in Italy*, Milan: IARD.
Mingione, E. (1988), *Sociologia della Vita Economica*, Rome: Nuova Italia Scientifica.
Reynieri, E. (1996), *Sociologia del Mercato del Lavoro*, Bologna: Il Mulino.
Solow, R.M. (1990), *The Labor Market as a Social Institution*, Cambridge, Mass.: Blackwell.
'The transformation of work and the future of labour law in Europe', paper presented at the conference on 'Transformation du Travail et Avenir du Droit du Travail en Europe', Nantes, 25 October 1997.

13. Changing patterns in the division of labour and in the segmentation of the labour force

Vittorio Rieser

CHANGES IN THE DIVISION OF LABOUR AS A KEY FEATURE OF THE 'POST-FORDIST' FIRM

Organizational changes of the firm, in its 'post-Fordist' phase,[1] may be classified as (a) changes within the firm, and (b) changes in its relationship with the environment. The environment in turn may be divided into the market environment, that is the customers and the competitors, and the productive environment, that is, the productive chain and networks involved in the production of the firm's final goods.

Leaving aside, as a direct object, the relationships with the market, we shall concentrate on the changes in the firm's organization, regarded both in its internal and its external aspects. These changes will be looked at as a (micro) part of a more general set of changes in the division of labour, which is a crucial feature of the present phase of 'global' capitalist development.

The chapter begins with an attempt to summarize these changes in a sort of 'ideal type scheme'. Given the specific features of Italian industry, which will be our main empirical reference, two ideal types are sketched: the first concerning the large firm, of which a typical example is the car producer, and the second concerning the small firm producing directly for the market (as distinct from the subcontractor).

The Large Firm

In talking about the large firm, Fiat serves as our implicit empirical referent, but what follows may easily be applied to other large firms. The changes are roughly classified into three sets.

Changes in the internal division of labour

These include changes in the horizontal division of labour among jobs, roles and functions – for example, the trend from separation to integration of functions within the production process – and changes in the vertical division of labour between the various levels of the organizational pyramid: see, for example, the flattening of the hierarchical ladder, aimed not at a more democratic command and control system, but at a speeding up and a partial dehierarchization of the flow of information within the firm, which amounts also to a speeding up of the decision processes (all this has of course to do with the functional imperative of flexibility, typical of the 'post-Fordist' firm).

The latter aspect is a part of a more general change in the division (or distribution) of information, running parallel to the changes in the division of labour.

Changes in the division between making and buying

Outsourcing of increasing portions of the organizational and production process, for example, of part of administration and accounting, or of logistic and transport systems, is one such change. Within productions that are already allotted to supplier firms, there is a shift in the balance of functions between the mother firm and the supplier, the latter becoming less and less a mere producer of pieces designed and controlled by the mother firm, and developing new functions related to project/design, certified quality and 'just-in-time' supply, which were previously centralized by the mother firm.

Changes within the network of suppliers

As regards new entries, new firms (and, sometimes, new kinds of self-employed workers) join the network, in positions ranging from very 'poor' ones to highly qualified ones. A typical example is the case of firms starting from elementary transport tasks and often ending up with the organization of integrated systems of logistics and transport both within and outside the mother firm.

There are changes in the organizational model of the front-line supplier firms (very often, but not always, the larger ones), related both to the shift in the balance of functions identified above and to the reorganization of the supply network into the supply of 'sub-systems' rather than individual component parts; but also in the (relatively smaller) 'second line' subcontractors, related, for example, to new needs for quality control and for 'just-in-time' organization of supplies.

These may be summarized as processes of organizational rationalization and differentiation, leading from artisan to industrial organizational patterns (incidentally, these processes may have different outcomes, ranging from 'neo-Taylorist' ones to new forms of rationalized flexibility).

Small Firms

As has already been said, we refer here to small firms with a final product of their own: a case in point may be that of firms producing specialist kinds of machinery, ordered by other firms in order to meet specific production needs.

Until the recent past, these firms operated in relatively protected market niches, often created by some kind of incremental product innovation. Now this relative protection may be eroded (a) by global competition with similar firms from other countries, and (b) by the growing flexibility of large firms that may allow them to enter these niches. The new competitive context may induce organizational changes showing basic analogies but also some differences *vis-à-vis* those of small supplier firms.

Changes within the firm

The processes of organizational change within the firm, as in the case of suppliers and subcontractors examined above, may be summarized under the label of 'organizational rationalization and differentiation', but with a different mix. For example, these small firms producing on their own already had an autonomous project/design function: but now this tends to become a more complex function including marketing, R&D and product projecting, connected with the transition from production on the basis of a specific order to an 'anticipation of future demand' based on market analysis and corresponding R&D activity. Beside this, as in the supplier firms, there is of course an increasing importance given to the calculation and planning of times and costs of production.

New balance between making and buying

Subcontracting has always been a common practice among small firms, but it may now follow a new pattern. In the past, it was often confined to special segments of the production process which, if performed within the firm, would have led to diseconomies of scale; or it was associated with peaks in production. Now we often see, even in the small firm, the logic of concentrating on the core business, subcontracting all the rest. This of course has a feedback effect on internal organization, for example on the growth and importance of the production planning function – as well as, more generally, on the overall shape of the firm's organizational structure, which tends to show a greater space occupied by 'indirect' functions connected with projecting, marketing and planning, as compared to the directly productive ones.

CONSEQUENCES FOR THE COMPOSITION OF THE LABOUR FORCE

Labour Force Diversification and Precarious Jobs

Changes in the division of labour among firms lead, at first sight, to two kinds of consequences. First, there is a new distribution of the labour force between different types of firms: first of all in terms of size (a rough scheme may be that of an increasing part of the labour force being employed in medium/small firms, and a decreasing part being employed in the largest and probably also in the smallest),[2] but also in terms of the kind of firm (see, for example, the new growth of cooperatives, and the various forms of self-employment).

Second, we see a new composition of the labour force within firms: for example, current organizational changes may determine a growing weight of white-collar workers in many small firms, while in the larger ones we may see the opposite trend, leading to a reduction in the share of the labour force not directly connected with production.

But all this does not take place in a context of stable and homogeneous employment relationships: on the contrary, there is a diversification of employment relationships, connected both with the diversification in types and sizes of firms, and with the growing market pressure towards a flexible use of the labour force. Thus, in the same plant, we may find, together with a core of wage-earners with a relatively stable employment relationship, other wage-earners with various kinds of temporary employment, workers with the special status connected with being members of a cooperative, and self-employed workers – all of these not only working within the same plant, but sometimes doing similar jobs.

The overall effect of such changes is not only a diversification in the composition of the labour force, but a growing proportion of more or less precarious jobs.

Changes in Skill Structure

At the same time, these organizational changes, along with technological ones, induce changes in the skill structure of the labour force.[3] Perhaps for the first time in a long period of capitalist history, they do not bring about a predominantly deskilling process but, on the contrary, a widespread (though much diversified) trend towards an increase in skill level, due to many factors, the most general and significant seeming to be the new and more active relationship between the worker and the firm's information system, as required by the new organizational models.[4]

At the same time, a number of factors – such as the already-mentioned active relationship with the information system (requiring knowledge of the appropriate languages), the speed and frequency of technological and organizational changes, and the specific features of the new technologies – lead to a growing importance of educational and training requisites.

But the distribution of this skill surplus and its implications in terms of worker strength on the labour market are the result of a complex interplay with other aspects, some of them already mentioned above.[5] Just to give a couple of examples: the employment of an increasing proportion of workers in medium/small firms may place them, in some cases, in a context of rich and increasing skill requirements, but, in other cases, in a 'neo-Taylorist' context. Again the degree of job precariousness may have significant consequences also for skills, because it may prevent processes of experience and skill accumulation.

New Patterns of Labour Force Segmentation

The overall effect of such phenomena amounts to a new and more complicated pattern of segmentation of the labour force and the labour market. We may say that changes in the division of labour inevitably imply changes in the division of the labour force, but the picture is complicated, not only by the interplay of many factors, but by the fact that relationships among these factors are not univocal, as we will try to demonstrate in the following section.

ALIENATION, CONTROL AND THE NEW PATTERNS OF SEGMENTATION

Alienation and Control

In trying to sum up some of these problems, we refer to a more general analytical framework, based on a conceptual pair: alienation and control. As they are used here, they are, so to speak, reciprocally defined. 'Alienation' is defined as lack of control; more specifically, in our context, this means lack of control by the worker over his/her working conditions and over his/her movements on the labour market.[6]

On the other hand, we have its opposite, 'control' (the degree of control) by the worker over the same set of conditions. Within this conceptual framework, trade union action may be seen as among the control strategies developed by workers to increase their degree of control and to reduce their basic condition of alienation. The strength or weakness of the worker on the labour market also becomes a part of this more general balance between alienation and control.

We may add that this picture sketched in the preceding sections may allow the hypothesis that, in the concrete condition of an increasing portion of the labour force, lack of control over the labour market is going to have a growing weight in comparison with the lack of control over working conditions.[7]

New Patterns of Segmentation

The picture becomes more complicated than before, and does not lend itself to definition either in terms of continuum or of dualism. This is due not only to the greater differentiation of the labour force and to the multiplicity of factors coming together to shape it, but also to other reasons.

First of all, no single factor can be assumed as a proxy for describing and explaining adequately the worker's position on the labour market or, more generally, his/her position within the framework of alienation and control. Let us take, for example, the formal (juridical) nature of the employment relationship. First of all, it is not an adequate proxy for the precariousness or stability of employment. A formally stable employment relationship in a building firm, or in certain kinds of small manufacturing firms, is far less stable than 'temporary contracts' (such as the 'Contratti di Formazione/Lavoro', which are one- or two-year contracts formally including a set number of hours of training) in the 'strong part' of firms and industries. Or, to take another example, to be a member of a cooperative firm may mean, in some cases, stronger guarantees of employment stability, but in other, more frequent, cases it means the opposite.

Nor is the formal nature of the employment relationship an adequate proxy for the degree of autonomy on the job; that is, for the degree of control over working content and conditions. Thus the condition of a self-employed worker may mean, in some cases, a high degree of autonomy (even if it may be counterbalanced by an equally high degree of precariousness), but in other cases it is associated with an extremely low degree of control over working conditions.

Moreover, certain 'subjective' features of the labour force, such as sex, age and educational level seem to be related to segmentation in ways that are partly different from those of the past. If, for example, we look at age, the strong segment seems now to be placed in a lower age range than before: the male worker in his forties, for instance, seems no longer to be in a privileged position. As to the educational level, its weight seems to be greater than before, but less closely connected with specific educational and/or training curricula.

On the whole, the port of entry seems to be increasingly important, but not so much as a port of entry into the firm's internal labour market, as relative to entry into specific networks of paths on the labour market in general (this, incidentally, gives increasing weight to the fabric of social relationships influencing the positions and movements of the individual on the labour market).

Finally, at the present stage of empirical analysis of workers' movements on the 'new' Italian labour markets, it is difficult to say whether the new patterns of segmentation are more or less rigid than the old ones.

A Larger and Diversified Area of Labour Depending on Capital

On the whole, the overall effect of the processes of change and diversification that we have tried to examine does not seem to be, as many people in Italy say, a spectacular growth of autonomous work, in particular of self-employed workers.

Italian statistics show, over the last 10 years, a moderate decrease in the share of wage-earners relative to total employment (let us say from about 75 per cent to about 70 per cent); all the rest, including self-employed, managers, entrepreneurs and so on, increasing correspondingly from about 25 per cent to something less than 30 per cent. But behind these aggregate figures a double process is taking place: the 'old' self-employed workers (such as retail traders) are rapidly declining in number, while there is a spectacular increase in what Sergio Bologna calls 'self-employment of the second generation', connected with the changes going on in many firms and industries.[8] But these self-employed workers of the second generation are in a sense a 'new edition' of the direct dependence on capital, typical of the traditional wage-earner. We may therefore say that, far from narrowing, the sector of labour depending on capital is becoming wider.

This, of course, is a quite different process from the old theories about 'proletarianization', as those theories (or ideologies) expected not only a larger but an increasingly homogeneous working class, while what we are witnessing is the growth of a deeply diversified, not to say fragmented, area of labour depending on capital.

NEW PROBLEMS FOR TRADE UNIONS

Factors of Crisis in Trade Unions' Strength and Representativeness

The dependence of labour on capital is, of course, the structural basis of the demand for union organization and collective bargaining. From this point of view, we might say that this demand is potentially larger than before, but actually the opposite is true: the range of workers actually represented by trade unions' collective bargaining is becoming narrower.

This is due first of all to well-known changes in the Italian employment structure that have been taking place since the 1970s: the reduction of the weight of industrial employment, and within it the increasing weight of employment in small firms, and the increasing weight of white-collar workers as compared with traditional blue-collar workers: all this has amounted to an increase in the share of employment located in areas of traditional trade union weakness.

But, besides this, the more recent changes we have tried to analyse play a significant role. Real dependence is scattered into many different patterns with different degrees and means of access to trade union bargaining action. Consider, for example, the following:

- the different bargaining positions of stable and temporary workers within a given firm;
- people working within the same plant, but belonging to different firms, may also refer not only to different kinds of bargaining at firm level, but also to different national collective agreements (relating to different industries);
- the increasing number of workers who are 'really dependent' but are not recognized as such, because they are formally members of cooperatives or self-employed, and who may have little or no access to the rules and conditions defined by collective bargaining.

Hence the present crisis in representativeness affecting Italian trade unions has a twofold dimension. On the one hand, it means that, for political and/or organizational reasons, trade unions do not succeed in representing workers whom they should and could represent, such as workers in small firms, white-collar workers, younger and more precarious workers or segments of the old working class dissatisfied with union policy.

On the other hand, it means that the unions cannot represent certain kinds of workers within the existing legal and bargaining framework; this is the case for a large number of cooperative members and for all the second-generation self-employed workers. This means that these workers are at present lacking any kind of union protection and representation.

No Ready-made Answer

There is no easy, ready-made global answer to this complex situation. The hypothesis of translating immediately the condition of real dependence into a unified organizational and bargaining pattern is a deceptive one, with the same shortcomings as the old ideologies of general proletarianization.

Equally deceptive is the temptation to invent some kind of universal character representing in itself the essence of labour in the new phase. This ideological operation did not work yesterday (or worked only in a very limited way) with the well-known 'mass worker' of the Fordist factory. Even less can it work today if it assumes the self-employed worker as the universal character of the post-Fordist worker: all the more so as, in this case, it includes – in the very definition of essence – a heavy element of 'appearance' (of *Erscheinung*, in its Marxian meaning).

More concretely, trade union action cannot resort to simplified solutions like the attempt to force inclusion of all kinds of workers under the category of wage-earners; or to more limited solutions like trying to include all workers in a given plant (but belonging to different firms) under one and the same collective agreement.

To this range of simplified and deceptive answers may also belong the tendencies to 'rediscover' and try to reproduce patterns and experiences of past workers' history, like the path leading from mutual aid societies to trade unions. These may have, at best, a useful suggestive function, but they are not 'the' answer to the problem.

As in other phases of big changes in class composition, the trade union movement should probably follow a less straightforward and more complicated or experimental path, trying to combine two basic elements: on the one hand, the building up, from the shop floor, of a number of experiences in organization, struggle and bargaining, corresponding to the specific needs of different kinds of workers, without too much fear of particularism and allowing a wide variety of approaches; and on the other hand, the unstinting attempt to connect these experiences into forms of representation and bargaining common to the various kinds of workers dependent on capital present on the 'post-Fordist' scene.

NOTES

1. I am in complete agreement with the critical remarks of Riccardo Bellofiore (see his contributions to this volume) on the use of 'post-Fordism' and of 'globalization', and on its ideological implications. I use the term 'post-Fordism' here, first of all, for the sake of brevity and, secondly, to stress the elements of novelty in the firm's organizational patterns – without accepting the theoretical (and ideological) implications very often associated with the use of these terms.

2. This hypothesis, of course, is derived, not only from the phenomena examined in this chapter, but from other empirical evidence on the evolution of Italian industry.

3. While organizational changes are (if very roughly) analysed in this chapter, technological changes are not; so their consequences for skill structures are in a sense taken for granted without illustrating and proving them.
4. Of course, this does not mean that the 'requirements of models' are always fully implemented by firms.
5. The frequent divergence between new models and their implementation may, moreover, both reduce the skill surplus and influence its distribution.
6. As one can easily see, there is an element of convergence on and one of divergence from the original Marxian definition. On the other hand, both terms are defined (as in Marx) from the worker's point of view and are seen as essential to it. But, on the other hand, the use I make of these concepts lacks any ontological implications, and this means, among other things, that it does not fit into an 'all-or-none' scheme, but rather into a scheme in which there may be degrees of control and, conversely, of alienation.
7. The new organizational models imply some increase in the autonomy at work (in varying degrees, often very limited) for a growing minority of the labour force; while, on the other hand, they imply a growing precariousness of employment for a growing majority of it.
8. See the essays collected in his (ed.) *Il lavoro autonomo di seconda generazione. Scenari del Postfordismo in Italia*, Milan: Feltrinelli, 1997.

Index